*Routledge Revivals*

# Thinking in Opposites

First published in 1952, *Thinking in Opposites* insists on the need for a carefully thought-out, rather than a merely authoritarian, basis for faith; but also insists that an indispensable preliminary is to know the laws which govern and limit the scope of human thinking in relation to three areas: the external world as it *is*; the internal world of *feeling*; and the *interrelation* of each of these with the other. This book is not a technical work in philosophy and the theory of knowledge; but it deals with problems in those fields which have usually been handled only in technical language. Therefore, this is a book both for the expert and for the intelligent and thoughtful layman: for the man who has a sense of responsibility for what he believes, and who is able to justify his faith amid the chaos of our times.

# Thinking in Opposites

an investigation of the nature of man as revealed by the nature of thinking

Paul Roubiczek

First published in 1952
By Routledge & Kegan Paul Ltd

This edition first published in 2024 by Routledge
4 Park Square, Milton Park, Abingdon, Oxon, OX14 4RN
and by Routledge
605 Third Avenue, New York, NY 10017

*Routledge is an imprint of the Taylor & Francis Group, an informa business*

© Paul Roubiczek 1952

All rights reserved. No part of this book may be reprinted or reproduced or utilised in any form or by any electronic, mechanical, or other means, now known or hereafter invented, including photocopying and recording, or in any information storage or retrieval system, without permission in writing from the publishers.

Publisher's Note
The publisher has gone to great lengths to ensure the quality of this reprint but points out that some imperfections in the original copies may be apparent.

Disclaimer
The publisher has made every effort to trace copyright holders and welcomes correspondence from those they have been unable to contact.

A Library of Congress record exists under LCCN: 53000180

ISBN: 978-1-032-73226-8 (hbk)
ISBN: 978-1-003-46317-7 (ebk)
ISBN: 978-1-032-73227-5 (pbk)

Book DOI 10.4324/9781003463177

# THINKING IN OPPOSITES

*an investigation of the nature of man*

*as revealed by the nature*

*of thinking*

by

PAUL ROUBICZEK

*Published in Great Britain
by Routledge & Kegan Paul Ltd
Published in the U.S.A. 1952
by The Beacon Press
Printed in Great Britain
by Butler & Tanner Ltd
Frome and London*

TO MY WIFE

whose constant devotion

and assistance

allowed me

to write this book

# PREFACE

THIS investigation is primarily a study of thinking, and this implies important limitations. Thought is neither the only nor the most important of those activities and powers which determine our lives; actions frequently spring from deeper layers of our existence than that of consciousness; feeling can influence us directly; and the most important of our decisions may surprise us because we are not aware of those urges and forces within us to which they give expression. Moreover, whatever the source of our actions, they are usually more significant than what we think. The concentration of this book on thinking, therefore, should not be mistaken for the claim that thinking is important beyond its own sphere or can achieve results beyond its own scope. It often proves powerless when confronted with these deeper layers of our personality, and the most correct thinking may avail us little. The positive achievements which we are going to describe can be brought about in a different way, or we may fail to reach them although we clearly know of them. There are other forces at work, determining us both from without and within, besides our conscious endeavours.

But when all is said that can be said against the relevance of thinking —and much of it has great weight—the real significance of an investigation of it probably emerges even more clearly.

Man's independence of thinking is never as complete as it may seem at first sight. Our existence is closely interconnected with language; human qualities do not grow in isolation, but depend for their development on relationships with other persons. All this forces man to become articulate—that is, to think. The development of personality, even in the simplest of men, involves the gradual raising of inner processes into the sphere of consciousness and their translation into thought. There is no stage in the history of man without some kind of wisdom. Feeling, too, has to be translated into thought to become a reliable guide for action. If, therefore, we cannot avoid thinking, it is obviously most important that we should think correctly. Though many achievements are more or less independent of thinking, wrong thinking can do the utmost harm. We need only look at the impasse which we have reached to see that the

# PREFACE

one-sided development of thinking during the last few centuries—the concentration on science and the neglect of man's emotional and spiritual nature—has had a profound, and profoundly disturbing, influence.

It remains true—to emphasize this once more—that thinking represents only part of our personality and that such important decisions and achievements as moral deeds or deeds of love can be reached at any intellectual level; thinking can even prove an obstacle. Nor is true wisdom necessarily connected with intellectual refinement; a peasant may —or may not—be wiser than a scholar. But so long as our right decisions are not conscious decisions, we are always in danger of succumbing to the wrong kind of argument. In any man, whether simple or sophisticated, instincts and desires employ very cunning arguments to lure him away from the path of virtue, and this danger has been immensely increased in our age, in which the wrong kind of rationalism seems to command the highest esteem. The only way of ensuring the right decisions is to make them conscious and to support them by thinking.

The irrational forces in man must needs be extremely attractive in an age in which such a one-sided rationalism seems to offer the only alternative. But there is no healthy development of man without the controlling power of thought, and this, in its turn, makes it once more imperative to develop the right kind of thinking which can offer an alternative even to those who are aware that there is much in the nature of man which escapes abstract statements. We may approve of the high development of consciousness in modern times, or we may fear that it cuts us off from the roots of our being; but the fact that it has been developed must be taken into account. It can hardly be doubted that the irrational reactions against it are at least as dangerous as exaggerated rationalism; the consequences of extreme Existentialism and Logical Positivism, of the deification of mere existence or of merely logical thought—to mention only philosophical examples—are equally fatal. The way out is to develop consciousness in the right direction and to counterbalance its one-sidedness.

*Thinking in Opposites*, the title of this book, will be explained at the end of the first chapter.[1] It is identical neither with any of the acknowledged meanings of dialectics nor with any kind of dualism. On the contrary, by disclosing the opposites at work within our thinking, we hope to be able to deal with some of those destructive external oppositions which threaten to split up that inner unity which is essential to our existence as persons.

Nor should the title suggest that this book is only concerned with the theory of knowledge. The study of thinking will serve as the basis of an investigation of the nature of man, thus taking up an implication of the

[1] See pp. 16–18.

## PREFACE

nature of our thinking to which little attention seems to have been paid. If it is true—as I hope this attempt will prove—that the nature of thinking (that is, the working of our minds as described by the theory of knowledge and not its psychological interpretation) can be more reliably stated than many other characteristics of man, should it not also be possible to derive from it a reliable knowledge of some aspects of our nature? The investigation, by including those effects of feeling which are relevant to thinking, shows that there is a direct relationship between the laws of thinking and ethics, and I hope to show that this approach to philosophy, which excludes metaphysics, can contribute essentially to our knowledge of man.

As a lifetime of reading has gone into the making of this book, it is impossible to refer to all the works which may have exercised some influence. It also seems that no useful purpose would be served by this, for, so far as I can see, no similar attempt has yet been undertaken. The references, therefore, have been chosen mainly from two points of view. On the one hand, I have tried to establish the relationship of this investigation with a few classical authors, particularly with Kant's teaching upon which this study partially rests; on the other hand, I have tried to show how this book can be related to some contemporary English philosophical and theological writings which point in a similar direction.

I have much pleasure in acknowledging my very great indebtedness to Professor H. H. Farmer, who never lost patience in reading and re-reading the different versions of my manuscript and discussing them with me in great detail, and to Professor C. E. Raven, whose constant help and encouragement enabled me to write this book.

Finally, I am more grateful than I can say to my friend Douglas Hewitt for the time and care he devoted to helping me find the right expression for my thoughts, and to Mr. K. G. Knight, who assisted him in this thankless task.

PAUL ROUBICZEK

CAMBRIDGE, *May 1952*

# CONTENTS

PREFACE  *page* vii

## PART I: EXTERNAL AND INTERNAL REALITY

I. CONTRADICTIONS AND OPPOSITES IN THOUGHT  3

  *1. The inevitability of contradictions, page* 3. *2. Opposites inherent in thought, page* 9. *3. Thinking in opposites, page* 16.

II. EXTERNAL AND INTERNAL REALITY  19

  *1. The concept 'reality', page* 19. *2. The necessary distinction between two realities, page* 20. *3. External reality, page* 24. *4. Internal reality, page* 33.

III. THE MAIN CHARACTERISTICS OF THE TWO REALITIES  41

  *1. The particular nature of internal reality, page* 41. *2. The need for a complete separation, page* 47. *3. Both realities must be taken into account, page* 55.

## PART II: THE EXTERNAL AND INTERNAL OPPOSITES

IV. THE NEED FOR OPPOSITES  65

  *1. The necessity for different kinds of opposites, page* 65. *2. The meaning of the concept 'opposite', page* 71.

V. THE EXTERNAL OPPOSITES  77

  *1. The main line of our investigation, page* 77. *2. Opposites indispensable for the knowledge of external reality, page* 80. *3. The special importance of the constructive concepts, page* 91.

VI. THE NATURE OF FEELING  98

VII. THE INTERNAL OPPOSITES  110

  *1. Means, ends and values, page* 110. *2. Intentions, aims*

## CONTENTS

*and principles, page* 116. *3. The constructive concepts, page* 124.

VIII. RIGHT AND WRONG DEVELOPMENT OF FEELING  *page* 136

*1. The intrusion of feeling into the realm of thought, page* 136. *2. The necessary concentration on values, page* 143.

### PART III: ABSOLUTE VALUES AND THE INTERCONNECTED OPPOSITES

IX. THE ABSOLUTE VALUES  153

*1. Truth, goodness and beauty, page* 153. *2. The major operations of thinking, page* 158. *3. The correct application of the absolute values, page* 163.

X. THE INTERCONNECTED OPPOSITES  169

*1. Their nature and purpose, page* 169. *2. Their main characteristics, page* 173.

XI. INTERCONNECTED OPPOSITES AND ABSOLUTE VALUES  179

*1. Space and time, page* 179. (*a*) *In external reality, page* 179. (*b*) *In internal reality, page* 182. (*c*) *Truth, page* 188.
*2. Necessity and freedom, page* 191. (*a*) *In external reality, page* 191. (*b*) *In internal reality, page* 195. (*c*) *Goodness, page* 203.
*3. The One and the Many, page* 208. (*a*) *In external reality, page* 208. (*b*) *In internal reality, page* 211. (*c*) *Beauty, page* 223.

XII. THE CREATION OF FURTHER INTERCONNECTED OPPOSITES  230

INDEX  241

# Part One
EXTERNAL AND INTERNAL REALITY

# Chapter I

## CONTRADICTIONS AND OPPOSITES IN THOUGHT

### 1. THE INEVITABILITY OF CONTRADICTIONS

IF we try to develop a comprehensive idea of the universe and man's position in it, we are inevitably driven towards contradictory conclusions, which we can neither avoid nor reconcile.

The modern development of the natural sciences has made us very conscious of the enormous magnitude of the external world, which seems to destroy any importance we may want to attach to our human existence. In previous ages, infinity and eternity were metaphysical terms; the earth and the heavens, comparatively small, were safely embedded in a transcendental reality which was interpreted in religious terms; in modern times, however, infinity and eternity have been transposed to the material universe so that man is robbed of his proper status in an external world which, at the same time, has increased in importance.[1] It is true that recent developments in physics seem to imply some new limitations in the realm of space and matter, but man still remains infinitesimally small even when compared with the earth alone, which is itself nothing but a speck among millions of stars. Similarly, man's life seems scarcely a moment compared with the endless course of time. How can we maintain that man has any importance in face of this overwhelming vastness of our world?

Yet even if he is clearly aware of the magnitude of the universe, man cannot escape the urge to attribute importance to human existence; he feels compelled to consider himself as the centre of his world. He experiences within himself a different world, that of thinking, feeling and willing, of moral laws, of truth and beauty, and this inner world seems as boundless as the universe. It seems, moreover, to point to another infinity, transcending the realm of space and time. But man's inner significance does not simply counterbalance his external

[1] Cf. Pascal, *Pensées*, Nos. 205-6.

insignificance, for these two infinities are not in equilibrium; he succumbs, time and again, to the impact of the external infinity, in spite of reassuring inner experiences whose importance is not diminished by knowledge of the external world.[1]

We cannot avoid this contradiction by restricting our thoughts to the consideration of life on this earth, for the concept of evolution leads eventually to a similar contradiction.

We find that we are subordinated to a development in which the single human life evidently has no value as such. Every step of this development, however small, sensible or senseless, destroys legions of human lives. The evolution of life in general implies an enormous waste of life; how many species have disappeared without even leaving a trace! The theory that this evolution is brought about by the cruel struggle for existence may no longer be of undoubted scientific validity, but none of the possible theories is able to establish the importance of the single individual. This waste continues throughout the history of mankind; entire races and great nations have been wiped out completely. All events pass blindly and regardlessly over the single man; he can escape from their murderous grip only by mere chance; the rule is that even the smallest change demands the sacrifice of innumerable human lives. We have to neglect the individual if we want to understand evolution.

Yet this life, so demonstrably worthless, remains for every man of unique value, and everything else depends on it. With its loss all reality vanishes for him, the whole world collapses. He has to reconcile himself to the fact of natural death, and he is able to develop a faith in values which transcend life, so that he can give a meaning to death. Therefore he can even sacrifice his life for a cause, but its meaningless destruction remains unbearable. If his life is deprived of all meaning by the processes of evolution which destroy him, then evolution itself must seem meaningless to him. It could be justified only by values which are based on respect for man. Thus the development which disposes so lavishly and carelessly of legions of human beings is yet unable to make man accept the wiping out of a single human life.

Nor can this contradiction be resolved by concentrating on the history of mankind in its narrower sense.

Born as the children of an epoch which believed that mankind is necessarily and automatically progressing, we have been forced to stop identifying scientific and technical progress with general human improvement, for any survey of our history shows us with appalling distinctness that there is no such improvement. Since the earliest times

---

[1] This contradiction is most beautifully stated in the Conclusion of Kant's *Critique of Practical Reason*, in the famous passage which contrasts 'the starry heavens above' with 'the moral law within'.

## CONTRADICTIONS AND OPPOSITES IN THOUGHT

humanity has tumbled from one terror into the other, from one war into the next, from destruction into destruction. Individual men or single epochs achieve grand and marvellous results, but even the religion of love unlooses the bloodiest wars, and the most overwhelming achievements of the natural sciences serve to make the age-old struggle for power enormously more destructive. There are, it is true, sporadic calm epochs in history, golden ages of culture, but even these seem to build up new strength for the barbarian evil instincts of man. By creating forms and rules which gradually become too rigid to serve human needs any longer, and by driving human thought into abstract regions, they clear the way for these instincts and enable them to break through just when we think they are overcome.

Yet in spite of these facts we are unable to believe that there is no progress at all. There is an enormous difference between primitive times and our highly developed civilization. The natural sciences, though they may not have changed man, have given him almost divine power over natural forces, they have abolished epidemics, prolonged human life and created technical possibilities which were unimaginable a short time ago. Apart from this, there is a slow accumulation of spiritual goods; whole worlds of art were inaccessible before Michelangelo and Shakespeare, before Rembrandt and Beethoven; the realm of thought has been transformed almost beyond recognition by such thinkers as Plato and Aristotle; and the religious possibilities of mankind were doubtless infinitely poorer before Buddha and Christ.

The life-story of the individual man, too, leads only to a further contradiction. Every man is compelled to recognize his own life as being a mere accident. His birth has placed him in a country, a people and family, which he could not choose; it has burdened him with a special heritage, with a mass of exterior and interior conditions from which he cannot escape; and this birth which he could not influence depended on the most fortuitous contingencies; the most insignificant circumstances could prevent it or change fundamentally the conditions of his life. This life, too, is full of accidents. He has survived the war although millions succumbed to the same dangers; he has escaped death, the train-smash, the mortal disease, only because he met some ridiculous hindrance or because he lingered for a second; a single step more and he would have been run over or fallen over a cliff. And he cannot believe that these saving incidents were the instruments of a purposeful selection; among those who died prematurely were men at the beginning of a career which promised to bring blessing to the whole of mankind; and among those who have survived are men who are only a burden to themselves and to others, men who do not know how to make use of their lives.

Yet, at the same time, nobody can escape the conviction that his life has a meaning. He is bound to look for a meaning in everything he experiences; he will find no peace unless he discovers a meaning in all these accidents. If he denies this meaning, if he gives up his search for it in disappointment or despair, or if he is forced to live purposelessly, he will find that he reproaches himself for living in a false manner, for not fulfilling his real task, for not trying to find a meaning in his life. Even if he struggles with all his logical mind against these reproaches, he will still be compelled to believe that every human life has its meaning. In so far as he succeeds in destroying this faith he will only destroy himself. Meaning represents an integral part of this apparently senseless life.

We could go on adding examples of such inevitable contradictions almost at will. We are confronted, for instance, with the problems of evil and of suffering. The Christian has the greatest confidence that this world serves the final realization of good, but it is he who will be forced, time and again, to exclaim: 'If God is all-knowing and all-powerful, and if He is love, why has He created a world which allows for evil, and why has He created men in such a way that they are bound to increase this evil infinitely?' We may be able to find convincing explanations for suffering, and many of these explanations carry great weight; yet if we are confronted with a woman who has lost her husband in the first and her children in the second world war, if we think of men who have been born with torturing diseases and yet grown old, or if we see that thousands of men are killed in an earthquake, and that the devastations due to man's lust for destruction or to his thoughtless indifference surpass the destruction wrought by nature; then even the most convincing explanation seems desperately inadequate and any answer we may be able to give will die on our lips.[1]

It is nevertheless undoubtedly true that we experience evil only because we know of good and because we believe in it. Our feelings may be blunted, we may become indifferent towards good and evil and destroy everything which is human within us. The pain, however, which we feel because of the evil and wickedness in the world presupposes the belief in goodness, in spite of the fact that the predominance of evil seems to rob this belief of its foundations. The recognition of evil, therefore, which cannot be reconciled with our belief in good, is yet impossible without it.

If we try to understand the facts on which our life is based and approach them without prejudice, we cannot escape fundamental contradictions which we are unable to resolve.

There are, of course, many unitary systems of thought, but all of them try to resolve these contradictions either by suppressing or by

---

[1] For a further elaboration of this conflict, cf. H. H. Farmer, *The World and God*, pp. 92–102, or Dostoevsky, *The Brothers Karamazov*, Book V, Chapter 4.

## CONTRADICTIONS AND OPPOSITES IN THOUGHT

re-interpreting one part of these contradictions. None of these attempts, however, succeeds in hiding the fact that our experience and our perception have been unduly simplified or impoverished in the process, and that it is only thus that the system has become possible.

The natural sciences which establish for us the most important of these unitary systems of thought have indeed transformed our world; they work so exactly that, in some spheres, we can predict the future with their help; and technical achievements prove their power beyond any doubt. But these sciences are only exact while they confine themselves to inanimate matter; they become insufficient and inexact when they have to deal with life or with the human mind. The theory of evolution has made an overwhelming impact on our age, but has not been definitely proved; in spite of great efforts it still contains serious gaps. Psychology is divided into many schools and we are unable to decide which of the different interpretations of psychological processes is correct. Physiology may perhaps one day succeed in explaining the formation of thoughts by corresponding movements of particles or electrical impulses in the brain, but this would not help us in the least to understand the content of these thoughts. Material processes and meaning are so different that they cannot even be compared.[1] No belief in an impersonal necessity, moreover, can ever completely destroy our inner knowledge that we are more than mere tools of blind forces.

Nevertheless, it would be equally wrong to renounce these sciences because of their shortcomings, and to look instead to the inner experiences of man to achieve a unitary system of thought. In trying to do so, we only populate the external world with projections from our internal world, with gods and demons, or we renounce explanations where they are still possible, thus endangering the consistency of our belief. It is wrong to rely entirely on mechanical explanations; but it was just as wrong to think, as the Middle Ages did, that if we believe in Christ the earth must be the centre of the world. We drag heaven down to earth or thrust ourselves up into heaven, and this makes any comprehension of either heaven or earth impossible. Nor can we replace the theory of evolution by laying stress on the importance of the single individual alone. Man is unable to free himself from external reality and he cannot escape from human society. If he tries to confine himself to his internal world, he will, in his neglect of the outer world, only impoverish those inner experiences which depend on his contact with nature, things and men. He will gradually destroy the life whose purpose he was trying to fulfil.

It is hardly necessary to explain at greater length that all unitary interpretations of human history also are bound to fail. We are unable

---

[1] See J. Oman, *The Natural and the Supernatural*, pp. 9, 169, and C. E. Raven, *Jesus and the Gospel of Love*, p. 440.

to re-create past events in every detail; we must simplify history and interpret it to make it intelligible, and because of this necessary simplification we may find a unitary explanation which seems convincing. But for this very reason history is open to all interpretations. One philosophy of history indeed demonstrates convincingly that nations and civilizations are doomed to perish, while another proves equally convincingly that progress is inevitable.

The most torturing contradictions in our lives make this impossibility of a comprehensive unitary system most clearly visible. The meaning of our lives is to be found neither in success nor in external consistency, for we are confronted with utter injustice time and again; do not the wicked prosper and the good fail? It is wrong to seek a confirmation of the inner meaning in external events, because such a confirmation can only be found if we shut our eyes to facts. But it is also wrong to believe in ultimate chaos, because to do so we must destroy the inner world which we so clearly experience. Nor can we simply restrict ourselves to the appreciation of positive values; if we increase our sensitiveness to good, to truth and beauty, we shall become more vulnerable at the same time and experience evil, lies and ugliness more painfully. An increase in our ability to appreciate positive values cannot be separated from a clearer and more poignant experience of their negative opposites, for it is the same ability.[1] It is for this reason that the highest forms of human striving, such as religion, are those which are exposed to the greatest corruption.[2] We must consider both these aspects of our lives and think two different thoughts at the same time, despite the fact that they contradict each other; it is only when we do not shun contradictions that we are able to do justice to the fullness of life.

Every man, however, in spite of these contradictions, longs to build up a unitary coherence of all his thoughts, feelings and actions. Every unsolved contradiction means mental discord and laceration and threatens, therefore, to destroy human life; it seems impossible that man could ever find peace except by establishing such a unitary coherence. Man craves for an explanation of all that he recognizes, feels, experiences, and an explanation seems satisfactory only if it means the fitting of each experience into a unitary system of thought.

This attitude seems to belong to man's very nature. On the one hand, it is based on the fact that he first perceives single objects; everything he can see and grasp appears to him as limited and as complete in itself. Even external events and inner experiences, although belonging to an unending flux of happenings, become intelligible by being isolated as unities. I see the tree in front of my window, a leaf falling slowly to

---

[1] See J. Macmurray, *Reason and Emotion*, pp. 45–6.
[2] See J. Oman, op. cit., pp. 374–5.

## CONTRADICTIONS AND OPPOSITES IN THOUGHT

the ground, I remember the last conversation with my friend—any such impression constitutes a unity, a whole. On the other hand, this impression is confirmed by our own personality. It is true that we experience ourselves as body and mind, and the body of whose organic and nervous activities we have no immediate knowledge is very different from our conscious activities; but both belong to our personality. We may be torn by contradictory intentions, thoughts and feelings and thus driven into painful conflicts, but all these experiences remain ours, even if we are unable to resolve their conflict, and this hurts us because it contradicts the unity of our personality. It is only because our being constitutes a unity that we are able to experience the most diverse impressions as our own, and to build up our lives and our knowledge with their help.

Yet we are only able to grasp finite unities, and the universe and our inner world are infinite. No unitary explanation, therefore, does justice to the whole of reality. But how can we reconcile the innumerable contradictions which we are unable to resolve with our longing for a unitary coherence which also seems an essential part of our true nature?

### 2. OPPOSITES INHERENT IN THOUGHT

Our longing for a unitary coherence of all our thoughts is prevented from reaching fulfilment, however, not only by the striking contradictions which we have considered, but also by some of the basic characteristics of our way of thinking, for we are forced to think with the help of opposites. This fact—the main subject of our investigation—will occupy us throughout the book; we shall return to most of the examples mentioned in this section and explain, too, our special use of the concept 'opposite'.[1] But even such a preliminary glimpse of this subject as does not need any special preparation, shows how many opposites in the ordinary meaning of this word are necessary to enable us to think clearly.

Let us begin with sense-impressions which are the natural starting point of our apprehension of reality and thus of thinking. A dazzling light will produce an overwhelming impression of brightness which neither contains nor needs any opposites, but we shall be unable to distinguish one object from another, or indeed to discern anything. If we are to see something clearly, the dazzling light must be pushed back with the help of darkness; we distinguish objects [2] only if contrasts

---

[1] See pp. 71 ff.

[2] Languages themselves seem to encourage us in our investigation. The words 'object' and 'subject' are derived from the Latin word for 'to throw', which presupposes an opposition. The German word 'Gegenstand' is even clearer, it comes from 'to stand against'.

within our field of vision enable us to perceive or to create boundaries. All the concrete objects we see become visible by some kind of opposition between different degrees of bright and dark.

Even if we want to clarify the undefined sensation originally produced by the dazzling light, we have to apply two different kinds of opposites. When light blinds us, the impression of brightness is intermixed with the pain of blinding. To conceive brightness itself, we must distinguish it from this pain; we have to oppose light as a pleasurable sensation to the pain which we feel at the same time. But this opposition is not yet complete, for both light and darkness can be associated either with pleasure or with pain. After a busy and harassing day we welcome the stillness and darkness of night as a great relief; after a sleepless night the first signs of daylight appear to us as a deliverance. Normal daylight, moreover, may produce neither pleasure nor pain. A clear conception of brightness will appear only after we have taken into account many such possibilities, and it will appear because 'bright' and 'dark' have emerged as the relevant opposites which enable us to concentrate upon this aspect of reality.

It may seem, however, that the clear apprehension of brightness and darkness, although originating in the contrast between them, eventually becomes independent of it, for we seem to be able to imagine brightness alone or darkness alone without the help of their opposites. Yet this is not correct, for we remain conscious of both. We can isolate brightness only because we have had the experience of darkness; we cannot exclude this experience at any time, even if we do not direct our attention to it; it always remains present in our mind. Darkness, on the other hand, cannot be seen at all; it seems visible and thus becomes imaginable only because the eye automatically opposes to it the usual experience of light.[1]

The necessity of applying opposites is hidden in this case, because light and darkness are so familiar to us, and because sight immediately provides us with the vision of something else which leads to further consideration. We cannot even realize that if we were uninterruptedly surrounded by the same degree of brightness we should not notice light at all. Yet this is exactly what would happen, if darkness were not such an inescapable experience, and this sense not so highly developed. This becomes clear when we think of the senses which are less highly developed. If we enter a room filled with a weak smell, we notice it at first, because it forms a contrast to the air outside, but if we stay in the room we cease to notice it. We usually become conscious of a smell or a taste only when it is replaced by a different smell or taste; we do not smell and taste the air which normally surrounds us,

[1] For the biological basis of this process see J. S. Haldane, *The Philosophical Basis of Biology*, p. 91.

## CONTRADICTIONS AND OPPOSITES IN THOUGHT

because there is no opposite to create a sensation and make us conscious of the normal smell and taste of air.

It is only when we leave the sphere of unclear sensations in this way that we can proceed to the creation of concepts which our thinking can use, for the creation of concepts is entirely dependent on such opposites. It is generally recognized that we need opposites in order to define concepts, but their function is far more fundamental. We cannot separate the two at all, for we can give meaning to the concepts only by opposing these opposites to one another; their use is implied in the creation of the concept.[1] We are unable to think of bright without thinking of dark at the same time, and this applies to all qualities whatsoever; we cannot think, for instance, of heavy without thinking of light, nor of warm without cold. We construct scales of degrees which seem to exclude the opposites; there are only degrees of hardness and not of softness. But these degrees, too, have been created with the help of opposites. We have to recognize that straw is hard when compared with cotton wool, but soft when compared with wood, before we can fit them into a single scale, and we have to return to these opposites if we want to understand the abstract degree of such a scale.[2]

We are also bound to use opposites when we try to get a clear idea of the object described by these qualities. It is an object within, and distinguished from, the space which surrounds it; we have to see it in opposition to the empty space. To make this distinction we have to recognize its boundaries, which we do by contrasting it with its surroundings. Inside the boundaries we find matter, and matter is nowadays explained by the theory of electrons. Here we must distinguish between positive and negative elements and consider their motion and the distance between their orbits, and for this purpose we have to apply scales of degrees founded upon the opposites of slow and quick, and of large and small. Each single electron, moreover, represents a part of

---

[1] How closely connected the opposites are is shown most clearly in the oldest languages. The opposites 'strong-weak', 'light-dark', 'large-small' are expressed in them by the same root-words. In old Egyptian, e.g. 'Ken' means strong and weak. In the spoken language, the two meanings were distinguished by the intonation, in writing by putting behind it either a standing or a sitting man. Later, 'ken' (strong) and 'kan' (weak) were derived from it. In Latin some such ambivalent words exist too, e.g. 'altus' meaning high and deep, 'sacer' meaning holy and sacrilegious. There are also derivations from the same root with opposite meanings, e.g. clamare (shout) and clam (soft); siccus (dry) and succus (juice). See K. Abel, *Der Gegensinn der Urworte*, pp. 6, 13 ff., 23, 31–2, 41 ff.

[2] 'We speak of getting hotter and hotter, and we think of what can be measured by a graduated scale of quantities. If, however, we isolate our sensations from the idea of a fire or a thermometer, the sensations of being frozen, chilly, tolerably warm, comfortably warm, hot, sweltering, burning are of different qualities, which, taken entirely by themselves, we could never have arranged in any scale of quantities.' J. Oman, *The Natural and the Supernatural*, p. 194.

a whole (whether of an object or of the entire material world) and one unit among many; and our concepts are based on both these opposites as well.

Each step forward in our thinking multiplies these opposites. If we consider the weight of an object, for instance, we not only need the opposites 'light' and 'heavy'; we also assume that two objects are in opposition to one another, for weight is the pressure exercised by one object upon another one, and it can only be measured if such an opposition is brought about. The pressure itself must be explained as a motion which has come to a stop, but which will continue as soon as the obstacle is removed; we have to apply the opposites 'rest' and 'motion', therefore, even if we are concerned with a state of rest. At the same time, the pressure is due to the power of attraction exercised by the earth; this is the cause and the weight is the effect—a further opposition. This power itself can be recognized only if there is something upon which it can exert an influence, and such a thing must be opposed to the forces working upon it, for it enables us to discern these forces by offering some kind of resistance. As soon as an object vanishes under the impact of a force, we cease to be able to detect the force.

Furthermore, all these concepts—motion, pressure, cause and effect, force—not only describe objects, but represent events. This leads to the recognition or application of further opposites. External events are based upon motions; we have just said that we think of motion even while thinking of rest, and we can see and measure it only if we are able to compare it with something which is at rest. We neither see nor feel the motion of the earth, for as we move with it, there is no opposition which would enable us to apprehend it directly. Yet we can recognize and measure it, because we are able, by indirect observation, to put it in opposition to other stars which move differently, especially because the fixed stars can be considered as being at rest when compared with the motion of the planets.

Modern scientific theories do not alter this position in the least. The theory of relativity, for instance, is based upon the speed of light which is considered as something which cannot change and remains absolutely constant—that is, it is used in exactly the same way as the concept 'at rest'. This theory, therefore, does not imply that everything is relative, but presupposes the opposites 'absolute' and 'relative'. Nor does the calculation based on probability, which is increasingly applied in physics, exclude opposites. We have to bring into opposition the cases which really happened and all the possible ones, and we do not abolish causality, for the single events have to be explained with the help of it. The concept of contingency must be interpreted and used as the opposite of that of causality.

Nor can we escape the application of opposites when we leave the

## CONTRADICTIONS AND OPPOSITES IN THOUGHT

realm of inanimate matter and try to understand man. As we ourselves are human beings, we might expect that we have a more direct knowledge in this sphere and thus become independent of any laws forced upon us by the nature of our thinking. Instead, however, we have to apply even more opposites here, and these opposites become even more complicated and involved as our knowledge progresses.

The activity of thinking itself is based on contradictory principles, on those of logic and mathematics on the one hand, which have to be applied to our external experience, and on values on the other, which often have to be accepted against all logical considerations, and we must apply both if we want to do justice to our lives. If we want to clarify our thoughts, we have to make clear distinctions between facts and theories, between sense-data and judgments, between knowledge and belief, and that means that we have to create a clear opposition between the thoughts due to our apprehension of external reality, and the thoughts due to the working of our minds or to our inner experiences. To understand thinking we have to separate our impressions from the laws of our thinking; to understand consciousness, we have to introduce the concept of the subconscious; to understand morality, we have to confront inner freedom with external causality or compulsion.

The realms of feeling and willing, too, do not make us free from the application of opposites. We speak quite automatically of pleasure and pain, of joy and sorrow, of love and hate. It seems that love can finally reconcile and transcend all opposites, but it presupposes them; it presupposes at least the confrontation of two separate entities. Our willing is determined by instincts and by intentions; the instinctive or conscious will to power struggles in each of us against our awareness of moral obligations; we experience in some ways the opposition between the impulses of our body and of our mind. Any action due to our willing, moreover, confronts us with the problem of necessity and freedom; we see that our human striving faces both external compulsion and a mysterious supernatural fate or providence. Actions themselves are useful or harmful, good or evil. Man, however, is not only active; he also succumbs to influences and events; nobody could understand his feelings and behaviour if he only paid attention to his activities without considering an opposite state of passivity or suffering.

The sciences dealing with life and with man are not so exact as those dealing with inanimate matter. This is partly due to the very fact that they cannot establish clear opposites. In biology, for instance, the boundaries between inanimate matter and living cells, or those between the animals and man, remain in many respects uncertain. In spite of this, however, we are bound to apply these opposites; no theory can stop us from seeing life in opposition to inanimate matter. Nor can we think of life without thinking of death, and we have to oppose death to mere dissolution; objects dissolve, living organisms die. Each single cell is a complete unit in itself, yet we have to see them, too, as parts of the whole of an organism which we have to oppose, in its turn, to some larger unit. It is true that the belief in a life force, representing life as a whole, has had to be abandoned, but our difficulties here are due to the fact that we are in need of such an opposite, without being able to describe it satisfactorily.

The transformation of our psychological knowledge into a reliable science is faced with similar difficulties. Most psychologists try to avoid them by excluding the possibilities of free choices and thus denying the moral nature of man. Yet no science can prevent us from regarding man as a sensual and a spiritual being, and from opposing his body to his mind or soul or spirit. We have great difficulties as the words themselves indicate, in defining these opposites properly, but, whatever words we choose, we have, if we want to understand man, to take into consideration some such opposition between his animal instincts and his moral impulses, or between external and internal compulsion and free decisions. Nor can we avoid seeing and applying the opposition between the single individual and society or mankind.

The development of philosophy confirms our belief that there is no acceptable unitary explanation. Neither an idealistic nor a materialistic or positivist philosophy can satisfactorily overcome these fundamental opposites; it is no accident that both these constant types of philosophical teaching continue simultaneously throughout the ages.

A perfect work of art, on the other hand, represents a complete unity which we cannot explain, but it remains inexplicable because we recognize, so far as we can analyse its composition, that it unites the most extreme opposites—opposites so contradictory that we are usually unable to reconcile them.

Any perfect work of art is conditioned by the period of its creation and yet valid far beyond it; to remain alive it must be firmly rooted in its contemporary world and yet transcend any temporal bondage. It is, at the same time, national and supranational, tied to both nationality and humanity; it expresses with equal strength the individuality of the artist and common human nature, and it is thus unique and yet general, an expression of general experiences and principles. It is conditioned by intuition which can be neither willed nor taught, and by intellectual intentions and endeavours; its technique is formally accessible to intellectual thinking and teaching and is, at the same time, the direct and inexplicable expression of feeling. It has entirely become part of the external reality, so that it can be grasped with our senses, and is, in spite of that, the frame of purely emotional or spiritual experiences. The artist has to be strong enough to comprehend external reality at once in its externals and its essence; he has to see it as external

## CONTRADICTIONS AND OPPOSITES IN THOUGHT

reality and yet to transform it into an expression of internal reality. It is thus that a unique work confined within narrow limits, a very strange and tiny particle of the universe, becomes in spite of its limits and its peculiarity the most complete symbol of the whole of reality.

The arts presuppose special gifts and talents; religion is based solely upon the fundamental conditions of human existence. But in the sphere of religion we are entirely dependent on the use of opposites. Here we need them, not only to express the results of our striving, but even to become aware of religious experiences. To find access to this spiritual reality, we must increase the power of our feelings with the help of the most extreme opposites; it is only thus that we catch a glimpse of this supernatural world whose part and opposite we are, and that we can understand what religion means. No intellectual interpretation, lacking the support of strong and developed feelings, could show us the meaning of any adequate statement about the nature of religion. For 'religion is the vision of something which stands beyond, behind, and within, the passing flux of immediate things; something which is real, and yet waiting to be realized; something which is a remote possibility, and yet the greatest of present facts; something that gives meaning to all that passes, and yet eludes apprehension; something whose possession is the final good, and yet is beyond all reach; something which is the ultimate ideal, and the hopeless quest'.[1]

For Christianity, God is the 'wholly other', the 'entirely incomprehensible', inspiring terror and awe,[2] and yet, at the same time, He is the Father whom we can approach with the simple love and trust of children. Any awareness of God is not only the awareness of 'an unconditional demand' which forces us to give up any shelter or security, but also that of the 'final succour' which gives us the certainty of salvation.[3] In the centre of Christianity stands the Cross, the most terrible catastrophe in human history, the most torturing defeat of the spirit, which nevertheless is a sign neither of tragedy nor of defeat, but on the contrary of the highest triumph of the spirit and the final expression of divine grace. Man is not severed from God and annihilated, but he is shown, by these extreme opposites, the real path to redemption.

Buddhism in its original form is the only one of the great religions which is not concerned with God, but with the striving for 'Nirvana'. Nirvana means the dissolution of everything that exists in 'the undivided eternal Whole' and is, therefore, freed from any opposition; it is 'extinction', 'a fire which has gone out for lack of fuel'; all its descriptions are attempts to describe nothingness.[4] It is not intended to be

[1] A. N. Whitehead, *Science and the Modern World* (1946), p. 238.
[2] Cf. R. Otto, *The Idea of the Holy*.
[3] H. H. Farmer, *The World and God*, p. 25.
[4] P. Deussen, *Die nachvedische Philosophie der Inder*, 3. Aufl., pp. 111–12.

nothingness, but to represent the highest state of blessedness, yet it reveals itself only as a negation of the world and as an overcoming of human existence, thus leading, in spite of its ecstasies and its high morality, to the complete destruction of all reality. It is no accident that the pure form of Buddhism has almost disappeared; because reality could not be excluded, Buddhism had to change its doctrines.

Neither external facts nor inner experiences, neither simple objects nor the sphere of our highest spiritual endeavours can be grasped and understood without the help of opposites. Nothing remains if we try to exclude them.

### 3. THINKING IN OPPOSITES

The following investigation tries to show in greater detail that we apply opposites whenever we think at all, and that accurate thinking, therefore, depends upon their correct application. We shall try to discover the nature of these opposites and to find out whether there are laws or rules which would enable us to apply them correctly.

*Thinking in Opposites*, the title of this book, has thus a twofold meaning. On the one hand, it points to the fact that our thinking is based upon opposites; on the other hand, it raises the demand that we should become aware of them and consciously apply them. This is no contradiction, for the fact that we are forced to think with the help of opposites does not imply that we consciously make use of them. On the contrary, it is chiefly by attempting to suppress, to exclude or to overcome them that we pay regard to this fact in most of our present methods of thinking. These attempts, however, never succeed completely; if we neglect the opposites, their influence passes unnoticed, but it falsifies our thoughts. We shall see that we must not try to weaken these opposites or to bridge them artificially; we must try to work them out clearly.

This abandonment of the hope of ever reaching an all-inclusive unitary explanation of reality may appear, at first, as a serious and painful loss, but in fact it leads to a great enrichment of our thinking. As we can, in fact, only think with the help of opposites, we do not lose anything if we apply them, but find how to make full use of our power of thought. Only if we are willing to acknowledge opposites are we prepared to consider all the many contradictions with which our lives are filled, and only then are we also ready to have regard to the many forms in which reality appears to us. We shall not attempt, therefore, to add yet another futile solution of the contradictions which we considered at the beginning of this chapter. These contradictions undermine any results which we may hope to achieve by building up a unity by thinking, but they increase our awareness of the manifold

## CONTRADICTIONS AND OPPOSITES IN THOUGHT

aspects of our lives, and become the clearest expression of our knowledge, if we accept the fundamental importance of opposites.

This thinking in opposites, however, does justice too to our longing for a unity which we also cannot exclude; it even promises to solve this seemingly insoluble problem in a more satisfactory way than any enforced unitary coherence of our thoughts. It does so, because it leads us to include in our investigation the sphere of feeling.

Thinking and feeling cannot be completely separated; they form opposites which always appear at the same time. Every feeling, to be understood, has to be translated into thought; every thought, on the other hand, produces a feeling; the more independent our thinking, the less we accept other people's way of thinking but really exercise our own power of thought, the more distinct is the feeling which accompanies our thought. Only if a thought has produced a feeling has it become a living property of the person who thought it. To-day most of us assume that thinking and feeling exclude one another; we are accustomed either to suppress our feelings in order to be able to think clearly, or to forego thinking so as not to weaken our feelings; we often use feelings as a means of escape or, in those regions to which our thoughts cannot penetrate, as a less reliable substitute for thinking. The clarification of opposites, however, helps also to free our feelings from their vagueness; it helps us to discipline them and to transform them into what they really should be, namely an organ of knowledge. It shows that we can increase, at the same time, both the intensity of our feelings and the clarity of our thoughts. It is this transformation of our feelings which, as we hope to show, satisfies our longing for a unity.

At the present time, the general tendency is to seek an all-inclusive unitary explanation. This leads to the setting of one part of our feelings against another, for no intellectual unity can ever be comprehensive enough to include the whole of reality, and therefore we have to reject whatever is inconsistent with it. This need to accept parts of reality and to reject others splits up our feelings and drives them in different directions, and thus we are prevented from re-establishing that unity which we originally experience. The struggle for an intellectual unity produces, not a unity, but inner discord and laceration, because this wrong way of thinking is not in accordance with our feelings.

The intention of this investigation is to reverse this process, in the belief that if we pursue these opposites to their conclusion we prepare the way for a synthesis of feeling which is really satisfactory, because it is with the feelings and not with the intellect that we can grasp the true unity of existence. We hope to show that, if we renounce the premature satisfaction of an intellectual unity and apply the real laws of our thinking, we can develop our feelings so as to lift up into consciousness that unity of existence which we cannot grasp by thinking alone. We must try, therefore, to recognize as clearly as possible the opposites which are the basis of our thinking; we must not shun the most extreme contradictions, but try, on the contrary, to discover them. Only thus shall we be able to overcome the dangers which we cannot escape by any artificial unification.

The fact that we accept opposites as the basis of our thoughts, and contradictions as the result, does not mean that we take refuge in some kind of dualism. On the contrary, it robs dualism of its foundations. As these opposites are the way by which we think, they cannot disclose the true nature of reality, and as they remain dependent upon one another, they never tear the world asunder. Those contradictions which might produce the belief that reality is determined by two independent principles, are shown to be the consequences of our thinking. The very acceptance of such opposites, therefore, prevents us from founding any kind of dualistic belief upon them. At the same time, it also prevents that unacknowledged dualism which is probably more common to-day, for if we are aware of these opposites there is no longer any need to keep our practical or scientific endeavours and our moral or religious convictions in two completely separate compartments.

As the investigation starts from the laws of thinking, it is primarily an epistemological one. Yet it transcends this sphere, not only because it includes feeling, but also because we believe that the knowledge of the conditions imposed upon our thinking can make an important contribution to our knowledge of the nature of man. By rejecting any attempt at a unitary or dualistic explanation of the whole of reality, we also reject metaphysical statements. But we shall try to show that the conditions of our thought, without the help of any metaphysical interpretation, express and clarify certain inner experiences, thus increasing our knowledge of truth and beauty, of morality, and of man's part in, and access to, that supernatural reality which is the concern of religion.

## Chapter II

### EXTERNAL AND INTERNAL REALITY

#### 1. THE CONCEPT 'REALITY'

Our purpose is to investigate the way in which we apprehend reality. But 'reality' is a very vague concept whose meaning seems to be clear so long as we use it without paying special attention to it, but which, as soon as we try to define it more exactly, seems to evade us. All attempts to define it have only led to many contradictory definitions, with the result that, in the end, the concept has become ambiguous and misleading. This failure is mainly due to the fact that all such attempts are wrong in themselves, because 'reality' is one of those basic concepts which cannot be defined; for it is impossible to find any simpler or more fundamental concepts to use in their definition. But since these definitions have been given and since, through them, the concept has become ambiguous, we need, if we wish to use it at all, some description at least of what we consider as real.[1]

There is, however, another reason to which very little attention has been paid, why it is hard to give even such a description. We are confronted, not with a single and coherent reality, but with two aspects of reality which are so different that they appear to us almost as two realities. This fact makes any general statement about reality impossible, for we have to think in two completely different ways if we want to apprehend both these aspects. We cannot, for instance, discover both the causal necessity and the moral value of an event by the same method of thinking. In science, we must avoid the application of values, but we have to apply them when judging our own actions. This fact, too, makes it impossible to find a definition; most of the usual definitions or descriptions are inadequate because, owing to our desire for a unitary explanation,

[1] Cf. F. R. Tennant, *Philosophical Theology*, I, pp. 371–2. He mentions there nine different definitions, but even this enumeration is not exhaustive. See, e.g., D. M. Emmet, *The Nature of Metaphysical Thinking*, p. 16. Tennant recommends avoiding this concept altogether. But this seems artificial and unsatisfactory, for we cannot really exclude it from our minds.

they do justice only to one of these aspects of reality and thus neglect or suppress the other which we are nevertheless bound to consider as real.

We shall start from the second difficulty. We shall not enter into the question of how the concept 'reality' could be defined, but shall try instead to describe these two aspects of reality. We do so in the hope that the description will enable us to use this concept in its common meaning, without running the risks caused by using ambiguous concepts. We hope to prove that this distinction between the two aspects of reality makes any further definition superfluous, because, as it solves many hitherto baffling problems, it makes what we mean by 'reality' sufficiently clear, although it does not provide a comprehensive definition of it.

For the sake of convenience, we shall consider these two aspects as different realities and call them 'external reality' and 'internal reality'. They are, in fact, so different that they seem to justify our considering them as two realities, but we do not imply such a separation. We shall try to show why reality appears to us under two aspects and describe them, and the very description will, we believe, confirm that there is but one indivisible reality, although its two aspects make it impossible for us to grasp it directly.

To indicate, moreover, that we do not assume that whatever exists is created by our thinking, but that there is a reality quite apart from our apprehension of it, a reality which is given to us and which we only transform by thinking, we shall use the term 'primary reality' whenever we want to refer to the reality underlying our apprehension.[1]

## 2. THE NECESSARY DISTINCTION BETWEEN TWO REALITIES

We are able to think because we can see a difference between ourselves and reality. We are part of reality, but a limited part which can

[1] I accept the fundamental theses of Kant as my starting point in this book. I do not doubt that there is a reality outside ourselves and that nevertheless our apprehension of it depends on the laws of our thinking. 'Knowledge is dependent on two conditions: first on the concept through which any object at all is thought of (the category), and secondly on the perception by which it is given.'—'Thoughts without content are empty, perceptions without concepts are blind.' (*Critique of Pure Reason*, pp. 146 and 75 of the original 2nd ed.) I believe Kant to be right when he says that we cannot apprehend anything unless primary reality, the 'thing per se', affects us, but that by our dependence on the laws of thinking and the application of *a priori* concepts we are cut off from any absolute knowledge of it. I further accept Kant's distinction between two completely different kinds of knowledge; my distinction between external and internal reality is roughly similar to that between Pure and Practical Reason. But there are, as will be seen, great differences in the foundation and development of these ideas. In my consideration of external reality I follow at some length Kant's treatment of space, time, and several of his categories (though by no means accepting his lists), but diverge from his application and interpretation of them, and my view of the way we acquire knowledge of internal reality develops along totally dissimilar lines.

be clearly separated from it; although we belong to reality, we can oppose ourselves to it. Only thus does thinking become possible; if we were completely submerged in reality, we could neither look upon it nor translate it into thought. Man's consciousness, the first condition of his thought, develops as he begins to differentiate himself from his surroundings and to see reality as an experience of his own. As soon as he becomes conscious of it, therefore, this reality is divided into two different spheres, and this division is inseparable from our consciousness, because consciousness depends on it.

This fundamental fact explains why there is a single concept of reality and why we yet know, not one, but at least two completely different realities. When we confront reality, we see that we are part of it; we are subject to the laws of nature; we are connected in manifold ways with things, plants and animals, and there are men like us within the reality which we are confronting. Thus we cannot exclude ourselves from it; there is a common basis which requires a unitary concept. But by the very act of confronting it we transform ourselves into another reality; in spite of the unitary concept, therefore, we have to acknowledge two different kinds of reality. We are able to think only when these two realities are clearly opposed to one another.

A mechanical division of reality into two parts of the same nature—that is, a simple distinction within one kind of knowledge—would not be sufficient; we have constantly to set them in opposition. We cannot merely consider man as one among other similar parts of reality, for we must develop activities of our own and use them to get at reality. If we want to think, we must transform ourselves into a centre of a different kind so as to be able to grasp the reality outside ourselves as something which is different from us. Man, it is true, remains part of reality, but his apprehension of it is the result of thinking, experiencing, feeling and willing, of activities, that is, which he has to exercise. He may exercise them intentionally or unintentionally, voluntarily or under some compulsion; they may give him a clear or a dim consciousness of what he is seeking, but in any case something must take place within ourselves which creates a distance and a difference between us and the rest of reality, so that our activities can be directed towards something foreign to them which they can grasp.

We can take our faculty of sight as a symbol of this opposition. We need our eyes in order to see the light, but the light and the eye are completely different. Yet we can only see the light and know that we see it because the light which is in movement meets a different body which is at rest, and because this body is equipped with nerves which produce sensations and inspire thoughts in a way which cannot even be compared with external events.

We shall investigate the nature of this opposition later. First we must make sure that we really cannot rely on a division within the primary reality, but have to create this distinction ourselves. This becomes evident when we try to define the boundaries between these two realities.

We must start to make this distinction from a realization of the difference between man and the other reality, a difference which can be easily recognized. With the development of life some kind of independent existence seems to begin for the single organism, and an increasingly clearer separation coincides with the development of its higher forms. We can discern the development of special organs, of the nerve-system and the brain, which make such an independence possible, and there is no doubt that highly developed animals possess intelligence which works in the same direction. But we can test this development in other beings only with great difficulty; we have to use analogies from our own experience and cannot be sure how far such conclusions are justified. In man, however, we clearly discern processes in his mind which distinguish him from any other reality and make him in certain respects independent of it. The most complete expression of this is his self-consciousness, but even if this is not yet fully developed, we know for certain that he thinks, feels and wills and that thus activities take place in his mind which separate him from the other reality.

Even with this clear differentiation, however, we cannot recognize the difference between the two realities which are created when we confront reality. It is impossible simply to allocate to these two realities two different spheres and to say that what we are going to call 'external reality' is the reality outside man, and 'internal reality' the reality within him. For every impression and every experience can be included in either of the two realities.

If we see a picture, for instance, we see it as a thing outside ourselves. It ought to belong, therefore, to external reality, and we can consider it so, as a thing of a certain size and weight, consisting of a frame, of canvas and of pigments. But this external appearance is usually taken for granted; we shall be more interested in finding out whether the picture is beautiful or not. The impression of beauty, however, although evoked in us by the picture, is a value, belonging to internal reality, and in our judgment the picture is considered, not as a part of external reality, but in its relation to internal reality. It is in fact included in internal reality. Any part of the reality outside man can be seen in the same way under two aspects; when we look at the starry sky, we can do so because we are interested in astronomy, but we can also be overwhelmed by its beauty. The difference between the two realities is not inherent in primary reality, but created by our attitude.

Psychological processes, on the other hand, take place within ourselves and seem to belong, therefore, to internal reality. They do so if we pay attention to the content of the thoughts, to our experience of feeling, and to the purposes behind our actions. But we can also regard psychological processes scientifically, excluding our own participation in them, our personal experience and our intentions, and so consider them in the same way as we consider the fall of a stone. Instead of trying to discover what they are and the meaning they have for us, we try to find in them cause and effect and the natural laws connecting them. Psychology, after all, belongs to the natural sciences. Similarly, we can either consider them as belonging to internal reality and judge them morally, or pay attention only to their practical causes and effects. Once more, the division depends upon the way in which we think.

There are certain phenomena which seem to belong only to one reality, because we can hardly succeed in including them in the other without falsifying them. We are unable, as the failure of astrology shows, to establish a close contact between the stars and ourselves, and there are also inner experiences which cannot be comprehended scientifically. Psychology does not help us to define a moral value; evil remains evil even if we discover its psychological causes. Such extreme cases show that the division between man and the world outside him is the starting point of the opposition of the two realities, but they do not change the situation. On the contrary, they too show that we cannot identify external and internal reality with the spheres outside and inside man, for, to apprehend them at all, we need to think about them in entirely different ways, and this cannot be explained by a mechanical division. We have to be aware, moreover, of both methods to be able to apply either of them correctly and to prevent valuing from intruding into science or science into valuing.

We can never completely separate the two realities from each other, but have to oppose them to one another in every impression and experience. It is this which proves most conclusively that the two realities do not coincide with any of the usual subdivisions of primary reality.

We can, it is true, concentrate entirely on external reality and forget that it is we who are dealing with it, but this suppression of indubitable facts does not alter the position. Even in science we grasp reality with the help of our minds and remain dependent on their nature. So long as we pay no attention to the working of our minds, reality appears to us as a unity, but as soon as this working also is considered, as it must be when we want to understand how we apprehend reality, it becomes the expression of another reality, and the original unity is divided into the two realities.[1] On the other hand, we can also enhance our spiritual

---

[1] 'Laplace swept the heavens with his telescope, and by doing so could find no trace of God, or of a spiritual world. Had he looked at both ends of his telescope, taking into account the activity of the observer as well as his physically interpreted observations, the result would have been different.' J. S. Haldane, *The Philosophical Basis of Biology*, p. 7.

life to such a degree that it seems to lose any connection with the reality represented by our bodies, but even then our thoughts have to be stimulated by something which is happening to our bodies and they cannot avoid remaining dependent on them. Just as the most impersonal knowledge of purely mechanical events cannot become independent of the laws of our thinking, so even the most abstract thinking or the complete self-surrender to mystical experiences cannot make thought independent of our material existence. If we investigate, honestly and without prejudice, how an impression or thought arises, we must find that both realities are involved in the process.

We are not confronted with two different worlds; the whole of reality, according to our attitude, is apprehended as external or as internal reality. Although we start, in the first case, from external impressions, and in the second from ourselves, we do not grasp two separate spheres. Natural laws and moral laws are valid, not in two different worlds, but in one and the same world, and the same reality is the subject of science and religion, of practical experience and of artistic representation, for all of them attempt to deal with the whole of reality.[1] External reality includes man, who is a material thing, an organism, and whose life depends on chemical processes. In internal reality, on the other hand, even the most personal feelings, if we develop and pursue them far enough, will lead us to ask the meaning of the universe. This unity of reality, however, does not alter the fact that we are unable to apprehend it as such; just because we always want to grasp the whole of reality, we must see it in the two ways we have described. The unity of reality only proves that it is our thinking which has to establish the opposition between the two realities.

The participation of both realities in any thought and the fact that both of them must thus be always present to our mind is characteristic of all our thought, whether we are conscious of it or not. We cannot know nature as it is apart from our thinking, nor can we know a realm of the spirit independent of man; the material world is accessible to us only through our minds, and the spiritual world only through our bodies. It is as impossible to grasp reality as a unity as it is to separate the two realities entirely from one another.

We have to investigate, therefore, how the division into the two realities is brought about and how they are opposed to one another.

### 3. EXTERNAL REALITY

The division into external and internal reality is not a primary one, but created by our thinking. In order to apprehend reality, therefore, we must transform it into external and internal reality. This division,

[1] J. Macmurray, *The Structure of Religious Experience*, p. 21.

without being itself conscious, arises simultaneously with our consciousness; if we are to think clearly, we must consciously repeat and develop this process.

Though external reality is the reality outside ourselves, this description must not be interpreted spatially, for it should be applicable to any part of reality whatsoever. We must therefore approach this reality from outside, so as to see it as external to us; it has to be external when compared with our own lives.

If we try, for instance, to grasp a thing as part of external reality, we try to apprehend it 'objectively', as it is in itself quite independent of our reaction to it. We compare different impressions to correct any mistake due to our senses or to our way of thinking; we try to apply measurements of general validity, so that we can measure and weigh it and exclude any personal factor in observations. We subordinate ourselves completely to the object, paying no attention to its meaning or importance for us, nor to the purposes for which we intend to use it; we exclude our feelings as well as our aims. We try only to apply concepts which do not appeal to any inner experiences, so that they can be understood by everybody in exactly the same way.

Similarly, if we try to grasp psychological processes scientifically, we endeavour to discover laws to which we are subordinated. We do not allow our investigation to be influenced by our wishes, judgments and interpretations, but try, on the contrary, to derive these from causes upon which we cannot exert any influence. We make all these processes as far as possible independent of ourselves, by seeing them as compulsions to which we have to submit. The introduction of the concept of the unconscious into psychology is one of the most characteristic features of this method. We assume that the conscious impulses, which we actually know, are based upon the unconscious, which we have to discover or even to assume, for it is thus that our impulses or actions can be regarded as out of our control and considered as the consequence of a necessity which is external to ourselves. We try to transform ourselves into an object which we can look at from outside, and although psychology cannot succeed completely in such an aim, it has been possible by this method to discover laws which govern some of our reactions in the same impersonal way in which external events are governed by natural laws.[1]

Any perfect apprehension of external reality has thus to fulfil the following three conditions, which can be considered as a definition of this kind of reality. External things or events (1) have to be independent of their relation to the person observing them; (2) they have to exist or take place in space and time; (3) they must be describable in terms of

[1] For a fuller explanation of why this method works see J. Macmurray, *The Boundaries of Science*, pp. 227, 236–7.

## EXTERNAL AND INTERNAL REALITY

general validity, so that, if they are correctly described, everybody can recognize them.

If I see a tree, for instance, I know that my seeing it has no influence upon the tree; and only if I succeed in discounting all the particular circumstances of my vision of it do I see it as it actually exists, as a part of external reality. If I have a wrong impression of it, moreover, I can rectify it, because the tree exists in space and time, quite independent of myself. I can measure it and define its component parts. I know, too, that other people see the tree in the same way as I do, and that they will recognize it if I give them a correct description of it.

The same is true of events. The tree grows and loses its leaves in autumn; all such events are independent of my watching them and take place whether or not I notice them. I can verify them, in space and time, with the help of sense-impressions, and other people are able to see them and to describe them in exactly the same way as I do.

The definition remains valid even for events which seem to be of a fundamentally different kind, for the phenomena of sound, for example. Sounds seem more dependent on the observer, because they seem to come into being only if corresponding events take place in our organs, but they are, nevertheless, independent of us. We can be sure, for instance, that a stroke of lightning, in normal circumstances, will be accompanied by thunder, even if nobody happens to hear it. It is for this reason that science can observe sounds as mere motions, without considering our hearing. They seem connected with time alone, but they can only be heard if they cause spatial events in our body, and science has to concentrate upon the motions in space which cause these events; it has discovered motions of the same nature which we are unable to hear. We can also be sure that, if the organs of another person work normally and if neither of us are subject to delusions, this other person will hear the same sounds as we do. It is for this reason that language and music become possible.

Psychological processes, when considered as external reality, are grasped in the same way. Certainly, inner experiences cannot be completely ignored, but the scientist tries to connect them with changes in the body, which take place whether we notice them or not and which can be observed in space and time. He tries, moreover, to discover those inner experiences which are common to all of us, or those reactions which must result in all cases from the corresponding conditions, so that they can be described in terms of general validity and their description understood by everybody, whatever his special individual experiences may be.

In all these cases, however, we are not dealing with an external reality which is unequivocally presented to us, but have to choose between different impressions and thoughts which have been evoked in us by the primary reality; we do not pay attention to all our reactions, but only to some of them. The definition does not define reality as such, but rather the choice we have to make and the direction we have to follow to grasp the reality to which we oppose ourselves. We can achieve, to a high degree, what the definition demands, but we achieve it by concentrating upon those thoughts which fulfil the conditions stated in the definition, and by excluding those which contradict it. We transform the primary reality into external reality by restricting ourselves to a certain aspect of it.

We can describe this transformation best by saying that we set the outward form of reality in opposition to its content, and grasp external reality by concentrating upon the form alone.

These two concepts—form and content—will be used here in the meaning which they acquire when we derive them from our own experience. We can derive them from it, because we apprehend ourselves both from outside and inside.

On the one hand, we know the human body and we are able to look at psychological processes as if they were exclusively subject to an external necessity; we are able to concentrate on the changes in our organism or on the abstract laws connecting our different reactions. If we do so, we grasp the outward form of our being, for we discover only those connections which may belong to very different experiences. They are purely formal, because they indicate the shapes or relationships which different things or events can assume, without being affected by our feelings or by any meaning which they have for us—that is, they do not disclose the nature of this content. We can describe exactly, for instance, the wound which somebody received and the disturbances caused by it in his organism and nerve-system, without knowing in the least what the pain he experiences is like, or what this experience means to him. If we had never experienced pain, we would not even know what pain is, in spite of all such descriptions.

On the other hand, the pain which we suffer ourselves is not a process which develops in a certain way, but is experienced as such; we know what this special pain feels like and what it means to be wounded, and thus we get to know the content of this experience. Similarly, while the knowledge of the movements of the particles in our brain or of psychological laws does not reveal a single actual thought, yet when we think, we know first what we think; we know, not the process of thinking, but our thoughts. We can be interested either in how or in what we think; in the first case we try to grasp the form, in the second the content of thinking.[1]

[1] The position of thinking may seem somewhat ambiguous, for, as it is concerned with external and internal reality, it may concentrate either on the form or on the content. But a confusion only arises if we mix up the consideration of thinking with

## EXTERNAL AND INTERNAL REALITY

It is in this sense alone that we apply these two concepts. They are mostly used in a more superficial way; one says, for instance, that the contents of pea pods are peas. In this investigation we speak of form if we know only the outline of a thing and its external structure, or some such connection as that between cause and effect, which can underlie very different events and have very different meanings; in short, anything which we grasp only from outside and which is not necessarily connected with one special thing or event, but can be applied to many of them. The content, however, is neither the peas in the pod nor the material of which things are made, for even if we know exactly the position of the electrons and their movements, or the chemical elements of which these things consist, we still know only their external structure, without being able to grasp them from inside. We can only apprehend content when we turn our attention to our own lives.

Here the opposition of which we speak immediately becomes clear, for it is quite obvious that our experience discloses a living content which is utterly different from anything material and from any knowledge of the structure of matter or of psychological processes and laws. The restriction of the meaning of the conception of 'content' to this kind of content is founded upon the fact that it is only by our own experience of objects and events that they become more than mere examples of general categories and thus disclose a meaning which we cannot reach in any other way.[1]

We shall have to deal with this content at greater length when we consider internal reality. It is quite clear, however, that we must acknowledge the existence of such a content even if we concentrate our attention on external reality.

Both form and content are already involved in the simplest sense-impressions, for the content is not the thing itself which always remains outside us and which we obviously cannot approach from inside, but the sensations, feelings and reactions which are evoked in us. If we see and feel a piece of iron, for instance, our mind grasps its shape and consistency, but the act of grasping may be easy or difficult, pleasant or painful, and the object beautiful or ugly. We apprehend external reality if we concentrate on shape or consistency, but we are only able to do this if we oppose them to the other elements, so that we can separate the form from the content and grasp the form alone. A shell-splinter

the apprehension of reality. The difference between form and content in the realm of reality becomes clear when we compare the different aspects of reality, the difference between form and content in thinking if we find out whether we grasp the process of thinking or what we think.

[1] This opposition becomes very clear when we consider a work of art. Here we can distinguish between its form and technique on the one hand, and its content, meaning and artistic value on the other. But this example will be considered later, for it implies some more difficult problems.

which hurts us seems larger and heavier than a similar piece of steel lying on the ground in front of us; we can form an accurate picture of it only if we concentrate exclusively on those elements in our sense-impression which convey its form, and exclude everything which, as a content of our own lives, has importance and meaning for us. But we must be aware of the content to grasp the form, for only thus can we prevent ourselves from overrating the size of the piece of iron because of the magnitude of our pain. Otherwise we might even be induced to project our anger into the iron and to ascribe hostile intentions to it. Even if we remain indifferent, we have to be conscious of the possibility of such reactions, so as to be able to exclude them should they arise.

The apprehension of external reality is always brought about, whether or not we are conscious of it, by opposing form to content and by renouncing knowledge of the content. We know a thing only after the sense-impression has caused an activity within ourselves, and this activity is its special content for us; without it no sense-impression would be possible. But it is this activity which we have to eliminate from our apprehension; we have to find out how far it is involved in our impression and to exclude it. It does not matter that the content of the thing itself and of the greater part of external reality remains inaccessible to us and that what we know is quite a different content, namely, that of our lives; the general knowledge of what we have to consider as content enables us to isolate any form as its opposite and to separate the two in any impression. It would be hopeless, in the case of the piece of iron, to try to discern something which we could call 'content' in the sense we have just defined, and yet we grasp its form by opposing it to the content of our reactions.

This opposition determines the character of external reality. If we grasp a thing as a thing, we always know in what form it is presented to us and what happens to it, but even if we know the changes in its structure which these happenings imply, we still do not know whether or not this process has inner aspects for the thing itself. When the shell splinter flies through space to hurt us, we know neither what significance this act has for the piece of steel or for the world nor indeed whether it has such a significance at all. We can discover a meaning only so far as we ourselves are involved, for this is the only way in which a content becomes accessible to us, but we must exclude this content. We must make the same effort if we want to grasp psychological processes scientifically; to recognize general laws, we have to forget what it means to experience pain or happiness or misery as the unique experiences which they are in our own experience. Here it would not be hopeless to try to discover the content, but we must concentrate on the formal elements if we want to treat psychological processes as part of external reality.

## EXTERNAL AND INTERNAL REALITY

This necessary concentration on form must not however mislead us; we must never deny the content altogether, though nowadays we often tend to. In contrast to previous ages when men endowed inanimate objects with a life or soul of their own, we endeavour to explain our very lives by purely material processes. Even to those who do not believe in such explanations, this attempt may seem to do justice to external reality and to endanger only the understanding of our own experience. Yet even this is not correct; any unprejudiced examination of external reality, too, shows quite clearly that to deny the content is fundamentally wrong. We cannot fully understand anything without opposing the form to the content; if we deny the existence of content in our own lives, we shall notice the lack of content even when we consider external reality alone. Even in the realm of the natural sciences we can see that this content is absolutely indispensable.

The natural sciences teach us systematically to exclude all feelings, all values and aims, and thus to renounce any knowledge of a content contributed by our own lives. Their immense success proves that the more we succeed in doing this, the better is our grasp of external reality, and this can lead us to overrate their methods and to think it impossible to grasp reality in any other way. This restriction, necessary for natural sciences, is no longer felt as a renunciation, but as a way of cutting out unnecessary thought and sentiments. Do not the explanations given by the natural sciences disclose a far more definite content within external reality itself? Although the knowledge of such a content, according to our definition, is purely formal, it makes it seem superfluous to pay any attention to internal reality at all. Yet such a conclusion is plainly superficial.

An explanation could be thought of as disclosing the content if something which cannot be understood was derived from something which we know and understand completely. We could say, for instance, that we knew the content of an event, if an effect which, as such, remains inexplicable were explained by a cause which we knew in all its details and aspects. We do not really know, however, the forces which explain the connection between external causes and effects, even if we call them electricity or gravity or by some more modern names; all these are mere names for something unknown. Nor do we know the nature of light, although it plays an increasingly important part in all physical explanations. At present we can only explain it by the two contradictory assumptions that it is a wave motion in which no matter is involved, and that it consists of material particles moving in a straight line across space. Nor do the explanations of the constitution of objects give us real knowledge; we divide molecules into atoms and atoms into electrons and shall probably continue this division still further; and then we gather them together again in quanta and fields, because, although we are able to restrict and limit the sphere of the unknown, we are unable to eliminate it altogether.

The process of explanation is, in fact, just the opposite of what we usually assume it to be. We do not explain the unknown by the known but, on the contrary, derive something we know from something unknown. We explain the objects and events which we observe in terms of forces and particles, and in the end we have to attribute a mysterious and arbitrary behaviour to the electrons, in order to account for their inexplicability.

Nevertheless, these explanations help us to give an account of external reality. Yet they help us, not by disclosing the content, but by pushing the unknown content further back, so that we can extend our knowledge of the form. They make external reality more and more external and thus we can describe it better and better. The separation of man from external reality is brought about gradually; we are inclined at first to endow it with a content and to judge it by analogies derived from our lives; we have to learn that we can grasp it more reliably when we give up any such attempt. We have learned, for instance, that we can protect ourselves against a stroke of lightning if we explain it, not as an instrument of gods or demons, but as a purely mechanical force. The real purpose of these explanations is to enable us to accept the form as such and to concentrate more and more on it, without being disturbed by the content; they push the content so far into the background that we can deal with external reality adequately although its content remains unknown. They help us, because they enable us to include an unknown content in our theories.

The correctness of this is shown by the fact that the progress of science is immediately endangered when we accept the concepts used in such explanations as the final content, that is as part of the reality which we really know. The sciences develop by destroying one theory after another; their development is not endangered if theories are treated as mere assumptions, but it is if these theories are prematurely accepted as final explanations. If, instead of endowing things with life, we believe that some of these forces or particles are the only content accessible, theories can neither be adjusted to fit in with new discoveries nor replaced. It is no accident that those sciences which are less exact because they cannot completely ignore the content, such as biology and psychology, are the most dogmatic.[1] The right use of such explanations,

[1] It should not be overlooked that the consequences of the two opposite attempts —to endow matter with life and to reduce life to material processes—are very similar to each other. If nature is considered as being alive in a similar way to human beings, the greater part of it must be regarded as evil and hostile. Any consistent materialistic explanation of the world, such as Marxism, has also to see part of the driving forces as evil, but as it does not want to endow matter with life, it has to declare the representatives of one class of people to be wicked and to transform this wickedness into

however, is only possible if we remain conscious of the real content, so that we neither deny it altogether nor look for it in the wrong place; for only thus shall we be able to accept external reality as mere form and therefore reliably without being forced to distort it by futile attempts to find some kind of content there.

Scientific explanations, it is true, are proved to be correct when the results of the theory agree with the observed events which were to be explained. It is for this reason that the concepts which in the explanation take the place of the unknown content seem to be the real content. But this need not disturb us, for, although science seems to start from its hypothesis and to lead up to the event, it starts in fact from the event, and the explanation is only accepted if it is successful in leading back to the event. We have said already that we explain the well known by the unknown. The fall of a stone, for instance, remains the same whether we explain it by the theory of gravitation or that of relativity, and all the theories agree with the actual fall; the theory therefore is clearly not the presupposition of, but an addition to, our apprehension of reality. Nor need it disturb us that theories make correct predictions possible, for the explanation of one event naturally enables us to explain similar events, even if we did not know them before. Theories can certainly also lead to technical inventions and thus create real objects, but these things become, in their turn, independent of the theory which was accepted at the time of their invention. Electric light is not affected by whether we believe that light consists purely of waves, or purely of particles, or of both. It does not even matter whether such explanations work with concepts derived from reality or with mere assumptions or constructions. Nobody claims that a model of the order of atoms in an organic molecule gives a true picture of that molecule, but it serves its purpose as satisfactorily as any other explanation.[1] The fact that an explanation proves correct does not mean, therefore, that it discloses a hidden content, but on the contrary that we grasp the form; if it did disclose the content, the explanation of the same event could not be changed, nor could it be based on assumptions.

Thus even scientific explanations demonstrate once more that we cannot consider the two realities as separate spheres which are simply presented to us as such. The necessity of a content can be seen in external reality too, although such a content is accessible only in internal reality, because both realities are created by our attitude to them and by

a natural law. Capitalist theory, less consistent, requires the belief in the struggle for the survival of the fittest, which is bound to be cruel, and forcibly identifies it with the good. In all such cases personal intentions are attributed to impersonal forces, and the boundaries between external and internal reality are blurred in an unwarranted and confusing way.

[1] See J. Macmurray, ibid.

a special selection among the different elements of our apprehension and experience. We have first to establish the opposition between form and content, for only then are we able to concentrate upon the form alone and to grasp external reality as such.

## 4. INTERNAL REALITY

The difference between external and internal reality can perhaps be better understood if we think of the following example.

Physicists apply to an increasing extent the calculus of probability, and in this way they achieve reliable results, although this kind of calculation claims only approximate, and not absolute, exactitude. The same kind of calculation is applied by insurance companies, and their calculations of accidents and deaths, too, is so reliable that the premium payments they fix produce the profits they expect. Certainly, the results of the insurance companies are not so exact as those of the physicists, but this is only because men are not so numerous as electrons; the calculations of the insurance companies would reach the same degree of exactitude if they could investigate the same number of events. Apart from that, their calculations are sometimes upset by catastrophes, but so are those of the physicists; neither of them can predict the consequences of, say, earthquakes. In principle, the two calculations are of the same nature and of equal validity.

Nevertheless, we are bound to consider them as very different. We are able to accept the physicists' calculations as a satisfactory representation of reality, but we are quite unwilling to accept those of the insurance companies as giving a significant view of reality. Although they are undoubtedly an extraordinarily exact prediction of the future, we cannot consider them as prophecy. They are unable either to predict who will die, or to make any statement about the infinite variety of the causes and circumstances of these deaths, and, as we are men, the calculation would only appear to us to represent reality if it told us these facts. In what we normally think of as inanimate nature we can be satisfied by purely formal numbers, but not where human lives are concerned, for we know that there the content should be accessible to us. We know that every single death finishes a human life with its varying fortunes in a different way, so that this reality is only grasped, therefore, when we know who dies, how he dies, and what effect his death has on other men.

On the one hand, this example shows how it is possible for us to grasp reality by restricting ourselves to the form. If such a purely external approach makes it possible to use even as complicated a process as men's deaths as a basis for accurate calculations, then it must be possible for such a formal simplification to do complete justice to

## EXTERNAL AND INTERNAL REALITY

reality wherever the content remains unknown, or wherever we are not interested in it. The only qualification is this condition that the content must be one that can be ignored. If we knew so little of man that his life and death appeared to us as the existence and the dissolution of atoms so much like one another that they could not be distinguished, then we would be convinced that here too this kind of calculation, in so far as its results are correct, does complete justice to reality.

On the other hand, it becomes clear that internal reality cannot be grasped in this way. As human lives have a content which makes them fundamentally different from external reality, we must apply to them a method which can take this content into account. The calculations of the insurance companies produce the expected profits; but even a person who seems exclusively interested in such dividends will refuse to think that these predictions are satisfactory as soon as he thinks of himself, of his family and of his friends.

Every object or event which we experience ourselves can be seen from two points of view. We can apprehend it as external reality, but this apprehension does not do justice to its other aspect, to internal reality, and therefore such an apprehension is bound to appear to us to be insufficient. If a falling stone hurts us, we can try to find out its weight, shape and consistency, or the laws governing its fall, yet what we experience is not these factors, but pain. We can also consider the pain as a psychological process which follows laws independent of us, but thus we once more fail to grasp the pain we experience. We can predict, not only that a stone falls if it is robbed of its support, but also that a man will be killed if he falls from a tower of sufficient height, but the latter statement will appear to us to be self-evident rather than important. The investigation of the laws of gravity, important as it is for our knowledge of external reality, is meaningless so far as internal reality is concerned. When we are stunned, so that the normal reactions of our body and consciousness cease, the natural laws alone are concerned with our fall; but normally, when we are not stunned, we do not enquire, while we fall or after we have fallen, what the natural laws of gravity are.

We can, of course, be interested also in the external course of the event, and we most probably shall be if we are hurt and if this experience influences our life in a surprising and unexpected manner. But even then we are not interested in natural laws; we ask rather why the stone had to fall just when we passed and not a second earlier or later; we ask why we alone had this accident while others passed by safely. We ask what this event means for us; we try to discover the connection between the external event and ourselves; we try to understand our fate. It is not the form of the event that matters but its content and value which have to be discovered. We may try once more to look for the content in

## EXTERNAL AND INTERNAL REALITY

external reality; but it remains impossible even in such a case to find the content here, and as this time its existence cannot be excluded, this attempt does not lead us to think about natural laws, but about problems of faith. If we want to cope with these, however, we have to apply quite a different way of thinking, one which can do justice to our inner experiences.

That we need a different way of thinking to grasp internal reality can be seen most clearly when we try to apply to it the definition which we gave of external reality. The main means by which we grasp internal reality are, as we shall see later, feelings, values and aims. All of them are undoubtedly real, we could not live without any of them; the mere fact that we live means that we feel and that we are forced to act, and we cannot act without applying values and striving for certain aims.[1] Yet feelings, values and aims flatly contradict each of the three conditions.[2]

If we want to know what we actually feel, and not merely the abstract process of feeling as it is described by psychology, we cannot even think of feelings as being 'independent of the observer', for they exist and become intelligible only within our inner experience, and they express, if they are due to external objects, a special relationship between the object and the observer. External objects, it is true, play an important part in our feelings as well, which, although they belong to our inner experience, need at the same time an object in order to become intelligible. We enjoy something or suffer something; we love a person or a thing. We shall see that, to know our feelings, we must always know their direction or their cause.[3] Certainly, there are vague feelings without any conceivable connection with any object or cause, and we can revel in such feelings, but we do not clearly understand them, and sooner or later they will awaken in us the desire to find a way out of this state of vagueness which cannot be permanently satisfying. Every naturally developing feeling forces upon us the wish for clarity and thus refers us to an object. Yet to understand our feelings, we have to give up any attempt to subordinate ourselves to external reality; we must, on the contrary, impose upon external reality the relationship between it and ourselves. We cannot regard the object as independent of us, but must concentrate on its relation to us.

The first statement, therefore, cannot be applied to internal reality, and neither can the second. It is true that feelings take place in time and, owing to their connection with our body, in space, but these facts do not help us to understand the values to which clear feelings lead.

Let us return, for instance, to an example already used: our looking at a picture.[4] If we consider a painting of a tree, the picture and

---

[1] See H. H. Farmer, *Towards Belief in God*, pp. 136, 139–40, and *Experience of God*, pp. 119–20.
[2] See pp. 25–6.   [3] See pp. 101–2.   [4] See p. 22.

its subject can easily be described as external objects. But we have said that the description of the picture as a material object is entirely irrelevant, and so is that of the tree; everything depends on how it is painted. We want to know whether the picture of the tree is beautiful or ugly or, in an æsthetic sense, good or bad. This once more invalidates the first statement, for beauty depends on the person who experiences it. The beholder can no longer be neglected or eliminated, for this special quality of the picture becomes accessible only if it awakens certain feelings in him. Beauty must be established by a judgment, and it can only be thus established when the picture is regarded as causing inner experiences. There is no such thing as beauty which exists somewhere in space and time, waiting for simple apprehension; for in order to come into being it presupposes the activity of the human mind. Thus, however, we cannot apply the second statement either. Space and time may have a secondary or accidental importance; spatial elements play their part in painting or sculpture, temporal elements in poetry and music, but neither can help us to find out what beauty is. It lies beyond their sphere, for the same elements, in different works, can be beautiful or ugly. We need other concepts than these if we are to describe beauty.

Nevertheless, in spite of these deviations from external reality, beauty is a real quality of the picture. We have to take into account the feelings of the beholder, but we cannot decide from his reactions alone whether it is good or bad, nor can we do so arbitrarily; it remains good even if we wrongly consider it to be bad. It is true that our conception of beauty has nowadays become so vague that we are inclined to assert that beauty is purely a matter of individual taste, but, though taste plays its part and leaves room for differences of judgment, it is quite impossible to accept this statement as a fundamental principle. If someone denies that Shakespeare's verse is beautiful, we do not believe merely that his taste is different, but that he has bad taste or that he does not understand poetry. Nor do we accept individual statements about goodness; if someone tells us that cruelty is good, we believe that he is wrong. Values, therefore, although they contradict the definition of external reality, are nevertheless real, but they belong to internal reality whose apprehension requires a different way of thinking.

The difference between the two realities can be seen best if we try to apply the third statement. If I am convinced that a picture is beautiful or a deed good, I claim general validity for my judgment, yet this, although we are using the same term, is not the kind of general validity asked for by the definition, but directly contradicts it.

If I am convinced that a picture is beautiful, I shall also be convinced that I am right, even if I am the only person to believe it, and even if I am unable to make anyone else discover the beauty which I clearly perceive. A correct description of beauty which makes all people see it cannot be given; it is possible for me to be the only person who discovers the beauty of the picture. Nevertheless, my conviction may be correct; many a great artist, even the old Rembrandt, was considered a bad artist by his contemporaries, but history has confirmed the judgment of those few who seemed wrong because they stood alone. My judgment can be of general validity, although it contradicts the general opinion, and although I am unable to describe beauty so that everybody recognizes it. General validity, in such a case, does not imply that everybody must come to the same conclusion. The same applies to goodness. Kant says that even if there had never been a sincere friend, yet pure sincerity in friendship would be required of every man.[1] But I shall be right only if I have the right inner experiences and if my feelings and thoughts correspond to reality. My feelings may be quite genuine and yet be wrong; neither their existence nor their intensity are a guarantee that my response to the qualities of the picture has been adequate or correct. We must establish the right relationship, and once again we need a different way of thinking to do so; we must be able to grasp internal reality.

The third statement, however, can also be completely contradicted. The process of valuing, it is true, always tends to drive us towards using some general terms. But my personal situation, my feelings, my difficulties are in many respects entirely my own; no individual is ever exactly like another. I am forced, therefore, to solve my problems in my own way, even if I am guided by values of general validity. When striving, for instance, for the common good, I still have to choose my particular contribution.

Even the sciences, if we look at them as human activities, prove that internal reality contradicts all three statements. No science would have come into being without personal intentions, and these presuppose feelings, values and aims. It is true that we must exclude all of them from the processes of science, yet it owes its existence to them. All our activities, including science, exist because they serve certain aims, and it is because certain scientific aims appeal most to the feelings of the scientist and because he values them most highly that he devotes his life to them. It may be that he has no special aim, but merely wishes to find out certain facts, but he will do so because knowledge and truth are his aims and are of the highest value to him. In this case, whether or not he is conscious of it, his aim is an absolute value, a value, that is, which is called absolute because it cannot be defined in external terms at all.[2]

If we want to find terms in which to describe this internal reality,

[1] *Fundamental Principles of the Metaphysics of Ethics*, translated by T. K. Abbott, 3rd ed., pp. 24–5.—See also J. Oman, *The Natural and the Supernatural*, p. 312.
[2] See J. Macmurray, *The Boundaries of Science*, pp. 73–4.

## EXTERNAL AND INTERNAL REALITY

we have first to realize again that we cannot rely on any mechanical division of reality into two parts, but have to establish internal reality, too, by choosing between different impressions and experiences, leaving out some and stressing others. The choice which we have to make can once more be stated best by opposing form and content; while we had to restrict ourselves to the form to apprehend external reality, we must concentrate on the content if we want to know internal reality. We no longer neglect the content for the sake of the form, but, on the contrary, use the form to express the content and to make it intelligible.

All internal reality is characterized by the fact that the content is experienced first. In our own lives—which, as we have shown, are the necessary starting point for the consideration of this reality—we can see this on three different levels.

First, our lives are never really empty. Even in moments which seem completely void we remain dimly conscious of our faculties and of their activities. Some fleeting thoughts which we neither intended nor can follow to their conclusions flash through our minds. Sensations and feelings appear and disappear before we are able to grasp them. Instincts and intentions press upon us, without leading to any action. Even when we sleep, the presence of these faculties makes itself felt in dreams. The smallest impulses suffice to bring about a vague stirring of thinking, feeling and willing, and the mere fact of living is normally sufficient to provide these impulses.

Secondly, when these faculties find a clearer expression, we do not at first know whether we grasp reality correctly nor whether we are thinking the right thoughts; but we do know that we think. We do not know whether or not our sensations and feelings correspond to their object or cause, but we do feel. Nor do we know whether we direct our wills towards a possible or an impossible aim, but we do know that we want something. The external or psychological description of these processes presupposes their artificial separation from ourselves, making an additional and conscious effort necessary. Only the content of all these activities is immediately experienced.

Thirdly, if we experience such a content, we need not make sure, as we do with external reality, that we really are grasping something. We know that the experience is undoubtedly present and real because of the immediacy of the content. Afterwards, we can try to find out whether we translated this content correctly into thought, and whether our feelings really correspond to their causes, but the experience as such is real in itself. In external reality, we have to find out if what we apprehend exists, but our apprehension, as part of internal reality, exists in any case, whether or not it really corresponds to external reality. If I feel pain, I do feel it, even if there is no reason for feeling it. We may find out that we were mistaken when we were frightened by some delusion, but this does not alter the fact that we were frightened.[1]

In spite of this immediate certainty with which we experience the content, however, we have to give it an external form, for only thus can we apprehend it distinctly and establish a reliable correspondence between our inner experiences and the reality they refer to. Our faculties are at first quite formless and vague; they cannot be recognized at all before they have been exercised; their content becomes accessible, clear and definite only by their being directed to, or determined by, a concrete object which is external to ourselves. Everything which takes place within us becomes a distinct experience by our finding an appropriate external expression for it.

We cannot think without thinking about some object or event; even if we want to think clearly of internal reality, we must either connect it with an object which is separated from us or partially transform it into external reality. We do not understand 'the good', for instance, without knowing a good person or some action which is good; nor can we think of love without knowing love between persons, or a person whom we love or who loves us. We have mentioned already that feelings, too, need an object. Abstractions can replace objects or events, but they are derived from them, and they frequently become dangerous because, owing to this need for an object, we are inclined to consider them as real things. Nor can we describe feelings without using some comparison with external events; if we have lost a person whom we love and if we want to describe our pain, we shall have to say something like 'it is heart-breaking'. Similarly, we have by nature a strong or a weak will, or our will may be strong in one respect and weak in another, but we shall not know which unless we actually try to do something.

As we are forced to identify the form with external reality, the search for the right form of internal reality means that we have to join external elements to it. In the sphere of external reality, we need explanations because we have to add to it an unknown content; in internal reality we need the external form to express the content, because it has itself no such form, and without form the content would remain vague. It is true that this adding of a form should not be overemphasized; as soon as we have ascertained the external elements, we must not concentrate our attention on them, but rather accept them as a way of expressing our thoughts or our feelings. The description of our pain by an external simile does not serve to describe the external event, but to express the feeling. We can grasp the content of such experiences only with the help of form, but it is the content and not the form which matters; the form

---

[1] Owing to our ignorance of feeling, it may sound strange that it can be correct or incorrect. But we do—or do not—feel in terms of the object. See J. Macmurray, *Reason and Emotion*, p. 25, and *The Boundaries of Science*, pp. 201-2.

## EXTERNAL AND INTERNAL REALITY

must serve the content and make it intelligible. We do not grasp external reality as such, but in its relation to ourselves. Yet all this does not free us from the necessity of apprehending external reality and from joining it to internal reality; we must see the tree as beautiful, but we must see the tree.

Internal reality thus proves once more that the two realities cannot be completely severed from one another. They are not different sections of reality which we have simply to accept, but they have to be separated by our opposing them one to another and by our apprehending them in quite different ways. They are created by our two different attitudes towards reality.

## Chapter III

## THE MAIN CHARACTERISTICS OF THE TWO REALITIES

### 1. THE PARTICULAR NATURE OF INTERNAL REALITY

BEFORE considering the laws of thinking in which the division into two realities finds its expression, we have still to describe internal reality in greater detail. A long tradition has forced us to concentrate on external reality, while the knowledge of internal reality is almost lost. It seems necessary, therefore, to elaborate the opposition between the two realities further, so that it becomes quite clear what we mean when we talk of internal reality.

When we are observing external reality, we have to try to eliminate all the personal peculiarities of our observations and to base our knowledge on those elements which can always be apprehended in the same way; our apprehension of this reality is only reliable if our observations can be repeated without the slightest alteration. External reality, therefore, appears to us as static and fixed; external events, even, are static in so far as we always presuppose that they follow laws which never change.

But it is impossible to exclude ourselves from internal reality; we must, on the contrary, establish a relationship between the objects and ourselves and concentrate on this relationship and on our own activities. In order to make internal reality accessible, we have to consider the activity of our minds and our influence upon the world, and as this internal reality is thus dependent on our actions, it becomes real to us only so far as we make it real. It cannot appear to us, therefore, as being static and fixed; it must always be experienced as something new. Even inner experiences which we have had before, or which we expected, have to be assimilated by means of renewed activity; even those contents which we believe we know have to be experienced in some new way, so that they can give rise to a new activity within us. Exact repetition, in this case, is not a help but a hindrance; if one of our reactions is repeated too often, our activities become purely mechanical; they no longer disclose internal reality, but make us unable to experience it.

It does not follow from this difference that both elements are not present in each of the two realities; but a different element determines the character of each. Our knowledge of external reality is dependent on ever changing theories and we are aware of incessant changes, but each theory must try to discover what remains constant in all these changes.[1] On the other hand, our knowledge of some elements of internal reality is far more firmly established than any natural law we know. The ten commandments, for instance, pronounced thousands of year ago, or the Sermon on the Mount, are in essence still valid, while their contemporary world has completely disappeared and scientific theories and methods have changed again and again. But we cannot simply rely on this stability, important as it is, if we want to grasp internal reality; we can only rightly obey the ten commandments if we constantly experience and interpret them anew.[2]

It is possible, of course, to attain greater security in feeling and valuation and in the setting up of one's aims; we can grow mature and learn by repeated experiences how to give expression to our inner knowledge by certain rules and laws, and thus how gradually to grasp the content better and more comprehensively. There are means of translating our inner knowledge into thought, and we shall look very thoroughly for all such opportunities, for it is the main purpose of this investigation to find definite ways in which we can reliably grasp internal reality. But all these possibilities do not alter the fundamental fact that the results thus achieved are bound to become meaningless and to cut us off from internal reality, unless they lead us from one new experience to the next. To make this reality real, we must constantly renew our experience of it. Previous experiences are fully remembered and further developed only at the moment of a similar new experience, and they become fruitful only by such a renewal. Even when experiences seem merely to be repeated, they must be transformed into something new; thanks to the previous experience the new one can become more fruitful, but our knowledge as such does not remain fruitful; it must be made fruitful by further activity. If the renewal does not take place, the repetition only deadens our former knowledge or ability.

[1] This remains true in modern physics, too, for though it has abandoned the belief in an unchanging causality, the theory of relativity is based on the assumption that the speed of light is constant, and the quantum theory on the discovery that energy can only exist in multiples of a fixed minimum quantum.

[2] I think it is because of this that we so frequently overlook the stability of the moral world. We believe in scientific results as if they were unchangeable and are inclined to regard moral laws as dependent on circumstances or even on fashion. We overlook the fact that the bulk of unchangeable knowledge in morality, common to all ages, religions and nations, is far greater than that in science.

## THE MAIN CHARACTERISTICS OF THE TWO REALITIES

The necessity of making internal reality real does not imply, however, that it is created by us; it has as independent an existence as external reality. We apprehend external reality by separating it from us as far as possible, and we grasp internal reality by connecting it closely with our reactions and activities. But this is only a difference in method, and the latter is neither less reliable, nor 'subjective' in that usual sense which indicates doubtful knowledge based on individual bias.[1] If we apprehend the content correctly, we soon discover that we grasp something which is independent of us, for our apprehension proves correct only if it is in accordance, not with our desires and purposes, but with the true nature of the content. In making the content real for ourselves, we do not create it, but make it accessible; it confronts us; we recognize that it exists quite independently of ourselves, even though we must pay attention to our most personal reactions to disclose it. The division of reality alone is our own creation, but as soon as we apply the two different ways of thinking which thus become possible and necessary, we grasp in both cases, despite the differences in method, an aspect of primary reality.

That the content has an existence independent of ourselves can be seen clearly if we consider the relationship between our activities and their aims. So far we have paid less attention to aims than to feelings and values; but although these usually determine our choice of aims, it is the aim which is most important for what we actually do. We need activities to disclose the content, and it is the aims which give rise to and direct our conscious activities. We frequently talk of aimless activities, but this usually means that they serve an aim which we do not consider important or of which we do not approve; completely aimless activities are rare and almost always an expression of an abnormal or desperate state of mind.[2]

Aims can either be imposed upon us or they can be chosen by ourselves. If they are our own choice, we ought to be satisfied when we achieve what we want, and disappointed when we fail. We can never predict, however, what an effect it will have on us if we reach, or fail to reach, our goal. The independence of internal reality is shown by the fact that it need not conform to our expectations at all and that we can yet do nothing but accept it as it presents itself to us. It is because of this independence that we so often experience painful disappointments when we achieve what we intended. We have exerted all our strength and put

---

[1] For this rehabilitation of the word 'subjective' cf. also the use made of it by Kierkegaard.

[2] People who sit in an office or work in a factory and do not like it probably talk of their aimless activity. But they want to earn their living, and so the office or factory serves some purpose. Even if we play a game of cards it is because we want pleasure, or at least to kill time. If we are very nervous, we may do something without knowing what we are doing; yet this is not normal activity, but an abnormal state of mind.

ourselves to exhausting trouble in order to reach the aim; we have pinned all our hopes on it; and yet, as we reach it, we meet a reality which destroys all our hopes. If we could alter this reality arbitrarily, according to our wishes, such disappointments would be impossible, but internal reality has to be accepted as it is.

We can strive, for instance, for external success, for money or fame. We may be extremely successful—and yet, how poor is the result for which we struggled with such expectations! It seems hardly possible to remain satisfied for long with such an aim, except by coming to take it for granted. Even the great industrialists or conquerors are driven restlessly onwards from one aim to the next, from one success to another. This shows that, as soon as they have reached their goal, they are suddenly forced to recognize that they have chosen an unsatisfactory aim; their activity as such was bound to make internal reality accessible, and they are eventually confronted with the fact that their aim does not do justice to this reality. Usually they are so completely absorbed in external reality that they cannot realize what has happened; they grow restless and go on trying to overcome their dissatisfaction by replacing their previous aims by others of the same kind which, surpassing the former in magnitude or difficulty, seem to promise better results and drive them once more in the wrong direction. They could only find satisfaction if they gave up their original intentions and used their success for different purposes, but then, too, the result would differ from their expectations. The independent existence of the content makes itself felt; the aim, once reached, has a different meaning from that of the aim striven for; if we do not want to recognize what we really experience, we have to pay the price for not doing so.

Our surprising experiences, however, need not end there; the independence of the content can make itself felt in another way too. The pain and the suffering which we thus undergo, and which seem bound to depress or even to destroy us, need not have this effect, but can become fruitful experiences; they can disclose to us new aspects of internal reality and thus give us quite unexpected peace of mind. We may fail to make our fortune, for instance, and as a result discover pleasures which our struggle concealed from us; we may fail to attain a position of power and thus discover good qualities in other people which power could never call out. Our failure does not have the effects which we feared because the content, owing to its being independent of our will, has a meaning of its own; it can overcome our sufferings by showing us their meaning. If we no longer defend ourselves against our inner experiences, but accept them as they really are, neither the disappointing success nor the painful failure need necessarily break us; on the contrary, they can inspire us by opening up to us further aspects of internal reality.

## THE MAIN CHARACTERISTICS OF THE TWO REALITIES

All this does not happen only when we set ourselves external aims. We can naturally also strive for aims which are chosen according to our knowledge of internal reality; we can aim, for instance, at a good deed. This we may achieve; yet we shall probably have to recognize that it has not done justice to internal reality, either because we have to confess, in face of the new experience of this reality, that we did not do the deed for the sake of the good but to serve hidden egoistic motives, or because our previous conception of internal reality now appears inadequate and has to be corrected. If we are completely satisfied with a good deed and proud of it, we can almost safely assume that we are denying our real inner experience and that we have not grasped the content. On the other hand, the failure which we feared need not be disappointing; it can serve the good better, lead to important new experiences, and thus be more satisfying than the success which we desired. But it can only become fruitful if we do not cling to our preconceptions.

We can never predict how the results of our activities will affect us; as soon as internal reality has become accessible, we are confronted with an independent reality which forces itself upon us, even against our will, and we can only cope with it if we acknowledge what we really experience.

This shows, and is due to, another important difference between the two realities—that between external and internal certainty. We can never, with the help of thinking alone, achieve complete certainty; what we gain is relative certainty in external reality and an incomplete absolute certainty in internal reality.

In external reality we aim at absolute certainty without being able to achieve it. We approach it gradually, by accumulating results and testing them again and again, but any certainty we may gain still remains open to further tests and corrections. We have seen that we must not even try to base our knowledge here upon any knowledge of the content; on the contrary, we must restrict ourselves to the form and eliminate the content as far as possible. We know how things are, but never what they are; we have to take into account an unknown content. To achieve any certainty at all, we must remain satisfied with the form alone; as we only know how to test our apprehension and our discoveries by means of our formal knowledge, we have to restrict ourselves to this sphere if we want to be able to test them. Yet whatever exists is determined by the content; our knowledge, therefore, can never be absolute. We remain dependent on further discoveries.

Internal reality forces itself upon us, even despite our intentions and preconceptions and aims. It is true that we constantly need new, and thus ever changing, experiences, but these changes only make us recognize, whenever we meet it, a reality which can no longer be changed. Then our certainty is absolute; neither our previous experiences nor the contradicting opinions of other people can shake it.[1] But we have to find the appropriate form to give expression to it, and as we do not find forms in internal reality, we have to use those forms which we have grasped in a different way in external reality. This is no obstacle; in the same way as the knowledge of the content of our lives was sufficient to isolate any form, these forms, even if originally foreign to the content, suffice to make it intelligible. But, to make up for their fundamental inadequacy, it is necessary constantly to apply them anew. As none of these forms is the necessary and complete form of the content, but only a means of enabling us to recognize it, we cannot find the final expression of the content, but must decide in each single case whether the form has really been completely filled by the content, so that each of the formal elements refers to it and makes it intelligible. If, for instance, we accept a religious teaching as a final embodiment of the content, we still have to make sure whether, in each particular case, we are filling the traditional forms with life or merely using them mechanically, thus depriving them of their meaning. If we apply the form correctly, we experience the content with absolute certainty, but it is only through such an immediate experience that we can decide whether or not the form has fulfilled its function. We remain unable, therefore, to transform our certainty into a comprehensive rational system of thought.

This difference between the two possibilities of gaining certainty corresponds exactly to the division into two realities. The content leads us to understand how the form is created and what it embodies, and the form enables us to grasp the content. If we were able to apprehend both simultaneously, our knowledge of external events would be absolute, because the knowledge of the content would give it an absolute foundation, and we could also grasp the content securely, because we could recognize the unique form which represents its final embodiment. By the division of reality we are cut off from such complete knowledge, for we must concentrate either on the form or on the content. Our certainty, therefore, is based either upon the form which cannot be fully understood, or upon an experience which is absolute, but which cannot definitely be embodied in any form. In external reality our knowledge of the form, not rooted in the content, remains purely formal and fits many different contents without disclosing them. In internal reality the content, whose form is never definitely grasped, has always to be experienced anew.

We are inclined to think that the certainty of our knowledge of external reality is greater than that of internal reality, because we can predict external events. We know that if we drop a stone it will fall, and the natural sciences have enormously enlarged the sphere of such reliable predictions. But we never know with certainty how we shall react to changed circumstances. The possibility and importance of predic-

[1] See pp. 36–7.

## THE MAIN CHARACTERISTICS OF THE TWO REALITIES

tions, however, make the difference between these two kinds of certainty still more clear.

To predict events in external reality, apart from the most common ones, is rather difficult and requires thorough investigation, because the sphere of our certainty is restricted; we have gradually to enlarge it and to make sure, at the same time, that we remain within its boundaries. But prediction is of the greatest importance; the unchangeable laws which we discover stand the test only so far as they enable us to predict; only thus far have we succeeded in penetrating to the static and fixed nature of this reality. We must endeavour, therefore, to make such predictions possible. But as the content is the determining factor, unforeseen events outside the sphere of our certainty may take place, and we can never exclude the possibility that they may require fundamental changes in our system of knowledge.

Prediction is in some ways very much easier in internal reality. As we experience absolute certainty, we know, too, that some aspects of the same content must be present in any new experience and that some elements of our previous experience will recur. We can be sure that our absolute certainty cannot be completely overthrown by unforeseen events, though we may be forced to develop or to re-interpret it. We have mentioned that our moral knowledge is far more static than our scientific knowledge. But this static element does not determine the character of internal reality, and for this reason the possibility of prediction is of no great importance here. Internal reality becomes real only so far as we experience it in a new way; whatever we can predict is known to us already; it cannot, therefore, directly serve to make this reality real. Even if we experience what we have predicted, the experience itself must in some important ways differ from our expectations; it will make the content accessible only if it becomes a new and unforeseen experience.

This peculiar nature of inner certainty, however, raises a further problem. We all know that we can succumb to wrong or even fatal beliefs and yet be firmly convinced that they are right; they can appear to us as absolutely certain. But the immediate experience of absolute certainty would become meaningless if we were unable to distinguish between what is correct and what is incorrect, between what is right and what is wrong in this sphere. This problem will occupy us later. First, to make the different nature of the two realities quite clear, we shall consider the two most important conditions of their apprehension which we are by now able to state.

### 2. THE NEED FOR A COMPLETE SEPARATION

The first main condition of apprehending the two realities clearly is that of separating them completely from each other. This condition is in fact so important that clear thinking is made easier if we talk of two realities, even though we consider them only as the two aspects of one primary reality, for we have to transform these two aspects into independent entities and to make them complete in themselves.

We can see now why this condition, which we have had to stress again and again, is so essential. The difference between the two realities is not the only reason for it; indeed they can both be described by the same set of terms. But it is just because we have to use the same concepts to describe both realities, so that several of the concepts we have used recur in the description of both, that we must separate them completely. For the same concepts have a different meaning in each of the two realities; they lead us in opposite directions and must be used in different contexts; to apply them properly, therefore, we have to think in two different ways, which requires a complete division of reality. Otherwise the concepts themselves would become contradictory and could not be used properly at all.

Let us take, for instance, the concepts form and content. In external reality, both form and content must be understood in a purely formal way. All the concepts we need to describe the external form of an event such as the falling of a stone—its shape, weight, consistency, and the concepts of distance, motion, speed and time—can be applied to any similar event; they must be emptied of any special content so that they can enable us to formulate a general law. The explanation, it is true, always assumes the existence of an unknown content, but the names we thus give to the different causes and forces are again purely formal; they replace the content by concepts which can again be applied on many occasions. It seems to us that we try to penetrate the external form which we first apprehend, and to find the content which is hidden; every new theory seems to lead deeper inside. But experience shows that the content is only being pushed further back; we must again and again suppress it for the sake of the form. Our endeavours are, in fact, directed towards grasping the form alone; we must try to get away from the content as far as possible.

In internal reality, we start from the content, and thus even the form loses its purely formal character. The experience of the content enables us to understand how the form is connected with it; one special form— a particular deed, a meeting with some person, an impression of a picture—becomes the expression or effect of one special experience of the content. The form, therefore, is no longer an abstraction; as the experience of the content must always be a new one—that is a unique event— the form can no longer be applied to many events, but is clearly linked with its content. It becomes, so to speak, an organic form; we see how it develops, why it takes the special shape which it has, and we see that the

## THE MAIN CHARACTERISTICS OF THE TWO REALITIES

relationships between its different parts conform to certain aspects or qualities of the content. The content, also, cannot be apprehended in a formal way at all; since it becomes accessible in our lives, no abstraction or simplification can do justice to our real experience. It is true that the process of our apprehension once again appears different to us, for the content is experienced first and the form joined to it; it seems, therefore, that we try to find the form. In fact, however, the form has to be subordinated to the content; although we have to find it, the form has to serve the content. Our endeavours must be directed towards grasping the content.

Thus we need to separate the two realities completely. We have to direct our thought in opposite directions, suppressing the content in one case and subordinating the form in the other, and this changes the meaning of the concepts themselves. Only if we follow two entirely different ways of thinking can we hope to avoid confusing what must be clearly distinguished. The more so as we are apt to misunderstand the two ways of apprehension, owing to the strange contradiction between the appearance of our activities and their real nature—a special difficulty which we shall discuss later.[1]

There are many other concepts and principles which have to be applied differently to each of the two realities and which thus confirm the need for their complete separation.

We have mentioned that external reality is apprehended most reliably when our observations can be exactly repeated, while such exact repetitions threaten to cut us off from internal reality, which is all the better grasped the more experiences, even recurring ones, are transformed into new ones. But we have mentioned, too, that this does not mean that the unrepeatable is not present in external reality nor that repetition is unimportant in internal reality.[2] On the contrary, both are so important for either reality that the process of apprehension may again seem to us to be the opposite of what it really is. We have to apply these principles once more in completely different ways.

External reality appears to us as static and fixed, but to apprehend it as such is a rather complicated process. We first meet single objects which are at rest and unrepeatable; as there can never be two objects in the same space, exact repetition seems impossible. But we are unable to understand these unique objects, for only the knowledge of the content could disclose their real nature to us. As we do not know it, we have to transform the objects into events which can be repeated, for these repetitions alone allow us to set up general laws upon which our knowledge of this static reality can be founded. Matter has to be explained by motion, because motion alone can be explained by general laws. We must get rid of whatever is unrepeatable; repetitions which confirm the

[1] See pp. 55 ff.    [2] See p. 42.

## EXTERNAL AND INTERNAL REALITY

same laws have to replace the knowledge of the unrepeatable content. Although we start from unique objects which are at rest, we attain to knowledge of their static nature only by transforming them into events which allow of constant and exact repetitions.

The reliability of the natural sciences, for instance, depends precisely on whether we are able to observe, or bring about, repetitions of the same events. Physics is the most reliable of all sciences, because, in its realm, there is almost always the possibility of numberless repetitions, but even physics occasionally loses in exactness, either if unique historical events such as the formation of new stars are to be considered, or in the spheres disclosed by its most recent developments, where inexplicable differences in behaviour of the same kind of particles make exact repetition uncertain. The less we are able to neglect the unrepeatable historical process and the differences of individual behaviour, the smaller the sphere of our reliable knowledge. Our biological knowledge in general is less certain, and it becomes particularly uncertain when dealing with the more developed organisms. In history we are faced with different interpretations without being able to decide which is the right one. In psychology, because we must pay attention to the many peculiarities of different men, several methods of explanation exist side by side, and we can neither reconcile them nor provide definite proofs for any of them.

Internal reality, on the other hand, is grasped by constant new experiences which exclude repetitions, but this process, too, is rather complicated, for repetitions play a most important part in it. One day of our lives may be very much like any other, and as our faculties and their functions remain fundamentally the same, even constant changes also involve repetitions, so that it might seem that this reality is characterized by repetitions. They also seem to be essential, for our senses with which we grasp external reality work the better the more often we have to perform a similar action. But the main source of our inner knowledge is feeling, because, though the content is accessible in internal reality, we are unable to find a definite form for it. We have seen that it remains linked with our activities, and as it becomes real to us only when we make it real, we cannot rely on results formulated as thoughts, but are dependent on our feelings to experience it. Owing to the nature of feeling, however, we do not grasp internal reality in the sphere of the repetitions which we meet first; we learn to understand it by finding an unrepeatable form for each single stage of these repetitions.

No feeling is ever entirely like another; we can neither preserve feelings, nor experience exactly the same feeling twice. Even if the same situation recurs, different feelings are bound to arise, for we ourselves have changed in the meantime. Observations of these repetitions would enable us to give a general description of feeling, but this only leads

## THE MAIN CHARACTERISTICS OF THE TWO REALITIES

back into the sphere of psychology and external reality; for, as our special personal reactions cannot be repeated, general statements force us to make the feelings impersonal, and this means returning to external reality. Mere repetitions, moreover, are bound to blunt our feelings; only by its unique quality can each single feeling be fully felt and thus become a new experience which makes internal reality real. The good, for instance, always remains essentially the same, but it becomes real to us only by new and unrepeatable experiences; if a good deed is repeated over and over again it is performed more and more mechanically, so that the good gradually becomes a purely formal law without any content, very similar to the natural laws. We must use such repetitions, therefore, to develop new and unique forms. In external reality, repetitions are substituted for the unrepeatable and represent it; in internal reality, they must be used too, but at the same time overcome for the sake of the unrepeatable.

This difference between the two realities implies another difference, and again the same concepts—those of accident and of necessity—acquire different meanings and have to be used in different ways.

External reality seems, at first sight, to be characterized by the accidental. We do not know why the world is as it is, nor why single objects are as they are and where they are. We shall never discover, for instance, why the earth, this tiny speck among multitudes of enormous stars, has become the place where we live. But we do not understand this reality so long as we continue to see it as accidental; we understand it only when we are able to see it as subject to necessity. We must be able to be sure, for example, that our desk will remain standing on the floor and not suddenly jump into the air, and as our understanding grows we formulate more and more general laws which serve to describe a necessary relationship between the different causes and their effects. External reality, so far as it is understood, is the sphere of exact repetitions, because it is the sphere of necessity. Single accidents only force us to look for further general laws, extending the sphere of necessity; we must presuppose that we shall find the necessity underlying them. In so far as we cannot hope to discard accidents, we have to give up the hope of understanding external reality.[1]

In internal reality, we experience necessity, for only there do we really know what compulsion means and what it means to be forced to do something. This is very important, for, as we experience the content with immediate certainty, such an experience always establishes some kind of compulsion, and this fact helps us considerably to recognize the content. But necessity does not help us to understand internal reality; as we have always to experience it anew, we must pay attention to the

[1] This seems to be the last position in physics. The more it leaves causality and necessity behind, the less able is it to establish reliable knowledge.

unique and thus to the accidental elements of the single event. We have to discover, not any abstract general laws, but the personal character of our experience and the concrete peculiarities which determine our reactions. We have mentioned previously that, when we fall, we are not interested in the general laws of gravity; we are not helped by concentrating upon the necessity which we might discover even in such an event; we must concentrate on the accidental elements which characterize this special event.[1] It is the accidental which enables us to find a special form for each single experience; contingency is the means by which to grasp internal reality.

In external reality, accidents are the starting point for discovering necessity; in internal reality, we have to break through the chain of necessity and to discover where the single case is not governed by the general necessity which we acknowledge in external reality. We have even to restrict the feeling of compulsion, evoked by the content, to the single event which creates it, so as to be able to grasp the unique character of this event through its accidental elements.[2]

This difference leads to another. In both realities, we are confronted with past, present and future, and have to grasp the present. But in external reality, we grasp it with the help of the past, and in internal reality with the help of the future. Once more we have to look in different directions.

We can apprehend a definite form only so far as it is finished and complete in itself; all formal knowledge, therefore, is based on events which have come to an end. Our knowledge of this reality is reliable only in so far as we can apply causality; we have to derive effects from causes which we must isolate in the past, and thus we explain the present by the past and include the past in it. We have to subordinate ourselves to external reality to apprehend it, and this we can only do when it already exists, that is when it has come into being in the past. We are able to predict because we know from the past what we are going to predict. Our biological knowledge is less certain because new forms arise which did not exist in the past and which, therefore, have to be explained by certain ends, that is by future causes; future results, instead of past events, become the cause of present events. This is so because we can no longer ignore the content completely, for the content can only be grasped with the help of the future.

To make internal reality real, we have to experience it in the present. In external reality we have to grasp the present too, but there it is only one instance of fundamentally static events or things which we appre-

---

[1] See p. 34.
[2] Christians explain all events by the personal will of God, that is by a necessity which cannot be fully understood, but only becomes obvious in single events—thus paying regard to the nature of internal reality.

## THE MAIN CHARACTERISTICS OF THE TWO REALITIES

hend as ever recurring. Internal reality, however, becomes real to us only so far as it is a new experience; we can never, therefore, consider the past as something finished; we must always have the possibility of giving a new meaning to the whole of our experience by a renewal of it in the present. But, at the same time, we cannot simply concentrate on the present, for it is most difficult to experience the present at all; we cannot prevent it from slipping incessantly back into the past; if we were to try to bring external reality into relationship with us in the present only, we should always be late, for, while we are making the attempt, the present has itself become the past. We must, therefore, establish such a relationship in advance, and make sure that the meaning of our experience, which will disclose internal reality, is recognized as soon as it becomes an experience of the present. Thus we must include the future.

It is for this reason that aims are so important for our apprehension of internal reality, for they alone enable us to judge the meeting with external reality when it occurs. Aims establish between ourselves and external reality a connection which depends on the future, for only when we reach, or fail to reach, our aim can we really understand the meaning of this connection, and for this reason this meaning can also become immediately clear to us, at the very moment when the future for which we strove becomes the present. To achieve exact results in the sciences we must try to eliminate all ends and aims; but, just because they depend on the future, both of them are the most important means of preparing our future experience in such a manner that, when it becomes the present, it can disclose internal reality to us. We have said that, to experience internal reality, we have to impose upon external reality some relationship to ourselves, and this we can only do by forcing it to serve future ends, or by imposing upon it our future aims.

It is true that the experience of internal reality can also come about suddenly and surprisingly; we frequently realize that something is good or beautiful without any previous intention of doing so, and without having had any special aim which might lead up to this experience. The absence of any ends even seems to be the condition of beauty. This, however, is due to another strange contradiction which we shall have to discuss later. Although we get to know internal reality only in so far as we make it real, we must, nevertheless, anticipate it to be able to understand it at all. Our experience of something good may seem completely new and unexpected to us, and it has to be new to be fully felt, but we shall be able to recognize it only if we already possess some knowledge of the good.[1] This need to anticipate, however, which alone explains such

---

[1] This does not only mean that we need the concept 'good' to call something good. This concept, as part of our common language, can be used without any correspond-

sudden experiences, does not deny the importance of aims, for when we recognize a positive value it becomes at the same time our aim. We experience such a value when it becomes valuable to us, and this means that it awakens in us the desire to strive for its realization; even if we try to deny this urge, we know that we ought to strive for it. The anticipation of a value, therefore, has a similar effect to the setting up of an aim. And while it is true that we can make values real only if we do not use them as means to other ends—we must not strive for the good for the sake of external reward, nor for the true or beautiful for the sake of usefulness or other advantages—this once more means, not that we have to renounce aims, but only that these values themselves must be accepted as aims without any reservations.

These examples all show how important it is to separate external and internal reality from each other completely. They are only a few instances, chosen rather arbitrarily to characterize the two realities; when we come to investigate the laws of thinking underlying their apprehension, we shall meet many more such concepts and principles. But there is another concept, that of the negative, which, though somewhat different in certain respects, is so important that it should probably be mentioned here.

In external reality, as we subordinate ourselves to whatever exists, complete negation is entirely meaningless. We know this reality only so far as we know something; nothingness remains an abstraction which does not correspond to any part of external reality. It would be embodied externally in complete emptiness, but emptiness can only be conceived in the framework of something which exists. In spite of the enormous enlargement of our universe, brought about by modern astronomy, physicists are extremely reluctant to admit the existence of empty spaces, for these indicate, above all, gaps in our knowledge; the limitation of our universe therefore leads immediately to the assumption that it is one among many. Negation, in external reality, has a purely logical function; it can help us to show what is incorrect or to limit what exists, but it has a meaning only when it refers to something positive. Any special emphasis on the negative involves the danger of losing sight of external reality, for it leads us away from it into the sphere of empty abstractions.

ing experience, and the good can also be experienced if we call it by another name. But the real meaning of goodness cannot be defined at all; it has a content which has to be experienced to be known, and it is this content which to a certain extent we must already know if we want to recognize it even in our very first experience of something good. Any experience of a value is a recognition of something we knew before, and the contradiction consists in the fact that we can recognize something which we meet for the first time, and which we can only get to know by meeting it. No explanation of internal reality can be convincing unless it accounts for this possibility of anticipation.

## THE MAIN CHARACTERISTICS OF THE TWO REALITIES

In internal reality, on the contrary, the negative has a meaning. It is one of the means by which we make this reality real, for this is done by any of our activities, including that of negation. We distinguish positive from negative values, and the negative values are neither meaningless nor unimportant; they correspond to certain feelings and represent internal reality in the same way as the positive values. Good and evil, friendship and enmity, love and hatred—any one of them has a content which it can disclose to us. The danger in considering internal reality is exactly the opposite of that in external reality; a special emphasis upon the negative values and feelings can make them so strong that they overwhelm us and cut us off from anything positive. But even then they are by no means abstract or empty, but rather so real that they may become for us the whole of internal reality. Even the idea of emptiness awakens such a strong feeling that it has become a very important symbol for the mystics.

Both dangers are increased if we mix up the two realities. We must not endow the negative in external reality with the strong feelings it can evoke in internal reality, for, as nothingness here really means nothing, this mistake is bound to destroy external reality altogether. This can be seen in many a metaphysical system.[1] Nor must the negative be considered as meaningless in internal reality. It must be checked by positive values and feelings, but never ignored; it is so important an element in this reality that, by ignoring it, we are in great danger of succumbing to a superficial optimism which makes the experience of internal reality extremely difficult.[2] If we want to apprehend the two realities correctly, we must separate them as clearly as possible.

### 3. BOTH REALITIES MUST BE TAKEN INTO ACCOUNT

The second main condition of our apprehending the two realities correctly is the recognition that they nevertheless cannot become entirely independent of each other. Although we must separate them so completely that it is best to call them two realities, we must never forget that they are only two interdependent aspects of a single primary reality. As we have mentioned before, we must always take into account the co-existence of the other reality.

The impossibility of any complete isolation of one of the two

---

[1] Schopenhauer, for instance, who in this respect follows Buddhism, considers any activity of the Will (which for him represents external reality) as bad, and thus he must wish to overcome this world completely. As in Buddhism, we must strive, according to him, for nothingness, so that this world ceases to exist. In Christianity, the more one insists on the Devil, the more the fundamental doctrine of Incarnation is robbed of its meaning.

[2] This is the particular danger of both Humanism and of conventional piety or goodness.

realities can be seen in the strange contradiction which we have pointed out—that our apprehension of each reality appears to us at first to be the opposite of what it really is. In external reality, we first met static objects which excluded the idea of exact repetitions, so that we seemed to grasp their static nature directly by means of what was unrepeatable; but in fact we have to dissolve the objects into events which are not static and can be repeated, and only these repetitions disclose its static nature. Internal reality, on the other hand, is not static, and as it appears to us first as a constant flux of repetitions, we could believe that this flux represents internal reality. But to grasp it correctly, we have to make use of these repetitions to discover what in it cannot be repeated, and only the constantly new experience of the unrepeatable helps us to make it real. This, however, ceases to be a contradiction if we recognize that the interdependence of the two realities is a further condition of our thinking.

In external reality, this necessity is shown by the fact that the main concepts which we need to grasp it are derived, not from our knowledge of this reality, but from inner experiences.

Such, for instance, are the two concepts of cause and effect, which we need to describe an external event. The cause itself cannot be seen and it is usually difficult to discover it. A stone falls if it is robbed of its support. This is all we see; the cause of this fall can only be discovered by careful investigation. We may ascertain that the stone fell because of a strong wind, but this is only a secondary element and not the real cause; a feather, blown off its support by the same wind, does not fall, but sails away. The real cause of the fall is the weight of the stone, that is the force of gravity, which we cannot apprehend directly. We discover it only because we assume the concept of causality and automatically regard any event as an effect of a cause; only these seemingly natural assumptions lead us to look for a cause and to discover it. We therefore also consider as effects those events of which we cannot clearly recognize the cause, such as the growing of a tree or life in general. We assume that there are forces which cause all events, but the concept of force, too, as we have already said,[1] is something quite incomprehensible; we obviously do not derive it from our knowledge of external reality, but discover it because we possess this concept beforehand and try to apply it.

In internal reality, however, all these concepts have a clear meaning for us; they are part of our experience and as such well known to us. Our life consists of activities; we are, that is, incessantly causing events. We need not even apply these concepts here, because the unity of willing and acting is quite self-evident to us. If we want to stretch out an arm, we normally do so; we are only forced to think about it if something

[1] See pp. 30–1.

## THE MAIN CHARACTERISTICS OF THE TWO REALITIES

goes wrong and our intention does not produce the normal effect. We know, too, without need of any investigation, what force means; we have to exert our strength to bring about certain actions, and we fail if the force we are able to produce is inadequate. The abstractions which we apply to make external reality accessible are, in internal reality, not abstractions at all, but part of our experience; we get to know their meaning, because we experience what they really mean. All these concepts are derived from our knowledge of internal reality and transferred to external reality.

The basic concept which enables us to connect causes and effects in such a way that they lead to a reliable knowledge of external reality is that of necessity, for only so far as we are able to rely upon the same causes necessarily producing the same effects are we able to rely upon this knowledge. But this concept, too, cannot be derived from external reality; our external experience is too limited to justify the concept of a comprehensive necessity valid beyond our actual experience.[1] It is in internal reality alone that we know the meaning of inescapable compulsion and from this, with the help of abstraction, we derive the concept of necessity. It is also in internal reality alone that we know complete freedom, and only this knowledge enables us to create the concept of that comprehensive necessity which we cannot experience.

The fact that all these concepts are not abstractions from external reality, but part of the laws of our thinking and thus additions to our knowledge of this reality, has been proved by Kant so conclusively that it seems superfluous to enter into a further discussion here. Though differing from Kant in the deduction of these concepts, our investigation accepts this basis of his teaching.[2]

Our knowledge of internal reality depends in the same way on elements which we have to transfer from external reality.

We have already mentioned that to understand our feelings we must direct them towards certain objects, because we have to find a definite form for them.[3] No objects, however, can be found in internal reality, nor can we apprehend forms there; we therefore have to connect external objects with these experiences to be able to give them form and thus to understand them. Who could explain beauty to anyone who had never felt that some impression made by nature or a person or a work of art was beautiful? We must have experienced love for somebody or love given by them before we are able to understand what the concept 'love' means, and only the knowledge of some good person or deed will tell us the meaning of 'the good'. Moral laws lose their meaning if they

---

[1] This has been sufficiently proved by Hume.
[2] Cf. especially Kant's *Prolegomena* and his *Critique of Pure Reason*, Part I and Introduction and first section of Part II. See p. 20, note.
[3] See p. 39.

remain pure convictions without ever being exercised in our real lives, within the context of external reality. All such concepts remain empty words so long as we cannot connect them with some experience which includes external reality, for it is only there that we meet our fellow-men.

This is even true of those concepts which can only be understood with the help of inner experiences and for which we are unable to find an adequate form in external reality. Certainly, such concepts as 'God' and 'immortality' are falsified if we connect them too closely with external facts. But, to grasp what these concepts mean, we have to describe their meaning in some way, and any such description will contain such concepts as those just mentioned to which we give meaning with the help of external objects and forms. Love, truth, goodness, beauty—these alone help us to understand whatever we are able to understand of the supernatural. We must be very careful not to take them too literally, but we must make use of these concepts to which we have given an external form to explain even those which acquire meaning only by corresponding to inner experiences.

The importance of this interconnection between the two realities is proved by the fact that our reliable knowledge of either of them is based upon the elements transferred from the other—the knowledge of external reality upon such concepts as cause and effect and particularly upon necessity, and the understanding of internal reality on the definite form which we create to embody it by means of external objects. We are confronted with the surprising fact that we grasp each reality best, not in those spheres where we seem to apprehend it directly, but on the contrary in so far as we are able to apply the laws of our thinking and to add to it elements which our minds provide by transferring them from the other reality.

In external reality the most reliable knowledge is achieved when mathematics, the most abstract laws of our thinking, can be applied.[1] These abstract laws, however, cannot be explained as abstractions derived from external reality. They start from assertions based on numbers, and the problem of numbers alone is a most difficult one. It is not possible to arrive at them with the help of abstraction—no abstraction from the numbers 5 and 7, for instance, could ever produce the number 12, as Kant has shown,[2] nor was it originally a simple process of thought to apply the same numbers to different things, such as apples and days.[3] Even if we abandon numbers, the relationship of

[1] This is usually taken for granted, but it is rather astonishing 'that as mathematics withdrew increasingly into the upper regions of ever greater extremes of abstract thought, it returned back to earth with a corresponding growth of importance for the analysis of concrete fact'. A. N. Whitehead, *Science and the Modern World* (1946), p. 41.

[2] *Prolegomena*, § 2, c.

[3] See A. N. Whitehead, op. cit., pp. 25-6.

## THE MAIN CHARACTERISTICS OF THE TWO REALITIES

mathematical laws to external reality remains puzzling, for they cannot be abstracted from this reality; no analysis of this reality can produce them.[1] We shall see later that these processes of thinking are also based on, and explained by, concepts transferred from internal reality.

In internal reality our most reliable knowledge is that of the good, embodied in the moral laws. But these laws are always in danger of degenerating into mere formal rules which can be fulfilled mechanically or even for quite immoral reasons, to avoid difficulties, for instance, or to acquire a good reputation. Because they concern our behaviour in external reality, we can regard them in a purely external way, and if this happens they become very similar to natural laws; they can be followed on many different occasions without telling us anything about their content. This danger can only be avoided when we transfer external elements into internal reality, and in considering this, we can also see more clearly what this transferring means.

It is not sufficient merely to relate the moral law to the external world; this can be very misleading and cut us off from the content in the way we have just mentioned. We are obliged to include individual external elements in internal reality; only a specific external event—such as seeing a man, under a dictatorship, helping a political opponent of the régime at great personal risk—can acquire the special significance which will enable us to attain knowledge of the good. The special character of the event must make it one definite and particular form of the good, which it therefore helps us to understand. The event must embody it so completely that the two can no longer be separated; any deeper knowledge of the action, that is, any better understanding of the form—for instance that the man helped the other although he was of a different political opinion, or although he did not know or did not like him, or that he avoided his thanks, or that it meant risking his life despite all logical considerations—must lead to a better understanding of the good. Only such experiences of single good or bad actions can give a moral meaning and content to the moral laws and prevent them from becoming formal rules; these experiences alone secure that constant renewal of our feeling which makes internal reality real. In this way the good may even become so real that we do the good deed without any further need for laws.[2]

We are so dependent, therefore, on the second condition of our apprehending the two realities correctly—that is on their interdependence—that the reliability of our knowledge of one reality is always secured by contributions from the other reality.

It is this fact, too, which explains the strange contradiction between the first impression we gain from each reality and its correct apprehension. In external reality we have to dissolve the static objects which we

[1] Kant, *Prolegomena*, § 6.  [2] 'By their fruits ye shall know them.'

meet first, for only their transformation into events enables us to apply the concepts on which our reliable knowledge depends; we have to transform our original impression so as to make room for the elements of the other reality which must be added. In internal reality we have to break away from the constant flux of repetitions which we experience first; for, to apprehend it clearly, we need those unrepeatable experiences which acquire a definite form with the help of accidental external objects. We have once more to abandon our original impression to be able to include elements from the other reality. Our final apprehension differs from our original impression, because our knowledge always depends on the elements from the other reality, and because these elements can only be included after our original impression has been transformed.

The second condition of our thinking, however, does not contradict the first. The elements from the other reality can be transferred without in the least impairing the complete separation of the two realities.

We have said before that we have to establish the opposition between external and internal reality in every impression and every experience.[1] By this process the elements which we transfer from the one reality acquire, before they are actually transferred, the character of the other reality, and thus they can be transferred without altering the character of the reality in which they are to be included. The transfer neither destroys nor lessens the difference between the two realities.

Our experience of cause and effect, of force and necessity is not included as such in external reality; on the contrary, we have to eliminate completely any meaning which these concepts may have for our own lives. We are able to do so because, in any inner experience, we oppose to the content which these experiences have for our lives the form which they take, thus deriving from them purely formal concepts which, unlike the content, fit many occasions. We think neither of our will nor of the stretching out of our arm when we talk of cause and effect, although these concepts originate in some such experiences. We transfer the concepts only after the abstraction has taken place. They have lost any personal meaning and represent that part of our inner experience which appears to us as its mere form. As they are won by abstraction, they can easily take their place among the abstractions which we are using in external reality, so easily that the difference between the two kinds of abstractions, which we shall discuss in a moment, is hardly ever noticed. Their inclusion in external reality, therefore, requires no effort and no change in the structure of this reality.

On the other hand, objects are not transferred unchanged into internal reality. We do not consider their external nature when they become causes or aims of inner experiences; we concentrate, in this case, on the meaning they have for us. We have already mentioned a

---

[1] See pp. 23–4.

## THE MAIN CHARACTERISTICS OF THE TWO REALITIES

few examples of this process. The falling stone which hurts us does not interest us as such; we do not ask what sort of stone or how heavy it is; we realize the impact of this event on us, and if we go on thinking we want to know the meaning of this event for our lives. If we see a picture, we are normally interested in its beauty and not in its weight; and its canvas, pigments and frame interest us only so far as they contribute to its beauty. Our interest in a good deed is governed by the conviction that it is good, and cause and effect are of interest only so far as they help us to understand what is good and how it can be achieved. We are no longer looking for impersonal abstractions, but for the manifestation of meaning, and though we must beware of seeing this meaning as part of external reality—values, for instance, do not exist somewhere in space and time, but are established by the relationship between external reality and ourselves—we are nevertheless bound to search for the meaning which objects and events have for us. For, to disclose internal reality, the form has to be used to make clear the content.

The process of abstraction and the search for a meaning—these two completely different methods of apprehension guarantee that the two realities remain completely separated and that, nevertheless, both realities can be taken into account simultaneously. But to apply these methods correctly, we must be aware of some frequent misunderstandings which tend to distort them and to blur the difference between the two realities.

We deal with external reality with the help of continuously progressing abstractions. The individual tree in front of our windows becomes 'the tree', consisting of 'trunk' and 'branches', of 'wood' and 'leaves', and we proceed from these abstractions to more general ones like 'plant' and 'life' which finally seem to allow us to derive general laws. But to be able to formulate these laws we need other concepts too, such as cause and effect, force and necessity, which, as we have seen, could never be won by abstraction from external facts, but have to be abstracted from internal reality. The failure to see this difference in the process of abstraction is one of the reasons why the influence of the laws of thinking is so easily overlooked; it leads us to believe that we can grasp external reality directly. We have seen that the division into two realities takes place automatically, and so does the transferring of the concepts from one reality to the other; we need not be conscious of all these processes in order to think. But we must become conscious of them if we want to judge our knowledge correctly.

This need to be conscious of them is especially important for our knowledge of internal reality. As we have to make use here of external objects and events, the knowledge of external reality must precede that of internal reality, and if we overlook the part played by our laws of thinking and thus by internal reality even in our knowledge of external reality, it may easily seem to us that external knowledge is direct and immediate, and therefore alone sufficient. Internal facts, then, appear as nothing but arbitrary and superfluous interpretations. We may, particularly in our age which stresses scientific knowledge so much, mistake what we emphasized as being two different methods of apprehension for the difference between 'objective' and 'subjective' in the usual sense. Or, if we do not want to dismiss internal facts altogether, we may make the opposite mistake; as abstraction from external reality alone seems to suffice for the formulation of laws, we may hope to discover the meaning of the universe by continuing with this abstraction. Whichever error we fall into, we shall never achieve an 'objective' knowledge of internal reality, nor shall we ever understand what we are able to know.

To avoid any such confusion, we shall in future call all the concepts which are transferred to one reality from the other 'constructive concepts'. This applies, in external reality, to those concepts which, although abstract, are not derived from this reality itself but from internal reality; in internal reality it applies to the concepts which help us to grasp the contribution of external reality. The latter are frequently the same as those used in external reality, but having a different meaning, as we have seen in the case of 'form' and 'content'; others are different as, for instance, 'means' and 'end' which are the internal equivalent of 'cause' and 'effect'. These distinctions will be discussed later. The term 'constructive concepts' has been chosen to stress the constructive part which the working of our minds plays in all our knowledge and to make sure that it is not overlooked. We are not originally conscious of it, but we must make it conscious if we are to think clearly. This, as we have mentioned already, is not a contradiction, for otherwise the automatic functioning of our mind tends to mislead us.[1]

The correct separation of external and internal reality therefore depends on two conditions. The two realities must be completely separated from each other, and yet we must never forget that they are only two interdependent aspects of one primary reality and that, therefore, the co-existence of the other reality must always be taken into account. We cannot gain a reliable knowledge of one reality without transferring to it elements from the other. This transfer, however, can be done without impairing their complete separation, because we have to establish the opposition between the two realities in every impression and experience, and thus the constructive concepts acquire beforehand the character of the other reality.

These fundamental conditions which govern our thinking create the need for further opposites and determine their application.

[1] See p. 16.

# Part Two
## THE EXTERNAL AND INTERNAL OPPOSITES

# Chapter IV

## THE NEED FOR OPPOSITES

### 1. THE NECESSITY FOR DIFFERENT KINDS OF OPPOSITES

THE division into two realities is the fundamental fact which underlies all our thinking. We experience primary reality as a unity, and therefore we also try to establish a unitary coherence in all our thought. But as soon as we become conscious of this reality and begin to think, we are confronted with two different realities. There is no way of escaping this division, for we have no other access to primary reality which we are unable to grasp directly. The opposition between the two realities is the condition of every thought, whatever the impression, experience, feeling or knowledge to which it may refer.

In the single impression or experience, however, the two realities are not opposed to each other as such; we do not always think of the fact that we are dealing with external reality, nor, indeed, that it is we who are dealing with it, nor of all that this implies. The opposition of the two realities is brought about by opposing to each other single elements from each reality; a certain object or event is made accessible by those special laws of our thinking which apply to it, and a particular feeling is directed towards a single object. We do not normally think of external and internal reality, but use automatically such opposites as 'dark and light' or 'cause and effect', as 'good and evil' or 'necessity and freedom'. The fundamental opposition between the two realities is indeed brought about in this way, but the two realities themselves remain in the background. We therefore translate this fundamental opposition into pairs of opposites composed of more limited concepts, to be able to apply them to the special occasion.

This statement hardly needs any further elaboration. When describing the two realities, we have been forced, again and again, to make use of such opposites composed of more limited concepts, and this has already shown us that such a translation takes place. The way in which the division into two realities gradually imposes upon our thinking a

## THE EXTERNAL AND INTERNAL OPPOSITES

general pattern of opposites can be seen best when we start from the constructive concepts.

The need for these concepts is due to the necessity of transferring concepts from one reality to the other without endangering their complete separation. This can be done, as we have seen, only by creating the opposition of the two realities in every impression and experience. We need more limited concepts, therefore, which can be applied within each reality, and these concepts have to form opposites to enable us to keep to the division into two realities. The examples which we have mentioned have already shown us that the constructive concepts always form pairs of opposites. We cannot think of effect without cause; the concept 'force' requires something upon which the force can exert an influence, that is the opposite 'matter'; necessity cannot be thought of without accident, and the idea of a comprehensive necessity cannot be arrived at without that of complete freedom.[1] Nor can we think of 'means' without 'ends' to be achieved by them, and the inner content remains inaccessible without a form. Thus, however, one concept always represents external and the other internal reality and we are compelled to think of each of these concepts simultaneously with its opposite, because they must refer to both realities.

In external reality, we really know only the results, the effects, and we have to make some division within them to be able to add a cause, the concept of which is taken from internal reality. The cause always appears as something which is hidden and has to be discovered by penetrating deeper into external reality; it can be disclosed only underneath the surface of things and events; it represents that internal reality from which the concept has been transferred. Moreover, we only know matter in external reality, and again the forces represent, so to speak, inner motives, the hidden impulse inside things or events; we cannot even fully understand them; once more the concept 'force' is being transferred from internal reality and represents it. The connection between cause and effect, between force and matter can only be understood with the help of necessity; the reign of necessity seems to embrace the whole of external reality; but this concept, too, is based upon an opposite which is taken from internal reality, for the concept of freedom is accessible only there.

In internal reality, we are confronted with a constant flux of vague inner activities which give us access to the content, but they could not become anything which we could call a content without a form which we have to transfer from external reality. To be able to find or create such a form, as we shall see, we have to impose on external reality ends which conform to internal reality; but no ends, not even the most

---

[1] We shall discuss later the difference between the opposition 'necessity and accident' and that of 'necessity and freedom'. See p. 194.

## THE NEED FOR OPPOSITES

spiritual ones, could be achieved without the help of external means. Forms and ends have to give expression to inner freedom which, after all, is the most important characteristic of internal reality; nevertheless, we could not grasp it without some kind of external compulsion or necessity.

The need for these opposites is confirmed and strengthened by the fact that we frequently have to use the same pairs of constructive concepts in both realities. We have seen that such characteristics as form and content, repetitions and the unrepeatable, necessity and accident, apply to both realities; the difference between them is established by taking one of these concepts as mere presupposition and by concentrating our attention upon the other. In external reality, the existence of an unknown content has to be assumed to enable us to understand the form; the unrepeatable has to be broken down as far as possible into what can be repeated; we have to discard accidents and to concentrate on necessity. In internal reality, on the contrary, the form has to serve the content; the repetitions have to help us to discover the unrepeatable; necessity must be restricted to disclose the accidental.[1] One of these concepts always becomes a mere presupposition, a mere means of concentrating on the other, and this can be achieved only when we apply opposites. In any unitary or purely logical way of thinking and in any causal connection either both concepts are bound to have the same importance, or the difference in their importance has to be carefully defined, which means once more that both have to be considered in the same way. Only if we use the concepts as opposites can we start from one of them and use it as the basis of the other without any conscious effort.

This advantage of using opposites can be seen in many ways. If, for instance, we try to concentrate on purely formal connections alone, as we do when we set up natural or mathematical laws, we need no effort to push the concept 'content' into the background; it is brought into our minds whenever we apply the concept 'form', but as the opposition is established automatically there is no need to dwell on it, no need, even, to be conscious of it. The natural workings of our minds make both concepts entirely clear, and thus we can easily concentrate on one of them. Similarly, we cannot think of freedom without thinking of necessity, but we can have the experience of inner freedom without being aware of the fact that the concept can only arise and be understood as the opposite of necessity. The one concept always contributes to the creation of the other and thus both have to be thought of together; but, owing to the division into two realities, their opposition is so self-evident and so firmly established that we can make use of them without any need for a conscious definition or explanation.

[1] See pp. 47 ff.

## THE EXTERNAL AND INTERNAL OPPOSITES

Yet there are other opposites among those which we have mentioned which refer either to external or to internal reality alone—such as light and dark or good and evil. Here the necessity for transferring concepts disappears. Why, then, do we need these further opposites?

Even these opposites are a consequence of the division into two realities, for they are inextricably connected with the constructive concepts. Whenever we translate any impression or experience into thought, we find that the constructive concepts have already ordered reality in such a way that we can use it as a foundation for thought. We should be quite unable to consider qualities such as dark and light, had not the concepts 'form' and 'content' enabled us to distinguish between the object and its qualities; we should be unable to count, had not the constructive concepts 'the One' and 'the Many' helped us to arrange reality into units which can be counted. The same applies to internal reality; the qualities 'good' and 'evil' presuppose the opposition between form and content as well as that between necessity and freedom. Our claim that we need constructive concepts may seem, at first sight, a rather superfluous subdivision of our real experience; but actually it is these concepts which are the indispensable basis of all our thought; only the order which they create while we think enables our thinking to work properly.

The constructive concepts, moreover, can only fulfil their indispensable function if further opposites are actually applied. If these concepts, for instance, separate the qualities from the object, they still leave the different qualities undistinguished, and we still have to single out the special quality which enables us to grasp reality. We can do this only by finding the right opposite which discards all the other qualities which would hinder us from recognizing this one quality clearly. We have already shown that it is only when we oppose 'light' to 'dark' and thus separate them from similar qualities that we can find the real meaning of 'light'.[1] Only the opposite 'dark' enables us to isolate the impression of light completely, because it is thought of automatically and thus need not be conscious. Any other connection or explanation gives other concepts the same importance as that of 'light'. The idea of waves or particles leads away from the real impression of light altogether, and the connection of light with the sun or some other source of light, or with the sense-impression and our eyes, mixes it up with other ideas which blur the pure concept.

Similar considerations apply to all the opposites which we have mentioned; there is no other way of apprehending the two realities accurately. In internal reality, for instance, such constructive concepts as means and ends help to give us access to the content, but they leave

[1] See pp. 9–10.

## THE NEED FOR OPPOSITES

its different possible meanings undefined, and we have to proceed to such opposites as good and evil to seize the meaning of a particular content. Any other approach—such as trying to explain the whole process psychologically or physiologically—makes us lose sight of the content altogether.

The division into two realities, therefore, imposes a general pattern upon our thinking and forces us always to form and to use opposites, whenever we think and of whatever we think.

But the difference between the opposites which we have considered points also to a further necessity in our thinking. There are different kinds of opposites—some which refer to one reality alone, either to external or internal reality, and others which are derived from the division itself and include both realities. In fact, the division into two realities forces us to use three different kinds of opposites:

(1) Those referring to external reality alone which we shall call *external opposites*.
(2) Those referring to internal reality alone which we shall call *internal opposites*.
(3) Those derived from the division itself and referring to both realities which we shall call *interconnected opposites*.

(1) In external reality, we have to subordinate ourselves to reality to such a degree that our knowledge appears to be entirely independent of ourselves; the influence of the observer and his special experiences have to be eliminated as far as possible.[1] We need opposites, therefore, which also seem independent of the working of our mind, opposites, that is, in which the single concepts seem to represent something which has an external existence independent of its opposite. Dark and light are automatically thought of together, but they seem to exist separately whether we think of them together or not; each of them seems to have an existence of its own. Even the constructive concepts, when we use them to apprehend external reality, are transformed in this way; though they clearly depend on each other, they are thought of as being independent entities. We have seen already that the form and the content are almost entirely separated, the form being so independent of its content that it fits many different occasions, and though it is very difficult to think of a cause without an effect, the forces which represent the causes are imagined as existing independently; they are regarded in the same way as single objects or events. The external opposites appear to us at first rather as an arbitrary combination of single elements which we find in external reality, and only the ever recurring necessity of applying the same opposites points to their close connection

[1] See pp. 24 ff.

## THE EXTERNAL AND INTERNAL OPPOSITES

with the working of our minds, and to the fact that they are not arbitrarily selected.

(2) In internal reality, we have to subordinate reality to ourselves and to impose its relationship to us upon external reality.[1] The opposites, therefore, are far more clearly dependent on our thinking and thus on each other; the single concepts do not even appear to represent anything which has an independent existence of its own. If we discard one concept, the other disappears as well. Nothing could be evil if there was no knowledge of good; nothing could ever be untrue if there was no truth. The constructive concepts, here, too, are far more obviously dependent on each other. We have already seen that the form becomes the expression of one special content from which it can no longer be separated, and similarly the accident, so important for our grasp of internal reality, creates a special combination of necessity and freedom which cannot be broken down. The internal opposites, therefore, always appear to us in their relationship as opposites; the single concepts are completely dependent on each other; we must either use both of them or none.

(3) The constructive concepts point to opposites which refer to both realities. If we do not use these concepts to grasp one reality alone, which makes it necessary to accommodate them to the nature of this reality, but try to penetrate to those elements in them which remain constant, we are led to discover comprehensive concepts which conform to the division into two realities. So long as we transfer one of these concepts from one reality to the other, we can, as we have seen, always concentrate only on one of them. But we can also use their opposition to help us to understand both concepts, and then we discover the interconnected opposites which allow us to understand not only either external or internal reality, but the relationship between them and the meaning of their division.

We call these opposites interconnected, because they combine the characteristics of the other two kinds. The two concepts forming these opposites appear to us as completely independent entities and yet, if we discard one of them, the other becomes completely meaningless. They thus conform to the two conditions of apprehending the two realities correctly—that they must be completely separated and yet both taken into account simultaneously.[2] They are the opposites which

[1] See pp. 33 ff.

[2] As the opposition between these opposites is not so obvious as that between the others, it would be rather misleading to mention examples at this stage of our investigation. We are confronted here with a difficulty, due to the necessity of starting from the two realities. For, as we thus cannot begin with the interconnected opposites, we have to include some of them—'necessity and freedom' and 'the One and the Many' —provisionally among the constructive concepts, and we shall only later be able to introduce clearer distinctions. (See p. 176.) But with such oppositions in mind one

matter most, for they lead us to understand the implications of the laws of our thinking.

We can penetrate to these opposites, however, only after we have considered the application of the constructive concepts to the two realities. The transferring of these concepts from one reality to the other serves their original function and makes them known to us, but thus we also know them at first merely as a formal means of apprehension. We have seen that the constructive concepts which are transferred from internal reality are mere abstractions, while those transferred from external reality acquire meaning when they become an expression of inner experiences. They have, therefore, no meaning apart from their application.[1] The form as such, for instance, cannot even be imagined, in spite of the fact that it appeals to our imagination; we have to know forms of objects and purely formal connections and also the form as the embodiment of an inner content before we can understand what the concept 'form' really means. We can, therefore, find the comprehensive concepts to which the constructive concepts point only after we have considered how they function as external and internal opposites.

## 2. THE MEANING OF THE CONCEPT 'OPPOSITE'

Until now we have been using the concept 'opposite' in the ordinary meaning of this word. Before starting the investigation of opposites, however, we have to try to define it more exactly; this is partly because the general usage of the word is not exact, and partly because, in this investigation, it is being used as a special term, different in some respects from its general usage. The whole scope and significance of this concept, it is true, can be recognized only after the different kinds of opposites have been considered. But without any definition, misunderstandings are bound to arise, and so we must at least try to compare the general usage of this word with our usage of it.

The concept 'opposite', as it is generally used, can have two different meanings. If two concepts are in opposition to one another, they can either—

(1) exclude one another and not be applicable to the same content at the same time; in this case we can call them contradictory opposites; or

(2) Condition and determine each other and refer to the same content at the same time; in this case we usually say that they form a contrast.

can more easily understand what has just been said, or one could also think of 'space and time', though in this case we shall have to show why they are considered as opposites. (See pp. 179 ff.)

[1] To these concepts applies what Kant says of all the concepts given *a priori*.

## THE EXTERNAL AND INTERNAL OPPOSITES

This book becomes readable because black letters are printed on white paper. In this case 'black' and 'white' are contradictory opposites, for it is impossible that the letters or the book should be both at the same time. But if we consider a page of the book as a whole, both black and white exist on it at the same time; they form a contrast and it is due to this contrast that we are able to read the book. The book as a solid body is in opposition to the air surrounding it which has the qualities of a gas. These opposites again contradict each other. But if we investigate a more comprehensive sphere, as for instance that of matter, the solid body and the air both appear to us as combinations of atoms or electrons; within this greater context their opposite states exist at the same time and only form a contrast.

These two meanings of the concept 'opposite', therefore, apply to the same facts; their difference refers only to two different ways of looking at them. Contradictory opposites become mere contrasts if we enlarge the sphere of our considerations; if we want to describe the book as such, we have to establish the concepts of a solid body and of a gas as contradictory opposites, but if we want to understand matter, we must find a common basis and characterize both the body and the gas as contrasts. Contrasts, on the other hand, become contradictory opposites when we restrict our attention. In the geometry of spheres, the plane is only a special case of the bent surfaces of spheres, because this geometry refers to the whole of space, but it would be nonsensical to consider the flat book therefore as being bent. We can only describe it when we use 'flat' and 'bent' as contradictory opposites.

When we leave the realm of sense-experiences and their immediate explanations and become dependent on judgments and conclusions, it may not always be possible to make such clear-cut statements. To this we shall return in a moment. But in this case, too, contrasts are transformed into contradictory opposites, this time whenever we are able to reach clarity or complete certainty. If we want to judge the value of an indifferent or tolerably good book, for instance, it will appear good to us if we compare it with a book which is worse, and bad if we compare it with a better book. Worse and better books provide us with contrasts which make it possible for us to judge such a book. But a book which is definitely bad will not appear good to us whatever book we compare it with, nor will a perfect masterpiece become bad by comparison. We have once more to leave the realm of contrasts and to apply contradictory opposites; comparisons will only make clearer either the worthlessness of the book or its real value.

Contradictory opposites are extreme cases of contrasts, and our usage of the concept 'opposite', therefore, will include both these meanings.

(3) We shall, moreover, include in our term a distinction which is

## THE NEED FOR OPPOSITES

usually not considered as consisting of opposites—that of differences of degree.

We have already seen that we need opposites when constructing scales of degrees or graduated scales of quantities.[1] The examples mentioned there have shown us that such scales are created by transforming contradictory opposites into contrasts and by arranging these in a certain order; but if we want to understand the abstract degree of such a scale, we have at least to re-establish a contrast which shows that they originate from opposites. This is clearly confirmed when we consider such a scale in greater detail.

If different objects have the same quality, but in a different degree, we usually create a unit which allows us to measure these differences, and it is this unit which enables us to consider them as degrees of the same kind within a unitary scale. Different objects, for instance, weigh one pound or several pounds. The unitary scale hides the dependence on opposites, for the opposite 'light' seems to disappear in it. We say that the object weighs such an amount and this means that it is heavy; we measure only heaviness and not lightness. We talk of the weight of the atom, of the weight of a book and of that of the earth; the book is no longer light, even if we find it so when we have to carry it, but heavy, for it weighs so and so many units. But the fact which we have stressed remains; we need opposites to create this scale and to recognize its degrees. The heaviness of a feather which the wind can blow off my palm and the heaviness of an iron bar which weighs me down if I try to lift it were originally quite different experiences, and only by bringing them into opposition can we find the common quality and thus the basis for the scale.[2] Nor can we dispense with the opposites when considering one degree of the scale alone; it always means that an object is lighter or heavier than another one. The application of the unit which we have created makes this even clearer; for it forces us to bring all the objects which we want to weigh into opposition to the unit. Even such a straightforward statement as that an object weighs eight pounds, therefore, implies the application of opposites and justifies us when we include differences of degree in our concept 'opposite'.

(4) With judgments and conclusions which cannot be definitely proved, contradictory opposites can become contradictions. Such contradictions arise when contradictory assertions which exclude each other remain nevertheless valid at the same time because we cannot decide which of them is correct.

[1] See p. 11.
[2] The children's trick question: 'Which is the heavier, a pound of feathers or a pound of lead?' points to the difficulty which we have overcome in regarding weight as a common quality. The single degree also presupposes the opposition between the One and the Many, but this we shall consider later.

## THE EXTERNAL AND INTERNAL OPPOSITES

Contradictions are of no importance in the realm of sense-experiences and their scientific explanations. The assertion that the letters of the book are white would be simply wrong, and the claim that they are both black and white at the same time nonsensical. Our senses can be deluded; it seems to us that the sun turns round the earth; if we touch liquid air we think it is hot; but such delusions can be rectified. We must presume that any contradiction in this sphere will finally be explained and thus resolved, even if we deal with completely abstract scientific theories which are contradictory.

Contradictions become important, however, as soon as human experience acquires decisive importance, for then the same facts allow different interpretations. The contradictions which we have considered at the beginning of this investigation provide us with many examples for this.[1] If I experience suffering as an expression of God's love and someone else as a confirmation of a blind mechanical necessity, this contradiction cannot be resolved by any proof; both convictions can be convincingly supported by conclusions based on indubitable facts. I can decide to accept one of these views, but my belief solves the contradiction for me alone and not generally, because I have to support it with my own experience. I may be very firm in my conviction, yet the contradiction remains, for others are as firm in theirs.

We can show some such contradictions to be founded upon opposites which are due to the fact that our thinking confronts us with two realities. 'The starry heaven above' and 'the moral law within' are for Kant the expression of necessity and freedom.[2] They seem to establish an insoluble contradiction, for how could everything which happens, on the one hand, be determined without any exception by necessity and yet, on the other hand, leave room for human freedom? But Kant shows that these two aspects of life can be reconciled if we take into account the laws of our thinking, and we have shown that they are based upon the opposition between external and internal reality which exist at the same time without forming a contradiction. Thus some such contradictions, but by no means all of them, can be considered as opposites.

In our investigation we shall always determine whether contradictions can be derived from opposites or have to be accepted as such.

(5) It may seem that the best example of opposites is provided by the opposition between 'Yes' and 'No', between 'positive' and 'negative', between affirmation and negation. We are inclined almost to identify opposites in general with the opposition between positive and negative and to call one of the related opposites 'positive' and the other 'negative'. This common usage, however, is not followed here as a rule because, as all the examples we have mentioned show, both opposites

[1] See Chapter I, Section 1.   [2] *Critique of Practical Reason*, Conclusion.

## THE NEED FOR OPPOSITES

always refer to something which exists and which, therefore, must in some sense be positive. But, to explain our usage of the terms, we must discuss this problem separately for each of the two realities, for we have seen that negation has a different meaning in external and internal reality.[1]

(a) In external reality, complete negation is entirely meaningless. As we know this reality only so far as we know something, nothingness, as we have seen, remains an empty abstraction; negation here has a purely logical function. If, in this reality, we call something negative, we can do so only because we do not use this word in its proper meaning. The negative electric pole, for instance, stands in opposition to the positive pole, but it exists in the same way as the positive pole; positive and negative are only names for different qualities. In the pairs of opposites which we have mentioned we could consider 'light' or 'freedom' as positive and 'dark' or 'necessity' as negative. But 'dark' is not a mere negation of light; it is a quality which we can experience as such; nor is necessity a mere negation of freedom, for it is much more than a lack or a denial of freedom. We need the opposite to form and to understand these concepts, but we do not need negation; we can apply them to reality without using any negative principle; we can refer directly to the negative electric pole, to a dark object, to a necessary relationship.

In this reality, therefore, we shall not include this kind of opposition in our use of the term 'opposite'. On the contrary, whenever we need a complete negation to form an opposite, we shall recognize that we have trespassed beyond the sphere of real opposites.

That negation is so frequently used in external reality only shows how important opposites are in enabling us to grasp it. Any thought needs an opposition to become possible at all; if it proves impossible to find an opposite in external reality, we create it artificially with the help of negation. Pure idealism must negate matter and pure materialism the spirit or even the mind, in order to acquire the appearance of referring to something real. Usually we are helped in this by the fact that negation has a positive meaning in internal reality. In order to make this external negation plausible, we mix up the two realities and unconsciously endow the negative with the content which it has in internal reality.[2]

(b) In internal reality the negative has a meaning, because feeling can give content to it. Here the negation helps to form opposites, but only because it creates and represents a real content which exists positively. Values, for instance, need negations; they can only be

[1] For this and the following, see pp. 54–5.
[2] Both Hegel's 'Spirit' and Marx's materialism have to be supported by logical negations which appeal to our feelings.

## THE EXTERNAL AND INTERNAL OPPOSITES

grasped as positive and negative values. But the negative value is still a value; it corresponds to a real feeling; it has a relation to something which exists; yet this time we must describe this real thing—a bad book, an evil deed—with the help of negation. The negative here can represent something which, in spite of the negation, is a positive part of internal reality. In this reality, therefore, we shall include the opposition between positive and negative in our usage of the term 'opposite'.

But even here we have to pay special attention to this kind of opposition, for we have seen that the very fact that the negative has an important meaning can endanger our grasp of this reality. A morality of mere prohibitions, for instance, can easily replace any other kind of morality; yet it is very different from one based on the positive principle of love, and only the latter guarantees a full grasp of internal reality. There is, moreover, the danger of mixing up the two realities again and, by mistaking the negative for part of external reality, of using it to explain the whole of reality, which can drive us, as we have seen before, into a wrong and one-sided pessimism. The nature of the negation in every case needs careful consideration.

If we compare our usage of the concept 'opposite' with its common meaning we can say, therefore, that it includes contradictory opposites, contrasts, differences of degree, contradictions which can be derived from opposites and, in certain cases in internal reality, the opposition between positive and negative. It does not include contradictions which cannot be resolved and the opposition between positive and negative in external reality.

One could perhaps raise against our usage of the term the objection that we consider as opposites what are, in fact, nothing but differences. The concept 'difference' is very vague; it can mean very small divergencies, such as differences in quantity or quality; but it can also mean extreme oppositions as those between good and evil which, for instance in psychology, are sometimes considered as mere differences of degree. As we nowadays try to achieve a unitary way of thinking, we are always prone to reduce opposites to mere differences, thus making the real oppositions appear of less importance than they are. We have already seen, however, that the differences of degree are based on opposites, and if this investigation proves correct we shall also see that we ought to apply the concept 'opposite' far more frequently than is usually done, instead of distorting the facts by talking of mere differences.[1]

[1] The danger of this can be seen when we actually consider the opposition between good and evil as mere difference of degree, for this makes the whole sphere of morality relative.

## Chapter V

## THE EXTERNAL OPPOSITES

### 1. THE MAIN LINE OF OUR INVESTIGATION

It has been recognized that our knowledge of external reality, including the laws which the natural sciences discover and which technical inventions seem to prove beyond dispute, is dependent on the laws of our thinking and that, therefore, all such knowledge represents an indirect and relative knowledge and does not give us direct access to the absolute nature of reality. This fundamental thesis was firmly established by Kant and held by many philosophers before and after; moreover, it has found support from the most unexpected quarter; the recent developments in physics have shaken belief in the unlimited validity of the law of causality and thus in an absolute external necessity within the very branch of the natural sciences which seemed to guarantee the greatest possible certainty. In fact, these recent developments confirm what Kant has taught.[1]

Yet in spite of such strong support, this thesis has had very little influence. Firm belief in all external knowledge in general and in the natural sciences in particular, though robbed of its basis, has hardly been shaken. We no longer try, as in the nineteenth century, to find the final cause with the help of these sciences, nor do many people consider one of the concepts used by them as the absolute principle which explains everything. We hardly hope for such final explanations; but as we rely entirely on the unitary way of thinking which the sciences seem to make possible, their methods and results form, whether or not we are conscious of it, the body of knowledge which satisfies us as completely as the belief in some absolute principle did. Any other knowledge, though accepted by many individuals, is neglected and powerless in comparison. Every one of us, even if he accepts the teaching that external knowledge has to be considered as relative, will find it difficult to shake his own belief in external reality and in the natural sciences,

---

[1] This will be discussed in detail. See pp. 86-8.

and to trust things which cannot be seen, touched, measured or, at least, scientifically explained.

There seem to be two reasons which mainly explain this failure. On the one hand, the theory of knowledge rarely offers an alternative. It has become a special branch of knowledge, developed by specialists who only show that the foundations in which we believe are not the right ones, without showing what kind of belief would be right. The scientist is hardly influenced by these epistemological investigations; it does not matter to him whether his theories are based on absolute truth or on relative assumptions; it is even better, as we have seen, if he treats all his discoveries as mere hypotheses.[1] As the theory of knowledge does not force him to take another kind of knowledge into account, he can go on as if this theory did not exist, and so the general public, not familiar with the teachings of the specialists, accepts his findings as if these other teachings did not exist. External knowledge remains the only knowledge upon which we can rely, the only one which seems to offer some satisfaction for our craving for certainty.

On the other hand, even if the theory of knowledge offers an alternative, which in some cases it does, the gulf between the sciences and morals or religion remains so deep that this does not alter the position, for the one cannot influence the other. We have seen that Kant offers such an alternative; his belief in the moral world is so strong as to make him believe that it is even 'a device of nature' to deprive us of any absolute knowledge in the realm of external reality, in order to force us to look for this knowledge for which we crave in the realm of morals. We believe that his teaching is true; it corresponds to our distinction between external and internal reality. But in his teaching, too, these two spheres exist as completely separated spheres which have no connection with one another; we must behave in one sphere as scientists and in the other as moral beings, without being shown how these two necessities are to be reconciled in our real lives. His teaching has been developed by both philosophers and theologians, but the gulf has only grown wider and the two spheres still exist side by side without influencing each other. If one meets an adherent of one of them, one hardly guesses the existence of the other.

If we now try to show that all our knowledge is based on opposites, we hope that this will bridge the gap and give to the important results of the theory of knowledge the influence which they so badly need, and this we hope for the following reasons.

(1) The necessity of applying opposites shows that the same principle is involved in all our thinking and that the one kind of knowledge cannot, therefore, be more or less valid than the other. The fact that all knowledge is dependent on the same laws of thinking destroys the ex-

[1] See pp. 31–2.

## THE EXTERNAL OPPOSITES

clusive claims usually made in favour of external knowledge. Thoughts referring to internal reality can neither be regarded as mere personal prejudice nor disregarded because this reality cannot be touched nor seen nor grasped with the help of science. They must be judged on their own merits, for the knowledge based on sense-experiences as well as the highest achievements of the sciences also depend on the correct application of opposites.

(2) As we have to make use of different kinds of opposites, the necessity of applying them also shows that any thought which is founded upon one kind alone must be incomplete. If we want to achieve comprehensive knowledge, therefore, we are forced to consider the whole realm of our knowledge and to pay attention to both realities. Any other claim is revealed as one-sided.

(3) Moreover, we cannot concentrate on external opposites alone, because the seemingly exclusive validity of external knowledge is made possible, as we shall see in greater detail in this chapter, by unconsciously introducing internal opposites. To make our outlook consistent, we are forced to introduce judgments of value without realizing that we do so, for we can ignore other aspects of experience, which clearly exist, only by judging them to be of no value. Even for the correct apprehension of external reality, therefore, the knowledge of internal reality is indispensable, for only if we apply the internal opposites consciously and correctly can we know that our knowledge of external reality is correct and remains unimpaired.

(4) Nor can we concentrate on internal reality alone, for the confusing of external and internal opposites must have very misleading consequences here too. If internal opposites are mistaken for statements about external facts, all our knowledge is fundamentally distorted.[1] This, again, makes it indispensable to distinguish between external and internal opposites, which can only be done if we know both.

(5) The danger which is greatest to-day—that of overlooking completely the existence of internal reality when dealing with external facts—is eliminated by the necessity of transferring concepts from one reality to the other. As the concepts on which our knowledge of external reality is based—cause and effect, force, necessity—are transferred from internal reality, they cannot be understood in external reality at all; if we know that we think in opposites, however, this will no longer puzzle us, for we also know that we have to look for their meaning in internal reality from which they have been transferred. Thus external knowledge even points towards internal reality, for we are bound to try to understand the meaning of the concepts which we apply.

(6) But again, this important and necessary emphasis upon the

[1] See pp. 7 and 55.

## THE EXTERNAL AND INTERNAL OPPOSITES

knowledge of internal reality does not lead to the temptation of concentrating on this reality alone (which may become the danger of tomorrow). As we need external forms to grasp internal reality, we must acquire a clear knowledge of external reality as well. The emphasis upon internal reality does not allow us, therefore, to renounce the correct application of external opposites; it does not even allow us, as we have seen, to renounce the development of the natural sciences.[1]

Thus, if we recognize the necessity of applying opposites, we can no longer confine ourselves to one way of thinking. The importance of internal reality becomes obvious even when we try to understand external reality, and the knowledge of internal reality needs the external opposites in order to become reliable and to lead to full knowledge. At the same time, the different kinds of knowledge are so closely interconnected that no gulf remains which might encourage us to restrict our thoughts to one reality alone.

(7) Finally, the necessity of applying opposites will also make us see that what matters most is to understand the division into two realities. Thus we are driven onwards until we reach the interconnected opposites, and these presuppose and test the correct application of all the different kinds of opposites. This will be discussed later.

The fact, however, that the knowledge of external reality has been overdeveloped and overestimated for a long time shows the line which we have to follow in our investigation of external opposites. When investigating internal opposites, we shall have to try to build up the knowledge of internal reality, for this knowledge has almost been lost. The knowledge of external reality does not require any such help; on the contrary it has to be prevented from invading other spheres. Here it is our main task, therefore, to prove that all our external knowledge is based on opposites, for this will enable us to confine this knowledge to its legitimate sphere and to make room for internal reality. In this way we shall also get to know the external opposites well enough to avoid any confusion of them with the other kinds of opposites. For, in spite of the general belief in a unitary external knowledge, these opposites can easily be recognized.

### 2. OPPOSITES INDISPENSABLE FOR THE KNOWLEDGE OF EXTERNAL REALITY

External things and events are correctly apprehended, according to our definition, when we perceive them as being independent of their relation to the person observing them; they have to exist in space and

---

[1] This does not mean, however, that a better knowledge of internal reality should not influence the sciences; it may prove very helpful in relating them again to human experience and moral principles.

## THE EXTERNAL OPPOSITES

time; and they must be describable in terms of general validity, so that, if they are correctly described, everybody can recognize them.[1]

The external opposites which help in the apprehension of this reality have to conform to these requirements. They seem, therefore, to be derived directly from external facts; they always refer to something which exists in space and time; they appear at first sight as a mere selection from facts which we find in external reality.[2] Their independence of the observer, moreover, finds its expression in their being independent of each other; each of the two parts of the opposites can be used by itself and seems to exist separately. If one part is taken away the other remains unimpaired. We can isolate the quality 'dark' as well as the quality 'light'; we can observe 'movement' without thinking consciously of 'rest'; we can concentrate on necessity and forget freedom. This independence of each other seems most strongly to confirm their external existence and their independence of the observer.

Nor can we alter arbitrarily the relationship between the two parts of the opposites; the light object is and always must be light in comparison with the dark object. The quality may appear different in different pairs of opposites; the light object may seem dark when compared with a lighter object; but such a change never takes place within the same pair of opposites, and within the new opposition the relationship is once more fixed. It is this impossibility of interchanging the parts at will which enables us to give a description of general validity.

The independence and the fixed relationship between these pairs of opposites makes it all too easy to overlook the part played by our thinking in external knowledge, and to consider this knowledge as a unitary system of thought. As the concepts forming the opposites seem to refer to something which has an independent existence of its own, they must create the impression that we apprehend this reality without forming special opposites. Yet it can easily be shown that there is no external knowledge whatever which is not based on opposites, and that this application of opposites is enforced by the laws of thinking.

We have already shown that our conception of qualities is dependent on opposites; the opposites 'light' and 'dark' have helped us to recognize that it is only by means of opposites that these and similar qualities can be apprehended at all.[3] To form any such concept we must look at the object solely from one point of view and exclude all other observations and considerations; to see it as bright, we must neglect

---

[1] See pp. 25-6.

[2] Language, however, encourages us once more in our investigation. The word 'fact' is derived from the Latin *facere*, to do; we must do something to create facts. The German word *Tatsache* makes this even clearer; it indicates that the matter (*Sache*) is dependent on our deed (*Tat*).

[3] See especially pp. 9-10 and 68.

## THE EXTERNAL AND INTERNAL OPPOSITES

its heaviness, size, coldness, and so on, and this isolation of one quality to the exclusion of all others and also of the object itself can be achieved only with the help of the opposite 'dark'. It is thus that we are enabled to concentrate on one quality alone.

This applies to qualities in general, but there seems to be one very striking exception. Yet this apparent exception, in fact, confirms most conclusively the necessity of applying opposites.

This exception is our apprehension of colours. It is not necessary, indeed it is hardly possible, to think of an opposite if we apprehend, for instance, red or green.[1] These concepts apply directly to a sense-impression which seems to be given without any opposition; we cannot explain the concept 'red' by calling 'green' its opposite; we can only explain it by pointing at something which is red. While in such cases as 'light' and 'dark' the opposite helps us to form the concept, it seems that, with colours, opposites enter our thought only when we proceed to their abstract explanation and base them on the number and length of light waves, thus creating a scale of degrees which implies opposites. But this explanation is quite obviously a later abstraction; it has nothing to do with our knowledge of the colours themselves which we apprehend independently of any such theory. The two rather exclude each other; we either see colours or observe wave motions.[2]

This exception, however, is due to the fact that the eye is the most highly developed organ we possess. We have already mentioned some characteristics of this high development when comparing it with other senses, and we have seen that it can by itself oppose light to outward darkness.[3] Owing to this high development, opposites are used by the eye when it creates the sense-impressions of colours. Every colour has a corresponding complementary colour which forms its opposite, and it is only because this opposition is brought about by the eye itself that we hardly consider it as an opposition at all and need not apply it in our thinking. In exceptional circumstances the opposition becomes obvious; if we are dazzled by a strong red light and close our eyes, we shall see the complementary colour green. The complementary colour also becomes visible when we compare different shadows, a shadow cast by candlelight, for instance, and that cast simultaneously by daylight, for the first appears blue and the second yellow—a phenomenon which cannot be explained by wavelengths at all, but only by these opposites.[4] It is also characteristic, moreover, that we cannot see both

[1] I say 'hardly possible' and not 'impossible' because painters, who have a more strongly developed sense of colours, experience and use them as opposites.

[2] See W. Heisenberg, *Wandlungen in den Grundlagen der Naturwissenschaft*, p. 36. This book confirms most of the conclusions of this chapter from the point of view of the physicist.

[3] See p. 10.

[4] See J. S. Haldane, *The Philosophical Basis of Biology*, pp. 90–1.

## THE EXTERNAL OPPOSITES

the shortest and the longest rays—ultra-violet and infra-red. This indicates that our faculty of seeing is limited by the ability of the eye to make use of opposites; it cannot embrace opposites which lie too far apart, and thus visibility ceases. Only abstract thought, using opposites of its own, can go beyond.

Colours are usually considered as 'secondary qualities'—that is, it has been recognized that they are as closely connected with our ways of apprehending them as with the objects themselves. People who are colour-blind see a different scale of colours, and other living beings, as far as we can say, may see in quite different ways, or even react to the light-waves as if they were radio-waves. Nevertheless, colours are the most general attribute of external reality as we perceive it; we do not see anything colourless, our whole world is completely steeped in colours. This shows once again the great importance of the high development of the eye, and thus the fact that its activity is based on the application of opposites is also one of the best proofs that the need for opposites is fundamental and comprehensive.[1]

When we proceed to the objects themselves, we must, as we have seen, apply opposites to apprehend and describe them.[2] Apart from their qualities, we need the opposition between the filled space and the empty space; we find out the boundaries of the object by contrasting it with its surroundings. We must oppose the form to the content, and we ascertain and describe the different materials with the help of different scales of degrees. But there seems to be once more an important exception—the fact that objects can be made known with the help of names.

There are unique objects and persons, countries and places, whose names do not imply any opposite at all. The name 'sun', for instance, undoubtedly applies directly to this single object; none of the abstractions which are based on opposites are required to form the name 'sun'. There are, of course, opposites which help to create our sense-impression, and we need these when we try to imagine or to describe the sun; but we leave them behind when we think of the name itself; the sun has no opposite. It is only a later discovery that it is a star, and only then do opposites enter our thinking once more; yet knowledge of the sun is quite independent of this discovery.

This fact would be a difficulty only if we assumed that our thinking created reality, and we have never doubted that reality has to make an impression upon us before we are able to think about it. It does not seem surprising that an impression can be given a name. But at the same time it is highly characteristic that we need opposites, so to speak, on both sides of the name. On the one hand, we need them to have a

---

[1] Something similar may apply to sound as well, for we never hear pure sounds, but always their overtones too. Music uses opposites to a very great extent.

[2] See pp. 11–12.

## THE EXTERNAL AND INTERNAL OPPOSITES

clear sense-impression; the senses must isolate the object with the help of opposites before we are able to fix it by a name. This can be seen when we try to describe the object; we must describe the sun by its qualities such as bright, round, hot, thus making use of opposites, and we can hardly imagine it without opposing it to the surrounding sky. On the other hand, the name remains independent of opposites only so long as we do not know the nature of the object; as soon as we discover that the sun is a star, opposites are needed to give form to and to explain this abstraction—in this case, at least, the opposition between form and content and that between movement and rest. All such names indicate, therefore, that our thinking, though able to apprehend and to describe these objects, cannot proceed further; we do not know why there is, for us, only one such object as the sun. The point where the application of opposites becomes impossible or superfluous shows exactly where our thinking is forced to stop.

The same applies to the more general names. It is true that, to form them, we need many abstractions which require the help of opposites. To obtain the general name applying to every tree, for instance, we have to eliminate all those characteristics which belong to individual trees, which we do by opposing different trees to one another, thus gradually discovering what is essential and what accidental. This we can do, because the opposition between form and content enables us to recognize the different forms as accidental and to separate them from the general concept. Nevertheless, all such general names contain an element of uniqueness which cannot be further broken down or explained, but must be taken for granted. Neither the tree nor the star have a direct opposite, and their further explanation which needs opposites does not dispense with these names altogether. But this does not mean that we are able to think without opposites; it shows, on the contrary, the boundaries of our thinking. It confirms that our thinking depends on the impression evoked by external reality and that we cannot consider thought as the creator of the world. Yet the activity of thinking as such depends on the application of opposites.

The contrary difficulty arises when reality itself seems to provide us with opposites, for then they appear no longer as laws of our thinking—as, for instance, in the case of men and women. But even there thinking plays a most important part in forming and applying the opposites. Both men and women are human beings; they have many characteristics in common; they are members of families and nations; they have each, moreover, individual characteristics which are independent of their being men and women. But we must forget all that and concentrate exclusively on those qualities which enable us to bring them into clear opposition; we must isolate these qualities like all others as soon as we want to use these concepts with precision. It may

## THE EXTERNAL OPPOSITES

or may not be surprising that nature contains such opposites; this question does not concern us here;[1] but, even if such opposites occur in external reality, thinking has to transform them so thoroughly that, in our final usage of the terms, they are not different from those external opposites which spring from thinking alone.

There are also, to take another example, positive and negative electrons, but here the case is simpler; we know so little about them that this abstract description which uses the opposites created by thinking seems to be sufficient. If we knew more we should no doubt soon discover how one-sided this view of them is and how little justice it does to the electrons so described.[2]

The more we proceed into the realm of abstraction, the more the opposites which we usually apply disappear; but it is easy to detect that the part which the thinking in opposites plays becomes even more important. Abstract thinking gradually breaks down the world as we know it through our senses. The table and the air, for instance, so completely opposed to each other in our actual perception, become different kinds of matter, different combinations of atoms and electrons; the stone which we see fall does so because of the power of attraction of the earth which we do not see; sun and earth become stars among the other stars with which originally we would hardly compare them. Abstract thinking creates a world of its own which cuts right across the world which we see and touch. This different world, however, can be created only because it is kept together by the laws of our thinking—that is, by concepts which are made real by their opposites. It is only because we can always fall back on an opposite that, in the void with which abstraction confronts us, we can find a basis which gradually enables us to become more and more independent of our senses.[3]

The abstract world depends mainly on our faculty of establishing between the phenomena connections which are different from those which we immediately perceive. We must see everything within space and time which, though conditions of our perception, are not directly grasped, as Kant has shown, but mere forms added to it.[4] We must bring into opposition different objects, such as the falling stone and the earth, and this opposition must be explained in terms of cause and effect. We must test the objects by the opposites of form and content,

---

[1] It would be fascinating—but a rather doubtful speculation—to follow up the principle of opposition in nature itself. However, as this is a metaphysical question, it does not come within the scope of this investigation.

[2] The fact that more and more kinds of electrons are being discovered seems to confirm this view.

[3] The void to which abstraction leads—formal mathematical calculations leading beyond the sphere of imagination—has become visible in modern physics. It hovers 'above a bottomless abyss'. See W. Heisenberg, op. cit., p. 95.

[4] This will be considered later. See pp. 179 ff.

## THE EXTERNAL AND INTERNAL OPPOSITES

and the causal connections by the opposition between necessity and accident, so as to be able to decide what is merely accidental and what can include other objects or events as well. We must see the whole of external reality as a multiplicity of single units, so that we can see the single objects or events as instances of general laws which may be applied to many such units. All this can be done because, from the very beginning of our perception, we find the world of the senses organized by the constructive concepts and thus can simply shift the emphasis from our sense-impressions to such opposites as space and time, cause and effect, matter and energy, form and content, the One and the Many—in short, to the concepts upon which the abstract world rests.

But does not, in the end, this progressive abstraction and the process of breaking down the seen reality also dissolve the constructive concepts themselves and base all knowledge on a single unitary principle of explanation? In modern physics, we hardly need any longer to differentiate between matter and energy, nor between space and time, and the more the different natural sciences advance, the more they are being unified, as happened for instance with physics and chemistry. Are we not able to think of a single natural science which would create an abstract world governed by one unitary principle, independent of all the opposites which we have mentioned?

We have already had several opportunities of pointing out that the advance of the sciences does not make them independent of opposites. On the contrary, the more they advance, the clearer their dependence on them becomes; it is when we renounce sensual apprehension completely that we come nearest to a pure and unmitigated application of opposites. It is clear, for instance, that the sciences are forced to use merely the bare opposites if the universe has to be considered as being infinite and yet limited, or if light has to be explained by the two contradictory assumptions that it consists both of pure waves which do not contain any matter and of material particles moving in a straight line across space. It is no accident that the electrons themselves have now to be considered in a similar way. That these contradictory assumptions, though they cannot be reconciled, have both to be accepted and both to be made the basis of calculation certainly shows clearly that we must conform to the requirements of our thinking. Similarly, the opposites come to the fore when matter is being broken down with the help of electrons into pure energy, for this energy has to be gathered again into quanta and fields.[1]

The opposites we normally use are reconciled, because they refer to the unitary impression of reality which is merely made accessible by them; these theories, however, are satisfied with the opposites as such. They are so difficult to understand just because most of them do not

[1] See also pp. 12, 30–1, 49–51.

## THE EXTERNAL OPPOSITES

even attempt to overcome the opposites, thus renouncing all relationship to the things we know and are able to imagine.

The most abstract theories, moreover, must start from the normal apprehension of reality and be tested by producing within it the effects desired, so that they can never free themselves completely from the opposites implied in our original perception. Their consequences only become discernible in the realms of the infinitely large or the infinitely small—of the stars or electrons; the world we live in remains a special case to which simpler theories apply, theories which are still based on the opposites used in perception, especially on the necessity of causal connections. As all theories have to start from this world and to return to it, no theory can escape entirely from the opposites which it seems to eliminate. Even if causality is no longer recognized as valid within the framework of the theory itself, the causal law has to guarantee a reliable relationship between the object under observation and the observed result, for otherwise experiments would be impossible. The same is true of measurements and technical application of scientific knowledge.[1] The new discoveries, far indeed from contradicting Kant's teaching that causality is merely a category of thinking, thus confirm it; they show that it belongs, not to reality as such, for the deeper we understand it the less we can adhere to a strict causality, but to the laws of our thinking, for despite all such theoretical knowledge the application of causality remains indispensable.

The abstract theories are usually founded upon higher mathematics and it is very difficult, therefore, to follow them in those spheres which transcend the world we know. Nor is this necessary for our purpose, for the mere fact that they need mathematics shows that the opposites are not being overcome even there and that the emphasis is once more only being shifted from our sense-impressions to abstract opposites and constructive concepts. We have mentioned before that Kant proved beyond doubt that numbers cannot be won by abstraction alone, his proof being so conclusive that there is no need to repeat it here. He proved the same for mathematical axioms and all 'synthetical' mathematical laws; none of them represent pure abstractions from reality, because all their basic elements, such as numbers, straight lines, regular triangles and spheres have to be constructed first before one can begin to base abstractions on them.[2] Opposites must help us to arrive at a regularity which can never be found complete in reality itself, for they are needed to exclude all accidental deviations, and constructive concepts must show that these deviations are accidental and must make it possible to apply the laws thus recognized to a reality which, without them, would not be accessible to such generalizations.

In particular there is, in the last resort, no escape from the opposi-

---
[1] See W. Heisenberg, op. cit., p. 17.   [2] See pp. 58–9.

## THE EXTERNAL AND INTERNAL OPPOSITES

tion between the One and the Many. Although we are unable to eliminate the forms of space and time from our perception, we may be able to abolish them, at least apparently, in certain mathematical calculations.[1] We may also be able, in general, to make the distinction between form and content seem unimportant when we replace that between matter and energy by mathematical formulæ. The calculus of probability may help us to bridge the gap between our practical dependence on the necessary working of causality or the necessity implied in mathematical laws on the one hand, and the recognition that such a causal necessity cannot be characteristic of primary reality on the other hand. But no scientific advance can ever free us from the opposition between the One and the Many, for all mathematics rests upon it, and no law, derived from a special case, could ever be applied to similar cases or to the whole of reality without it. Our knowledge would be reduced to single names, applying to unique things, if we were not able to establish this relationship within reality, and only so far as we are able to establish it are we able to get beyond the realm of mere impressions. This forms a last barrier which no science can possibly surmount.

But there is also another consideration which shows conclusively that the sciences cannot finally overcome the opposites on which all our knowledge is based. We have mentioned, so far, only the results of modern physics, because this science has made the greatest advances into the realm of the hitherto unknown, and because any complete unification of the different natural sciences would have to accept these most revealing discoveries as its final foundation. Such a unification would also be one of the conditions of any really unitary system; but this unification, too, cannot possibly succeed completely.

We have had to stress before that external and internal reality do not represent different parts of reality, but that both include the whole of reality, which is seen each time from a different point of view.[2] The same is true, though perhaps to a lesser extent, of the different branches of the natural sciences; all of them investigate almost the whole of reality from their special point of view. Physics includes man and living beings so far as they are matter and solid objects; in many respects, as with weight for instance, physical considerations are very important for us, though we are living beings. Biology has to include the whole environment of living beings; it has to deal with their physical surroundings and dwellings, with the chemical analysis of their food, with the climate and even the sun, but it must look at all these from

[1] Time is being considered as a fourth dimension, but as more and completely abstract dimensions have to be assumed as well, this transformation has little to do with the time which we experience.

[2] See pp. 21-4.

## THE EXTERNAL OPPOSITES

the biological point of view. All these elements are also important for psychology, which in its turn has to deal with the whole environment of man, although only so far as it produces psychological effects. It is true that physics will hardly deal with purely biological or psychological phenomena, though the boundaries between molecules and cells have become doubtful and though attempts are being made to explain thoughts by movements of particles in the brain, and it is also true that biology or psychology will hardly deal with the stars and galaxies, though astrology seems to satisfy a deep seated longing of mankind. Nevertheless, the phenomena which form the common subject of all the sciences and which have to be considered from different points of view, thus excluding complete unification, undoubtedly cover the greater part of external reality.[1]

This overlapping of the sciences cannot possibly be overcome by their unification. Any unification rests on an advance in abstraction and has to be based on the most abstract theories; this, however, leaves some spheres completely untouched, and to these different methods have to be applied. The old differentiation between the sciences is, therefore, preserved. Even in the very realm of physics we still need a description of the different stars, and have to try to discover their history which, as it represents something which cannot be repeated, can never be replaced by purely abstract theory. Chemistry has been based on physical laws, but no abstract observation can make superfluous the observation of chemical processes by chemical methods. The lack of advance in our knowledge of colours is most probably due to the fact that no attention has been paid to the necessity for applying different principles to this sphere, for abstract knowledge, as we have just said, cannot help us to know the colours as such.[2] The same is true of biology, where no theories will ever abolish botany or zoology or physiology, and psychology will have to describe our actual thoughts and feelings whether or not science succeeds in explaining them by purely mechanical processes in the nerve-system. It would be an immense impoverishment of our knowledge if a super-science tried to destroy all these old-established branches of the sciences.

All this shows once more that no advance in science can ever free us from the opposites which are the condition of our natural perception. We may advance still farther than seems possible to-day; we shall still have to pay attention to the stones and the trees, to the stars and the countries, to flowers and animals and men, if we want to have knowledge of them at all. The renunciation of opposites means loss of knowledge.

[1] This has been thoroughly elaborated in J. S. Haldane, *The Philosophical Basis of Biology*.
[2] See p. 82.

## THE EXTERNAL AND INTERNAL OPPOSITES

The advance of the sciences, moreover, though it seems to enable us to dream of their final unification, has in fact led to an ever increasing specialization. While the unification seems to come within reach, scientific work has to be split up into more and more special branches. This indicates that we cannot even reduce the number of opposites. As soon as some oppositions give way to a unitary principle, new oppositions and differentiations spring into being; the differences between physics and chemistry, between animate and inanimate matter, may disappear, but each of the different kinds of molecules and atoms, of electrons and rays requires a different approach and technique and thus a new special branch within the unified science.[1] It is true that this specialization rests on a far greater unity of method than the different older branches of the sciences. But this unity does not alter the position, for wherever unity could be strengthened, the impoverishment we have just had to mention took place, and only so far as new differentiations and oppositions were established has our knowledge been enriched. Nuclear physics, for instance, has enlarged our field of understanding, but we had to renounce the hope of understanding the qualities themselves; if the quicker or slower movement of the atom produces warmth, it cannot itself be warm, and the atom-theory cannot deal with warmth as such.[2]

Again, it would certainly be very difficult to follow up this specialization and to investigate in every case whether mere differences or the familiar opposites are being stressed, or whether new opposites are being created. But there can hardly be any doubt that such an investigation would disclose the application of the familiar opposites and the creation of new ones. In any case, it would confirm what has been said before. Any isolation of a group of phenomena requires the help of opposites, all experiments must make use of the opposites of our normal perception, and specializations also increase the importance of mathematics, thus pointing to the final barrier of opposites which no abstraction can surmount.

The difficulty lies rather in another direction; to investigate specialization, the philosopher himself would have to become a specialist in all sciences and thus cease to be a philosopher. Each of the special different departments of science presents so many difficulties that it is hardly possible to change over from one to the other, and the mass of special knowledge has grown so large that no single mind can hope any longer to grasp even the bare results of all the sciences, in spite of the considerable unity of method and of all prospects of a final unification. So far as thinking is concerned, we are not really overpowering external reality, but being overpowered by it; as we are unable to grasp it as a whole, we are lost in a maze of unconnected and meaningless details.

[1] See W. Heisenberg, op. cit., p. 22.   [2] Ibid., pp. 24, 27.

## THE EXTERNAL OPPOSITES

If specialization had to be taken into account, therefore, philosophy would cease to be possible.

Yet this difficulty is hardly important, because such an investigation would not serve an important purpose. The fundamental facts are what matters; philosophy is not called on to follow the details of the natural sciences, but to disclose their nature, so as to be able to show their significance and their right place in the general ordering of human life. That philosophy has lost its influence to such a degree seems mainly due to the fact that it has been overwhelmed by the natural sciences and given way to specialization, instead of dealing with the sciences from a philosophical point of view. It is the fundamental facts which must help us to decide how far science can reveal truth.

These fundamental facts have been established. There is no knowledge of external reality which is not based on external opposites, and the sciences are unable to break them down, for they cannot get away from the original opposites of our perceptions, nor can mathematics, which even the greatest abstractions must use, dispense with all the constructive concepts. All this is confirmed when the striving for unification, instead of leading to unity, brings about specialization.

The constructive concepts, however, by defining the boundaries of external knowledge, show us that we must apply internal opposites, too, if we want to do justice to our experience.

### 3. THE SPECIAL IMPORTANCE OF THE CONSTRUCTIVE CONCEPTS

One of the most important factors in scientific thinking is the boundaries of the subject which is to be investigated. So long as men thought that there was an edge to the earth, the sky remained a half-sphere and the sun a flat disk. It was only when it had been discovered that the earth is a ball—that is, when its real boundaries became known—that the heavens could be transformed into a universe and that the shape and movements of the celestial bodies could be described correctly. Recent progress in physics has been possible because the boundaries of the physical world have once more been shifted and the infinitely large and the infinitely small have gradually been more and more included in its scope. The knowledge of life has similarly been dependent on the length of time taken into consideration; so long as thinking was confined to the present, single species existed without any connection with each other; the theory of evolution presupposed the breaking down of these time-limits and became possible only after the past had been made accessible as well.

The erecting of correct boundaries becomes even more important when we consider external reality as a whole.

## THE EXTERNAL AND INTERNAL OPPOSITES

So long as a stroke of lightning was considered as an evil demon or as divine judgment, it was impossible to gain knowledge which could protect man against nature; yet, at the same time, morality remained dependent on reward and punishment, instead of being based on the good as such. So long as it was considered essential for the Christian belief that the earth should be the centre of the world, all progress in the realm of the natural sciences was impossible; yet, at the same time, religion seemed to be dependent on an assumption which has no bearing upon true faith, a dependence which had fateful consequences when knowledge finally developed. To-day we are no longer in danger of personifying natural forces or events, but rather in the opposite danger of excluding from serious consideration everything which cannot be explained mechanically, and of believing the working of man's mind to be a purely mechanical process. The consequences are even more dangerous; because internal reality is being completely suppressed, man can no longer counterbalance this scientific development, and now it is this development itself which threatens him with destruction.

It is possible, of course, that the individual person experiences the consequences of a stroke of lightning as divine judgment, but this is an inner experience and does not give us any knowledge of external reality. Similarly some mechanical explanations of human behaviour may be of importance for certain impersonal aspects of our lives, but they provide no knowledge of internal reality. We can include, as we have seen, any part of reality either in external or internal reality, but we must not try to explain the one by the other. It is just in such cases as these where the object referred to seems to belong, not to the reality which is actually being considered, but to the other—lightning to external, psychological processes to internal reality—that the drawing of the right boundaries is of the utmost importance. We must clearly recognize what our conclusions mean; otherwise knowledge of both realities is destroyed.

The erecting of wrong boundaries creates this danger because it allows arbitrariness. We can test our knowledge of reality only by finding out whether the laws of thinking have been applied correctly, and test these laws by finding out whether the results correspond to our real experience.[1] The proof that the test has been successful consists in the establishing of a necessary relationship between the two. If, however, we extend the realm of internal reality into external reality, or that of external into internal reality, no such certainty can be achieved. The possible personal interpretations of a stroke of lightning are as many as the possible scientific explanations of the sub-conscious elements in psychology. No interpretations of this kind can ever be proved beyond doubt; it will always be possible to replace them by others, according

[1] See p. 20, note.

## THE EXTERNAL OPPOSITES

to the intentions or opinions of the different interpreters. Our knowledge remains insecure and open to distortions.

The task of setting boundaries is that of the constructive concepts. Our knowledge of each reality needs elements from the other, and only these concepts transfer them in such a way that the character of external or internal reality is not impaired. If we now consider only the external reality with which we are concerned here—all such concepts as cause, force, time, freedom, though belonging to internal reality, are transferred as purely formal concepts which do not disclose the content as such, but give only its abstraction, thus enabling us to gain that formal knowledge which is adequate for external reality. By giving a firm foundation to their opposites which are the main characteristics of external reality—to effect, matter, space, necessity—they enable us to concentrate on external reality itself without any further reference to internal reality. These concepts, therefore, represent boundaries, for, by the way in which the transferring is done, they force our attention in one direction only. We have seen that they have to be used in quite a different way when referring to internal reality; we have to start from them, as from any other boundary, in two different directions if we want to enter either the one or the other realm.

The urge for unity must sweep across these boundaries because they would exclude a large part of primary reality from external reality, and thus this urge is mainly directed against the application of constructive concepts. We have just said that the modern development of science transcends some of them; though it cannot succeed in eliminating all, a great deal of confusion is brought about by wrong generalizations, based on theories which have been partially successful in this respect.[1] These conclusions seem to have a certain justification, because the constructive concepts are being replaced by negations; matter does not exist, causality is negated, and, above all, inner processes are eliminated by being reduced to material ones. There seems to be nothing left outside the sphere of these theories upon which we could base any objections to them, and it is this very fact which creates the confusion.

The part which negation plays in external reality has already been explained. The negative as such has been recognized as meaningless in it, for we know this reality only so far as we know something. External negation, therefore, must remain a purely formal principle, helping us to deny errors, to limit special spheres in external reality and to focus attention upon them. Its most important task consists in making abstraction possible; if we progress, for instance, from the concept of a beech-tree to that of a tree, and then further to such concepts as plant, organism, wood, matter, we have always to use negation to eliminate some particular characteristics which belong only to the more concrete

[1] See pp. 85 ff.

concepts and no longer to the more abstract ones. But we have also seen that the constructive concepts cannot be derived in this way; no abstraction from external reality could ever lead to such concepts as cause and effect. They are based on abstractions from internal reality and have to be added to external reality to enable us to grasp it. They are not part of the external reality which we apprehend, but presuppositions of our apprehension. Hence negation must not interfere with them; as it has a purely logical function, it can make possible abstractions within external reality, but must not be allowed to effect changes in the premises themselves, which it would do if it touched these concepts. Negation must be halted before it affects the constructive concepts, for otherwise it would rob external reality of its foundations.[1]

We have had to mention before that we ought to see this difference in the process of abstraction. Negation only makes the importance of this difference more obvious. So long as it makes possible those abstractions which can be derived from external reality, as, for instance, when we proceed from 'tree' to 'matter', only particular characteristics are gradually excluded, but the connection with reality is never lost; we can go back even from the most abstract concept to reality and point at things which represent matter. This, therefore, is the legitimate use of negation, for here it has purely logical functions; it creates simpler concepts which allow us to deal with external reality more easily. Yet if we negate such concepts as 'cause' and 'effect', they are eliminated altogether; there is either causality or no causality. We do not create a new and simpler concept, but effect changes in the fundamental structure, thus transcending the legitimate sphere of negation. As nothingness has no meaning in external reality, this kind of negation is pure destruction and we must beware of it. It is justified so far as errors have to be destroyed, but not in the process of abstraction.

If negation transcends these limits and is used to satisfy the urge for unity, correct thinking is inevitably falsified in at least four ways.

(1) Abstraction from the constructive concepts confronts us with that nothingness which has no meaning in external reality and thus really destroys it. Recent developments in physics, for instance, by depriving space and time of all those characteristics which make them different, exclude the world of our perception from scientific theory; by negating causality, they leave the world of our actual experience behind; the only things which have remained intact are mathematical formulæ, because the One and the Many are the only constructive concepts which have not been negated.

(2) Our thinking is necessarily falsified, because it is this very nothingness which is required to make the knowledge of external reality

---
[1] For this and the following, see pp. 54–5, 56–9, 75.

## THE EXTERNAL OPPOSITES

our only and comprehensive knowledge. The negative as such must show that there is nothing beyond external reality which asks for further investigation and thereby contradicts unity. The claim that scientific knowledge can explain the whole of reality implies that everything which has to be grasped by other methods is either not real or not true —that is, that it is nothing at all. The elimination of contradictory elements such as values, feelings, meaning and inner experiences, does not rest upon a thorough investigation, for science cannot grasp them; it rests on pure negation, for the claim that nothing can possibly escape scientific investigation can only be upheld when all those things which actually do escape are negated, so as to appear as nothing. Naturally, the results of such a method of thinking must be distorted.

(3) Negation, thus employed, is also bound to falsify the opposites upon which our thinking rests. The claim that external reality is all-inclusive only appears convincing because a real opposition seems to be established, an opposition which adds to the many other opposites a last and fundamental one—external reality, representing everything, is confronted with complete nothingness. But from all we have said it is already clear that negation cannot create a real opposite to external reality. The main characteristic of all fruitful opposites is that both parts are in some sense positive; they allow us to understand reality because both parts refer to it. Nothingness, however, does not exist; it comes into being only by the denial of elements of reality which do exist. The opposition is wrong, because its negative part represents only a negation of positive elements of reality. The thinking in opposites, therefore, is not applied, but misused; it lends the appearance of truth to an opposition which does not consist of real opposites.

(4) In fact—and this is the most dangerous falsification—this meaningless and wrong opposition is only accepted because the two realities have been mixed up and unacknowledged value-judgments have been introduced into external reality. We have seen that negation has a meaning in internal reality and that positive and negative values are both positive, in so far as they both refer to a real experience; it is only because a negative value can be attached to everything outside the scope of scientific investigation that the crude negation of existing elements of reality becomes acceptable. The statement that nothing can escape such an investigation means, in fact, that all other experiences and all other knowledge are of no value for our knowledge of reality; their apparently complete negation represents nothing but a negation of their value. They are not really considered as non-existent, but as worthless or wrong. A value-judgment, meaningless in external reality, borrows meaning from internal reality in order to give an appearance of meaning to nothingness which otherwise would have no meaning in external reality.

## THE EXTERNAL AND INTERNAL OPPOSITES

Thus, however, negation interferes with the fundamental conditions of our thinking which we have stated. It becomes impossible to fulfil the two main conditions of a correct division into two realities—namely, that they have to be completely separated and yet to be taken into account simultaneously. The separation is destroyed, and as the participation of internal reality is not even acknowledged, it can no longer be taken into account. But in this way we see that negation confirms most strikingly the need to insist on the fulfilment of these conditions, for now indeed all possibility of correct thinking vanishes. Supported by such a method, arbitrariness reigns supreme. Unacknowledged value-judgments enable the modern scientific mind, alive in all of us, to attack everything which threatens to disturb unitary scientific thinking.

This arbitrariness becomes particularly obvious when science tries to deal with internal reality, as in psychology and sociology. There results are so insecure that, if one wants to accept one of the systems of theories which exist side by side, there is no way but arbitrary choice. Moreover, as the inner phenomena can be considered only in their external aspects and thus not fully understood, there is always a tendency to attack—more directly and violently than in other sciences—anyone who believes in the existence of an internal reality.

Finally—and this is by far the most important distortion—the meaning of all inner experiences, of the absolute values, of belief can no longer be understood. As unconscious value-judgments are used to exclude conscious valuation, the values as such disappear, and even the occasional discovery of such an illegitimate value-judgment only adds to their bad reputation. Negation, freed from all necessary limitations, drives abstraction into the regions of nothingness, and human life, deprived of its values, becomes abstract too, which makes man the more willing to support this development with perverted value-judgments. They do not succeed in giving meaning to external nothingness, but they do succeed, to a most dangerous degree, in supplying negation with human energy. Nothingness finally seems to acquire meaning, because it becomes real as an inner void in man, and because this void, by creating intense dissatisfaction, turns as a destructive force against all reality.

Conscious thinking in opposites could do a great deal to counter these disastrous consequences of wrong thinking. It is the urge for unity which drives us onwards into more and more abstract regions and makes us overlook the obvious consequences of an unrestricted negation. Truth seems to lie in this direction alone. If we knew from the beginning that we could never get away from the opposites altogether and that their final exclusion could only lead to a complete void, we could prevent ourselves from supporting science by a false nothingness

## THE EXTERNAL OPPOSITES

which alone creates the appearance of a unitary method of thinking. As we always need opposites, truth must be different from the knowledge of external reality, for the mere fact that we must apply opposites forces upon us conclusions of a different kind. The constructive concepts in particular, applying to both realities, but with a different meaning in each, can best enable us to understand the significance of external reality and of scientific knowledge and to see their relationship to other kinds of knowing.

## Chapter VI

### THE NATURE OF FEELING

AMONG the human faculties it is feeling which is the main source of our knowledge of internal reality. Neither thinking nor willing need necessarily refer to that reality; thinking can serve the apprehension of external reality or purely practical purposes or make us conscious of inner experiences, and willing can be determined either by thinking or by feeling. Both will only disclose internal reality if feeling is the determining factor. It is true that feeling, in its turn, can be influenced by acts of thinking or willing which do not spring from feeling, but even then the participation of feeling will disclose internal reality. Feeling, moreover, is the decisive factor in value-judgments which, as we have seen, are our main help in making this reality real for us.

This is due to the fact which we have explained before—that, to disclose internal reality, external reality has to be subordinated to ourselves. A secure knowledge of external reality as such requires that the influence of the observer is eliminated so far as possible; but to know internal reality we must, on the contrary, establish the relationship with ourselves; here external reality has to become the form which helps us to make the content accessible.[1] All impressions and experiences must, so to speak, force internal reality into the open; to be able to do this, they must most definitely be our own impressions and experiences, for only if our participation is complete can their full meaning for us become obvious. Yet it is feeling alone which secures such a participation, for only what has evoked feeling has really become our own.[2]

This can be seen even in the most abstract thoughts. If we do not merely learn and accept them indifferently, but try to understand and acquire them thoroughly, so as to make them our own, they are bound to evoke at least interest, which is a feeling. This means that feeling

[1] See pp. 27, 35.
[2] 'Allen gehört, was du denkst, dein Eigen ist nur, was du fühlst.
Soll er dein Eigentum sein, fühle den Gott, den du denkst.'
SCHILLER.

inevitably takes part in all thoughts which are of importance to us. It is this fact which explains why the scientist so easily mistakes external knowledge as absolute and why negation, based on feelings, can be used to make this kind of knowledge appear comprehensive; his interest focuses his attention exclusively on external knowledge and, as feeling is already involved, contempt for all other kinds of knowing can also creep in.

Thus, however, we also see once again how important it is to distinguish clearly between external and internal reality. That the scientist pays no attention to the positive support of his knowledge by feeling is correct in so far as feeling must not influence this kind of knowledge. But he is wrong when he considers interest as nothing but an unimportant accompaniment of his thinking which can in no way lead to any knowledge, for there are aspects of reality which can only be disclosed by the right kind of interest.[1] It is because he does not understand his feelings that he remains unaware of the fact that he also makes use of the negative counterpart of his interest, of contempt. We must indeed exclude feeling entirely from our external knowledge, but to be able to do this we have to know it, to allot it its proper place and to develop it in accordance with its true nature—that is, we have to pay attention to internal reality and to use feeling to make it real for us.

Yet the mere concept 'feeling' already proves how insufficient our knowledge of internal reality is, for its meaning is extremely vague. If we want to use this concept properly, we have to be aware that it has at least three different meanings.

(1) Feeling as a human faculty. This needs no further explanation; we can use the word in the same way as 'thinking' and 'willing', to denote in general our ability to feel.

(2) Single emotions which arise on particular occasions. We talk of joy as a feeling, or of sorrow, or of love, and in such a case the word does not refer to our general faculty of feeling, but to single experiences of certain distinct feelings. The concept serves no longer to describe the common nature of man, but refers to a special state of mind of single individuals.[2]

(3) Feeling as an organ of knowledge. There is knowledge which can only be acquired with the help of feeling; our knowledge of values, for instance, such as good and evil, though it can be elaborated by thinking,

---

[1] 'Unconcerned detachment in matters of religion implies an a priori rejection of the religious demand to be ultimately concerned. It denies the object which it is supposed to approach "objectively".' P. Tillich, *The Protestant Era*, p. xi. See also H. H. Farmer, *The World and God*, p. 37.

[2] Unfortunately, the meaning of the concept 'emotion' is so little different from that of 'feeling' that we can only occasionally use it to make certain contexts clearer, but not in general to separate this second meaning of the concept 'feeling' from the others.

is finally based on feeling. But this kind of feeling is neither identical with the general faculty, for it can be extremely weak in persons who feel passionately, nor with the emotions which arise on special occasions, such as joy and sorrow, for the knowledge of good and evil, if present at all, is lasting. Occasional single feelings, moreover, do not provide us with a knowledge of principles as this kind of feeling obviously does.

This is a rather unexpected transition. Single emotions remain subjective in the usual sense of the word; if we are happy or in despair, we are inclined to see everything in the light of this mood; the whole world is probably seen in a rosy light or veiled in darkness. Though love or anger may sharpen our awareness, these emotions, on the whole, tend to distort our knowledge; we do not recognize things as such by love or anger, but have to control their influence. Yet, as an organ of knowledge, feeling suddenly reveals itself as cognitive; it leads directly to objective knowledge of general validity.

In a certain respect, the common name is justified. It is the peculiarity of feeling that the single emotions can never be completely separated from the general faculty of feeling; while single thoughts represent results to which we can give a definite form and which can be preserved in isolation, feelings cannot be preserved; they have to be actually felt to be real and understandable at all. This means that our force of feeling has to flow into them to keep them alive. The presence of our faculty of feeling is always felt as well; it is either so absorbed by one special emotion that we feel that our whole being is taken up in it, or we feel that there are powers dormant in us, or experience a conflict because the single emotion does not occupy our faculty of feeling entirely. Every single feeling remains related to the whole power of feeling. Even such a knowledge as that of good and evil, though here principles can be stated, has to become, as we have seen, an actual feeling, for only thus is this knowledge kept alive and saved from degenerating into empty formulæ. Even this different kind of feeling, therefore, is in this respect similar to all other feelings and related, as they are, to the general faculty of feeling.[1]

The importance of this common basis of all feelings is unquestionable and must always be taken into account. The distinction between the different kinds of feeling, however, is nevertheless of greater importance.

Unless we recognize that the general faculty of feeling is only the common denominator of two different kinds of feelings, the fact that they spring from the same source can all too easily be misused to blur the difference between them, and this makes it so simple to dismiss feeling from the realm of knowledge altogether. We have to see that the

[1] For this and the following, see pp. 17–18, 35, 39, 41–2, 59.

## THE NATURE OF FEELING

knowledge acquired by feeling is fundamentally different from subjective single emotions, for otherwise it must seem impossible to achieve, with the help of feeling, any objective knowledge of general validity at all. This, however, is an extremely serious loss, for it is feeling which opens the way to the most important knowledge we possess—to the values, including the absolute values, and to all those regions which we can only grasp with the help of faith. There is no access to absolute knowledge if we eliminate feeling as merely subjective. It is of the utmost importance, therefore, to distinguish between the different meanings of the concept 'feeling', for only if we separate them will the knowledge thus acquired be distinguished from the general faculty and protected from distortion by subjective emotions.

The importance of a better knowledge of our feelings can also be seen from another point of view. There has to be some kind of relationship between feeling and thinking, and here again three completely different possibilities exist, though we hardly ever distinguish between them.

(1) We can experience very many different single feelings, for whatever interests us, appeals to us or displeases us is bound to awaken a feeling. These feelings are different from each other, according to the occasion on which they arise; there are, in fact, far more differences between feelings than we usually realize. The names we give to them, such as 'interest', 'joy', 'sorrow', 'love', 'hatred', fall very short of the real wealth we actually experience. Each of the many emotions which we generally call joy, for instance, can be different, their difference being determined by the different objects or events to which they refer as well as by our state of mind. We talk of joy only, but the joy may be due to looking at a rose, or to a success, or to a good deed, and the actual feeling will be different in each case. Even the emotions of joy due to looking at a rose, or a sunset, or a work of art, are considerably different, and each of these feelings will vary at different times. Feelings can never recur in exactly the same way or as exactly the same, even if our language suggests mere repetition.

As there is hardly any impression or experience which is not connected with feeling, these different feelings accompany our thought, influence it and are, in their turn, influenced by thinking. This interaction between feeling and thinking is natural, for every feeling, so long as it is not distorted, tries to force its way into consciousness; if we feel, we want to know what we feel and why we feel it. But this interaction is also of the greatest importance, for to understand a feeling we need, as we have seen, the help of external objects and events, and thus a feeling can become clearly conscious only with the help of thought. The participation of feeling forces us to establish the relationship between external reality and ourselves and thereby discloses internal reality, and as soon as this relationship has been established, every increase in such a knowledge of external reality must also develop our feelings and thus once more widen our knowledge of internal reality. If this interplay between feeling and thinking remains undisturbed, moreover, so that every feeling remains related to a corresponding experience which clarifies it, we shall also be able to distinguish between single subjective emotions due to actual impressions or experiences, and the knowledge which we can acquire through that kind of feeling which is constantly present within us.

To make feeling an organ of knowledge, therefore, we have to develop the wealth of feelings and the differentiation between them. We must learn to feel most exactly in terms of the object, partly to be able to relate the object entirely to internal reality, and partly to distinguish between right and wrong feelings and thus between internal reality and mere imagination, which has been misled by accidental emotions. The admiration frequently felt for warriors or great criminals shows how easily a single emotion (admiration) can make us forget the facts (the killing of men or a brutal crime). The relationship to the object is particularly important in view of the fact that feelings, though real in themselves, can be created by delusions.[1] If we feel in terms of the object, moreover, we shall also experience every feeling as a new feeling and so fulfil another of the conditions of making internal reality real—that every experience must in some sense be a new experience.

The development of the wealth of feelings, of course, also has its dangers. We can be too willing to follow up every impression and every impulse, so that we finally succumb to every impulse. In this case, the wealth of feelings is transformed into a maze which robs us of any possibility of finding a central position from which to govern our feelings and to lead the process of thinking to the right conclusions. But, so long as thinking plays its part properly, this danger is comparatively small, the more so as any knowledge acquired by feeling points towards the right central position. Yet this danger can become great if our feeling is developed with the help of the second way in which we can establish the relationship between feeling and thinking, for this way excludes their fruitful interaction.

(2) This second way could perhaps be best described by saying that we stress the passive reactions instead of active feelings.

Every feeling, whether joy or love or hatred, is also pleasurable or painful, and it is this accompanying pleasure or pain, or similar purely subjective states of our minds like tension, excitement and relaxation, which we here understand by the term passive reactions. While active feelings—which can be of any of the three kinds just described—can become a clear experience with a definite content and thus enable us to

[1] See pp. 38–9.

## THE NATURE OF FEELING

grasp almost any part of reality, these merely passive reactions within the sphere of feeling have a far smaller range, because they only indicate whether our senses or nerves produce a positive or negative response, so that the same response can accompany very different feelings. This difference is difficult to define,[1] but it can occasionally become very distinct, for the nature of the feeling and of the simultaneous reaction need by no means be the same. A great joy can be very painful, in so far as it disturbs our peace of mind; a new discovery which makes us extremely happy will at first, like a dazzling light which blinds us, create pain, and the shock we experience may not be very different from that due to a catastrophe. Every strong impact, whether due to sudden happiness or to sudden misery, will at first be painful. On the other hand, we can enjoy experiences which make us unhappy, for instance when they free us from an activity or responsibility which we shun, or if they secure pity and care for us.

It is true that it is not always easy to distinguish between the two; if we enjoy our pain, for instance, it is sometimes difficult to say which is the active feeling and which the passive reaction, and this becomes even more difficult if such a reaction accompanies a similar feeling; pleasure, joy; or pain, sorrow. As feelings are always linked with passive reactions, it is hardly possible to achieve their complete separation. Nevertheless, the distinction is not artificial nor meaningless, for we can quite clearly recognize that we are able to develop feeling in two different directions—either away from the passive reactions so that their importance decreases, or towards them so that their importance increases.

The way of developing our feelings which we have just described diminishes the influence of these reactions. So long as our feelings are vague, our reactions are the stronger of the two, for pleasure and pain are immediately and clearly experienced; but if feeling is directed towards the object and developed with its help, we forget our pleasurable or painful reactions, because our interest is focused upon reality and because the active feelings become clearer. We do not try to experience our feelings as such, which would direct our attention to our own state of mind and thus to the passive reactions which are its expression, but try, with the help of feeling, to grasp the object. This must push these reactions into the background, for as they are, so to speak, nothing but the private side of our feelings and cannot lead to any knowledge of objects, they can no longer help us.[2] Feelings directed

---

[1] The German concepts 'Lust' and 'Unlust'—which denote only such reactions—make the distinction clearer than 'pleasure' and 'pain' which can also be active feelings.

[2] 'Suppose we are listening to the playing of a violin . . . these sounds we may be aware of as pleasing, but, when we are rapt in the music, we cease to be conscious of

towards the object, moreover, serve the knowledge of internal reality, thus disclosing to us the meaning of all our experience, and this is so infinitely more important to us than our individual moods that we are bound to outgrow the sphere of mere reactions almost completely.

The development of feeling in this direction, however, is only possible if thinking is used in accordance with feeling—that is, when it takes internal reality into account. If, on the contrary, we accept external knowledge alone as knowledge and believe that the apprehending of external reality is the only way of thinking, then the danger of overemphasizing our passive reactions arises. External knowledge must, as we have seen, exclude feelings, and therefore the other kind of thinking which could help us to understand and develop our feelings is suppressed. Feeling and thinking can no longer be reconciled, no longer influence and stimulate each other, but must needs become hostile and conflicting forces.

This struggle can take two different forms. We can take sides with external knowledge and try to concentrate on it alone; in this case we must disregard feeling so far as possible and deprive it of its value, strength and importance. This is usually done by all those who try to adopt a purely practical or rational or scientific attitude. But then feeling does not simply disappear, and as we do not want to develop it, all our feelings remain vague and the passive reactions grow stronger. This leaves the two inextricably intermixed, so that we can no longer understand our feelings at all. On the other hand, we may want to preserve our feelings and emphasize them, despite the fact that we believe in external thinking alone. In this case we must separate feeling from thinking completely, interrupt the interaction between them, and secure for feeling a sphere of its own where thinking cannot interfere with it. This is characteristic of Romanticism and sentimentality, both of which we shall discuss in a moment. Though this time the feeling is not weakened but kept strong, the effect upon its character is very similar. In order to strengthen our feelings, even though we have cut off their natural development, we can only try to feel whatever we feel more strongly, and as there is no way of including our experience of reality, we can only do so by increasing the strength of our first reactions. The mixture of feelings and passive reactions is brought about, no matter how feeling is divorced from thinking, and again, although we now feel more strongly, we are unable to understand what we feel.

The transformation which our feelings thus undergo can be best seen in their relation to their object. There is, still, an object towards which the feeling is directed; there is no feeling without a cause, though it may frequently be difficult to recognize it. But now we do not try to

the pleasure of the sounds, and are conscious of the music only as continuous melodious meaning.' J. Oman, *The Natural and the Supernatural*, pp. 174-5.

discover it, to get to know it well and to make the object of feeling a definite form which would help us to grasp its content. On the contrary, as the knowledge of the object is left entirely to a way of thinking which contradicts feeling, we avoid this knowledge or weaken it as far as possible. We come to cherish the feeling which does not know its object, and even if the knowledge of the object cannot be entirely avoided, the connection with it is loosened or broken, so as to make the feeling independent of everything outside itself. As thinking seems bound to destroy feeling, feeling must be saved from the influence of anything about which we could also think.

Examples of this way of dealing with the feelings abound. It is often astonishing, for instance, how easily scientists, outstanding in their field, accept evidence in other fields which they would scorn if it concerned their own research, merely so as to maintain this separation of thinking and feeling. On the other hand, if the main intention is to preserve feeling, its connection with the object is frequently artificially severed. What is usually called 'romantic love' is a good example of this kind of separation of thinking and feeling. This love is no longer love for somebody, but a vague feeling which cannot be destroyed (nor, moreover, developed) by any contact with reality. We do not love a person, but experience a pleasurable emotion.[1] This romantic love is closely related to the characteristically romantic emotion of yearning or longing. Normally longing means longing for something and forces us to try to reach its goal. Thus it would bring us into contact with reality and, as reality is the realm of a hostile way of thinking, it would put an end to feeling. Therefore, the aim is suppressed; longing is transformed into a vague and aimless feeling which we can enjoy endlessly as a constant state of our mind—as melancholy if pain, or as enthusiasm if pleasure prevails.

This strengthening of a single emotion is very easy if it has no strong or obvious cause; we then merely strengthen pleasure and pain so as to make everything outside ourselves seem unimportant. If we cannot help acknowledging a cause, however, we accept whatever can be accepted without much thinking as appropriate thoughts and feelings on such an occasion, and once more strengthen pleasure and pain by dwelling on these conventional reactions, and even by adorning the object quite arbitrarily with qualities which are apt to justify and to increase these reactions. Romantic longing or love can be attached now to this, now to that object, but this does not really matter, for the object is seen in a certain light and adorned with certain preconceived qualities, so that it can increase either the pleasure and pain which, in any case, we happen or want to feel, or a mixture of both which most successfully guarantees the sterility of the feeling. Our feelings serve to create moods

[1] See J. Macmurray, *Reason and Emotion*, pp. 31–2.

which can underlie or replace or paralyse thinking; they can become, according to our state of mind, intoxication or despair; but they cannot possibly lead to any knowledge nor to any helpful experience of reality. Everything is done to enable us to enjoy our feelings and to revel in them, so as to save us from the necessity of thinking.[1]

This divorce between feeling and thinking is so common to-day that hardly any of us can escape completely from it. Certainly we very often hardly notice how much we rely on moods and conventional formulae; do we know, for instance, what we really feel when we attend the funeral of a person whom we hardly knew or whom we disliked? Do we care to break through the conventions so as to experience the feeling which would really be genuine and appropriate?

(3) The third way of establishing the relationship between feeling and thinking is closely connected with the second. If there is hostility and struggle, the result need not be the defeat of feeling nor its separation from thinking; feeling can also overwhelm thinking. It can break into the realm of thought and subjugate even that kind of thinking which normally enables us to apprehend external reality.

The intrusion of feeling into the realm of thought is, as we shall see in a moment, very dangerous and must therefore be clearly distinguished from the fruitful interaction of the two. This, however, can be easily done, despite their superficial similarity, for this wrong and disastrous victory of feeling always has two characteristics. First, it is not due to a development of the wealth of many different feelings, but to one single emotion which either suppresses all the others or subjugates and transforms them. Secondly, thinking, once more, is not concerned with internal reality, but concentrates solely on external knowledge; it is used by the feeling to build up an elaborate external knowledge in support of it.

Let us take, for instance, the feeling of nationalism. This tends to become passionate, but even before real passion arises, the nation which is the object of the feeling is not only credited with qualities which justify nationalism; the national character—which, in fact, can only be described with the greatest difficulty and most unreliably—is elaborated in the greatest detail and becomes the basis of all valuations. All other values are appreciated only so far as they seem to agree with this character, or because they embellish it.[2] 'Faithfulness' becomes German and 'fair-mindedness' typically English, and they are praised, not for their own sake, but because one wants to be a good German or

[1] This seems to be the true nature of what is usually called sentimentality. See J. Macmurray, *Freedom in the Modern World*, p. 152.

[2] This element of embellishment explains why the Romantic Movement has played an important part in the development of modern nationalism. But the intrusion of nationalistic passion into thinking is very different from the romantic revelling in vague feelings.

## THE NATURE OF FEELING

a good Englishman. When the state of passion is reached, however, very complicated theories, dealing exclusively with external reality, are at once developed; a new kind of science, referring to external reality, but determined by feeling, sweeps away all proper thinking. A one-sided philosophy of history is supported by belief in race and blood or at least by the belief in a special mission, which makes the one nation infinitely more valuable and important than all others; thinking is exclusively used to support and to increase the passion.

There are innumerable examples of this relationship between feeling and thinking; every individual falling in love or overwhelmed by some new experience or taken in by some political creed or mass-movement is in danger of going this way. Even mystics are inclined to translate their ecstasies either into complicated and purely intellectual theories or into another kind of external reality whose smallest detail they claim to know.[1]

The dangers which arise are twofold. On the one hand, external knowledge becomes unreliable, for the influence of the observer is no longer excluded; on the contrary, external reality is made to support whatever error we choose to embrace. On the other hand, feeling does not disclose internal reality, but is split into irreconcilable opposites referring to external reality. The first danger is fairly obvious; it is, even if we are obsessed by a feeling, only thinly veiled; it does not need special consideration. But we must dwell for a moment on the second danger, because this kind of succumbing to feeling must not be mistaken for a realization of internal reality.

If we merely sever the connection between feeling and thinking, we are still able to enjoy our feelings in a positive way. But it is very conspicuous that, when feeling overruns thinking completely, this enjoyment almost always vanishes; passion tends to become a torture, and this negative counterpart usually becomes stronger than the passion itself. Nationalism and communism find a stronger expression in hatred than in love, and passionate love can be very near to hatred.[2] This agrees with the nature of feeling in so far as we can never develop positive feelings in isolation; if we become more sensitive to beauty and goodness, our awareness of ugliness and wickedness is bound to increase as well. But it is this very quality of our feeling which is fundamentally distorted. Ugliness and wickedness normally evoke feelings which take their place among many others; they increase our faculty of discrimination and thereby contribute considerably to the development

---

[1] Cf., for example, the theology of late scholasticism or of late Buddhism, or Swedenborg's homely pictures of life in heaven. Or, to give a more recent example, Aldous Huxley's representation of life hereafter in *Time Must Have a Stop*.

[2] Only mysticism is usually free from this, because this kind of ecstasy must remain connected with internal reality.

## THE EXTERNAL AND INTERNAL OPPOSITES

of the wealth of our feelings. But if passion creates hatred and hatred strengthens passion, the wealth of different feelings is destroyed; our entire ability to feel is now dominated by the opposition between positive and negative; it has either to support the passion or to attack whatever contradicts it. Every feeling which arises has, as it were, to take its place in one of these two camps and to accept the domination of the determining passion. We have become unable to feel naturally; every feeling is transformed either into passionate approval or passionate disapproval; instead of developing many feelings we are forced to collect them all into two groups, so that they can all be absorbed in this irreconcilable opposition. We shall see that this opposition has nothing in common with the true internal opposites, for feeling is forced to acquire the nature of the passive reactions and thus can no longer help us to understand our experience.

This effect of passion becomes understandable when we remember that single feelings remain closely connected with our faculty of feeling and that some of our entire force of feeling must always flow into each single emotion. The passion tries to absorb our power of feeling completely, but this remains impossible, for the passion is directed towards external reality and the feeling, however distorted, still represents internal reality; this reality, therefore, cannot be completely neglected. To occupy the force of feeling which is not absorbed, negation has to be summoned up; we can at least deny and attack what we cannot suppress. This denial of internal reality need not become obvious or conscious; in the same way as a part of external reality is adorned so as to be able to attract all our passion, a distorted part of external reality can be made to attract all our hatred. By this, however, we are forced to suppress the greater part of reality, for we must suppress all that in external reality which does not fall in with our passion and almost the whole of internal reality, and thus negation must also become stronger than the positive feeling.

This splitting up of feeling into violent acceptance and rejection usually starts by affecting only that range of feeling which determines actions which we regard as fundamentally important; minor likes and dislikes can exist unaffected. Nowadays we may be inclined to believe that the fully developed dominating passion belongs only to romance and legendary ages, conveniently forgetting that even a consistent bias shows that feeling has triumphed over thinking. But the effects of passion can be seen also in modern national and political creeds which always give great prominence to the embodied opponent and tend to diminish the range of feelings which can remain unaffected. The power of the negative element is so strong that the creation of such an opponent may even hide the lack of a real belief, while the feelings and thoughts which remain unbiassed become more and more insignificant.

## THE NATURE OF FEELING

Feeling, therefore, can also destroy every possibility of knowledge, instead of leading to the most important knowledge which we possess. We have always to remember that the mere strength of feeling or its dominating position by no means guarantee that it has been developed in the right way.

To escape all these distortions, feeling must be supported and protected by thinking. But it must be the right kind of thinking, a thinking which can help us to develop the natural wealth of our feelings and to distinguish between accidental emotions and the knowledge disclosed by feeling. In order to fulfil this task, thinking must be able to apprehend, not only external, but also internal reality—that is, we must apply not only external, but also internal opposites.

## Chapter VII

### THE INTERNAL OPPOSITES

#### 1. MEANS, ENDS AND VALUES

WE have seen that, to make internal reality real for us, we have to subordinate external reality to ourselves. The influence of the observer can no longer be eliminated; on the contrary, only if we establish a relationship between external reality and ourselves are we able to discover internal reality at all.

The internal opposites which serve this purpose must in the nature of things conform to these conditions. They are, therefore, completely different from the external opposites.[1] They are not derived from external facts, but seem to be created solely by our thinking, for they refer, not to something which we could consider as existing independently of our thought, but to our intentions, or to ideas and ideals, or to inner experiences. Their dependence on the observer, moreover, finds its expression in their being dependent on each other; as they have no equivalent in external reality, but are created as opposites by thinking, we must apply either both their parts or none. If one part is taken away, the other becomes meaningless. There is no sense in talking of means, for instance, if there are no ends to be achieved with their help; we cannot talk of badness or ugliness unless we also acknowledge the idea of the good or beautiful; nothing can be seen as an aim if there is no intention of striving for it. This dependence on each other seems strongly to confirm that these opposites are nothing but our own creation and that they do not refer to anything which has an independent existence of its own.

Nor is it impossible, in this case, arbitrarily to alter the relationship between the two parts of the opposites; on the contrary, they change places according to the point of view from which we happen to look at them. We can view a means and its end with different purposes in mind or judge deeds by the application of different standards, and this

[1] Cf. p. 81.

## THE INTERNAL OPPOSITES

can lead to an interchange of the two parts within the same opposition. For the army, for instance, the production of iron is the means which makes armament possible; for the businessman the armament is the means which makes the production of iron possible. For the follower of heroic ideals it is good to kill one's enemy and bad not to resist evil; for the Christian killing is bad and non-resistance good. The relationship always depends on our way of establishing it.

The dependence and the possibility of interchange within these pairs of opposites are the reason why it seems so easy to dismiss internal reality as non-existent. But their examination soon discloses that here, too, we are dealing with an aspect of primary reality which is as real as external reality, and that the internal opposites play the same part in our grasping of this reality as the external opposites in the apprehension of external reality. Just as the external opposites are not entirely independent of our thinking, the internal opposites are not entirely dependent on it.

We can hardly consider internal opposites as arbitrary creations of our mind because, first of all, we are compelled to apply them. We have to achieve certain practical ends to be able to live, and this necessity forces us incessantly to impose certain ends upon external reality and to find the means to achieve what we must achieve. It is true that this takes place mainly in the realm of external reality, but we have to apply internal opposites to be able to perform this task. It is the simplest way of establishing a relationship between external reality and ourselves, and just because it still refers mainly to external reality, this opposition can do most to help us to recognize the difference between the two kinds of opposites.

The opposition between a means and its end is similar to that between a cause and its effect. There seems to be only a small difference. When we progress from a cause to its effect, we are led from the past to the present or future, for the effect follows the cause. The end represents a future event, but it also becomes, by awakening our intention of achieving it, the cause of our activity. It is true that we are led this time from the future to the present or to the past; nevertheless, the end seems to be just another kind of cause which lies ahead.

There, however, the similarity ends, for the different nature of the internal opposites becomes visible at once. If we discover, for instance, that the force of gravity causes the falling of the stone, this discovery is either correct or not; we can discover a cause once and for all and cannot choose between different causes at will. To achieve our end, however, we can normally choose between different means and our choice has no final validity; every alteration in the circumstances will influence it. The idea of the force of gravity, moreover, is quite foreign to that of valuing; but to make the right choice between different means we have to value them. If we want light in our rooms, we can probably choose between candles, gas-light and electric light; we shall try to choose the most appropriate, and to be able to do this, we shall have to recognize that each of them is of different value for our purpose. But every new invention or change of price will force us to revise our judgment. The introduction of a future element implies the possibility of constant choice.

Now it could seem that our judgment is still entirely based on external facts, for we can find out, if necessary with the help of experiments, which means serves its purpose best. There are scales of degrees worked out by scientists which indicate with scientific exactitude the suitability of certain means, for instance that of metals for different functions. In such cases it seems possible, therefore, to make values largely independent of the observer. But this is in fact true only within narrow limits, and this limitation is entirely dependent on our intentions. We can find out by tests how to get the brightest light, but we do not always want this; we probably choose it for our study or for the factory, but we dim it in our sitting-room, and for the Christmas tree or on other festive occasions we may prefer candles and value them most highly, despite the ascertained highest practical value of electric light. As we are still moving within the realm of external reality, external qualities play their part, but they do so only within the scales of values; the choice of the scale itself depends entirely on our intentions. External reality remains subordinated to man.

But are we not able to discover the relationship between means and ends also in external reality itself, where there is no connection with man, and does this not prove that this opposition can be independent of the observer? Biology, for instance, can hardly dispense with these terms. The feeding of many insects serves to fertilize flowers; organs are developed to satisfy certain needs; plants and animals adapt themselves to their surroundings. In all these cases the end has not been imposed upon external reality by man; we cannot even talk of a conscious intention; yet neither can we assume a mere coincidence.

In fact, however, none of these instances can wipe out the difference between external and internal opposites. It is no accident that the biologists strive to exclude teleological thinking from their science and try to introduce causality wherever possible. It seems probable to-day that they cannot completely succeed in this; ends and means have still to be presupposed to enable us to explain certain processes which otherwise would remain inexplicable. But whether or not teleological thinking can be dismissed, it is certain that biology can only become an exact science if and in so far as causality can be applied. The introduction of ends, even if seen in the past—as a cause of organs, for instance, which have developed—creates an element of uncertainty just because these

## THE INTERNAL OPPOSITES

internal opposites cannot be made completely independent of the observer.

To understand the reason for this uncertainty, we must clearly distinguish between conclusions based on the transferring of concepts from internal reality and those based on analogies.

The transferring of the constructive concepts from internal to external reality takes place, as we have shown, without any conscious effort on our part; we cannot help applying such concepts as 'cause' and 'effect' and discover only afterwards—if at all—that they have been derived from our knowledge of internal reality. They appear to us at first as an objective knowledge of processes within external reality; it needs an effort to realize that they belong to the laws of our thinking. As they have been completely adapted to the other reality, they become the indispensable basis of our knowledge; they belong to the working of our mind and we cannot remove them without endangering its functioning.

Analogies, on the other hand, though often very useful for our approach to phenomena which we could not otherwise approach, show that we are applying knowledge, acquired in another field, to a sphere in which it can be neither acquired nor tested. We consciously apply terms and experiences to facts with which we cannot prove that they are connected; the derivation of the attributes of God from human qualities is the most common example. Teleological thinking, too, is based on such analogies. In the instances mentioned we interpret biological processes in human terms—organs have been developed to satisfy certain needs—but remain aware all the time that the application of terms derived from our intentional behaviour to processes which lack intentions may not be justified. Hence the attempt to replace this interpretation by causal laws. As it is quite impossible to approach the working of nature from inside, all external signs and symptoms have to be interpreted with the help of such analogies from internal reality. But this also makes all these interpretations arbitrary—an unmistakable indication that we have not applied the laws of our thinking correctly. No such arbitrariness is attached to the constructive concepts. Analogies, therefore, can never be completely justified in the realm to which they are applied; they remain expedients, very good expedients sometimes, but cannot claim to establish certain external knowledge. Thus, however, they can never prove that the opposition between means and ends exists independently of the observer.

We have seen that to start from the future is essential for the grasping of internal reality.[1] At first sight, the difference between causes and ends seems slight, for both cause events, and yet it is impossible to start from the future when we want reliably to apprehend external reality. The seemingly small difference indicates fundamental divergencies.

[1] See pp. 52–3.

## THE EXTERNAL AND INTERNAL OPPOSITES

There are indeed further differences between external and internal opposites which become obvious in the opposition between means and ends, even though this opposition still mainly refers to external reality.

We have just mentioned that the usefulness of means can sometimes be tested by experiments, and that there are scales of degrees of certain practical values which can be applied with scientific exactitude. Does it really matter that the actual application of these scales depends on our intentions? Is there any fundamental difference between these experiments and scales and other scientific discoveries? Other experiments, after all, also serve a certain purpose, and the certainty achieved with the two kinds of experiments seems the same. Yet the fundamental difference becomes obvious here, too, for contradictory scales of values exist side by side and their contradictions raise no problem. They remain independent of each other.

Naturally, we can look at certain external processes from different points of view and different scientific explanations can exist side by side without our being able to bridge the gap between them. We can, for instance, explain processes in the human body in physical, chemical, physiological and even psychological ways. But the mere coexistence of these explanations raises a problem; the scientists try to find a unitary explanation. The problem, moreover, becomes urgent if there are contradictions, for this always proves that the two contradictory theories cannot both be correct. There exist complete contradictions, for instance, between the view of the physiologist, who regards processes in the body as causing effects in the mind, and that of the psychologist, who regards processes in the mind as causes of disturbances in the body. But such complete contradictions merely prove that no satisfactory results have yet been achieved. No such contradictions could be left in existence in one special branch of science; there the scientists cannot rest until they have solved them.

Internal opposites, as we have just said, can change their places within the same opposition, and thus these contradictions are the natural rule in the sphere of valuation, even if we are dealing with the same kind of objects from a very similar point of view. When, after the introduction of electric light, the value of candles for the purpose of lighting is reduced, their price may nevertheless go up, because less candles than before are being produced. Electric light, the most valuable means of lighting, may at the same time be the cheapest. The same things can take opposite places in different scales of values; for lighting purposes, candles are of value, but diamonds valueless; yet if we consider their worth in money, diamonds are certainly more valuable. They are also valuable if we want to cut glass, but valueless if we want to cut wood. The scientific scale of the values of metals for certain purposes may be completely reversed by the introduction of a different end. But

## THE INTERNAL OPPOSITES

no such contradiction invalidates or even endangers any scale of values, for they depend entirely on the purpose which they serve, and the different scales remain valid for the different purposes.

There are, of course, attempts to unify these different scales of values, too, and at least one of these attempts, the creation of money, has been very successful. Diamonds are, in fact, no longer useless for any practical purpose, for we can most probably sell them and acquire with the money we receive a great quantity of other means, of candles or electric bulbs or whatever we need. But this unification, though of great practical importance, is nothing more. On the one hand, the unification cannot be compared with that in the realm of science, for it remains artificial, dependent as it is on a general recognition which can be withheld, for instance, when the currency of a country is inflated or not accepted in others, and it is shaken by every political and economic disturbance. On the other hand, despite its almost general acceptance, its sphere remains limited. Usefulness for a special purpose must still be decided in other terms and need not have any connection with the price. Air costs nothing, bread is cheap and perfectly superfluous things can be most expensive. We need not even think of truth, goodness and beauty or of personal relationships, to all of which this scale of values does not apply; money expresses none of those qualities which directly serve a definite purpose. Nor can any other unification bring about a comprehensive unity.

Thus, however, this opposition between means and ends, although it represents only the first step into the realm of internal opposites and still mainly refers to external reality, is already most important for our grasping of internal reality. It covers external reality with a net of relationships which make this reality accessible by a quite different approach; by including the same objects in many different scales of values, these objects are made amenable, so to speak, to a different kind of treatment. The resistance of external reality is gradually broken down; the facts are prepared in such a way that we can use them within the context of a different kind of thinking and change them into that form which we need for grasping their content. Nor can we remain satisfied with this first step; as all values depend on our intentions, they must lead to a consideration of these intentions and thus we are necessarily driven on to recognize more and more of internal reality. That we are inevitably forced to use means to achieve ends implies, therefore, that we are forced to progress from external to internal reality.

This can also be seen when we remember the way in which abstraction makes external reality accessible. It creates relationships which cut right across this reality and almost represent the creation of a different world.[1] These relationships make external reality simpler than it really

[1] See p. 85.

## THE EXTERNAL AND INTERNAL OPPOSITES

is; they enable us to apply the laws of our thinking, so that we can grasp this reality more easily and more reliably. By eliminating from our thinking the complicated details of the concrete objects and events and the differences between them, they enable us to concentrate on their common qualities and forms. The net cast over external reality by the different scales of values could be mistaken for such an abstract pattern; but it is, in fact, completely different. It makes external reality far more complicated than it could appear from any external point of view; as every single object or event can find its place in different scales, the differentiations are not eliminated, but multiplied; the concrete details are stressed and increased by their manifold connections with different values. Clearly, if we want to discover order in this sphere, we can no longer restrict our attention to external reality alone; we must start from internal reality, for it is there that we can deal with our intentions and find the principles which determine the different scales of values.

It is true that our thinking can always take a wrong turn; we are able to escape any compulsion, even if it appears as an inescapable necessity when we consider the working of our minds from outside. But that the necessity exists can easily be seen, for, if we neglect or do not recognize it, we are bound to come to wrong conclusions. In this case, we need not become conscious of what these simple kinds of internal opposites already imply; we can neglect valuation and thus halt our progress towards internal reality. But as, nevertheless, we must value, this is clearly wrong and means that we are overlooking facts. This progress can also be disturbed by a wrong development of feeling. The net of which we have spoken is closely interconnected with the wealth of different feelings; its purpose can be frustrated if we develop our feelings in a different way. Yet we shall consider the possible disturbances of this progress later; first we want to show where the natural consequences of this first step in the application of the internal opposites lead.

### 2. INTENTIONS, AIMS AND PRINCIPLES

The discussion of the—still rather external—opposition between means and ends has already forced us to refer to intentions. That this implies that we cannot restrict our attention to external reality, but have to proceed towards internal reality, can be seen when we consider the following example.

Let us assume that there are four people who want to earn money. They are businessmen, applying exactly the same methods, and yet their intentions are completely different. The first wants to earn money in order to become rich; he is attracted by money as such, because it seems to guarantee his own worth; though he hardly knows how to use it, the increasing figures in his bank account give him intense pleasure. The second wants money to be able to build up an industrial enterprise; he wants to create something; he is interested in his factory and in the increase and improvement of his production. The third wants money to enable him to live a leisurely life later; money should secure him freedom from drudgery; he wants to become independent with its help, to enjoy life, to follow his inclinations. The fourth does not want anything for himself, but needs money to be able to help others; he wants to do what he considers as good.

Now the opposition between means and ends cannot help us to recognize the differences between these four men. Each of them has to value things and actions according to their ability to help him in earning money; none of them can remain satisfied with inadequate profits; all have to do something which provides them with a surplus in money. To achieve their aims, they have to make a quite considerable profit, and so they have to apply the methods which guarantee a profit. We could perhaps say that, for the first, money represents an end in itself, while, for the three others, it is only a means of achieving other ends. But this does not show the differences between the three others, nor is it quite satisfactory to describe the wishes of the first, for he wants the money because it gives him pleasure. It is only when we consider their intentions that the differences between them can be clearly recognized and stated.

This example is important in several respects.

(1) It shows that it is useful to distinguish between the concepts 'means' and 'end' on the one hand and 'intention' and 'aim' on the other more clearly than is usually done. In the common usage of these words we can say (as we have just tried) that the one end (the earning of money) becomes the means to another end (the gaining of freedom); we can also say that it is our intention to earn money and that the means serves our intention, and there is hardly any clear-cut difference between 'intention' and 'aim', though these two concepts obviously ought to mean something different. This common usage would make it rather difficult to describe the processes of thought which we have in mind. We shall, therefore, use these concepts in the following ways:

(*a*) The opposition between means and ends will be used to refer to external reality, and its main characteristic, therefore, will be that it depends only to a small degree on our personal choice. We can choose the end, but once we have chosen it we are very restricted in the choice of means, and the limits of our choice are determined by external reality. If we want light, we have to choose means which can produce it; we cannot expect stones to burn. There are, of course, different means of different value for achieving the same end, and we can choose between them according to the special end we aim at—electric light for the study, candles for the Christmas tree. But the choice remains dependent on the ability of the means to serve our end.

(*b*) We shall talk of intentions where the personal element determines the choice completely, and therefore we can use this concept only when referring to the choice of ends. The concept 'end' points backwards to the choice of the means; the concept 'intention' refers to the choice of an end for the sake of a further purpose and thus points forwards to a more comprehensive aim.

(*c*) The differentiation between 'end' and 'aim' is less definite. There is, as it were, a sliding scale of ends and aims: we want light in the evening because we want to work; we want to work because we want to earn money; we want money because we want to be rich; we want to be rich, because we want to live a life of leisure. The freedom of choice, too, can be of a different degree; we can hardly help wanting light in the evening, but it depends on us whether or not we want a life of leisure. In all these cases we shall talk of an end when we restrict our attention to the limited practical purpose and want to find means which enable us to achieve it; we shall talk of an aim when we refer to the intention which subordinates this end to a more comprehensive purpose or when we leave the sphere of limited practical purpose altogether. In the instances mentioned, light is only an end, work and money can be either ends or aims, according to the point of view from which we look at them, and to be rich and to live a life of leisure are only aims.

(*d*) Intentions and aims are similar in so far as both are based on plans for the future. The differentiation between them will be used to isolate the final and essential goal of our intentions from all other elements. We want light in order to work, work in order to earn money, money for a life of leisure—all this is our intention, but the aim is only a life of leisure. The intention refers to the whole process (to *become* rich in such and such a way), the aim to the result (to *be* rich); it indicates the farthest point which thinking reaches. The two can be distinguished because they can be independent of each other. When I can do my work in daylight, I no longer need artificial light; when I become rich by an unexpected inheritance, my intentions will vanish because I have reached the aim, although I could not intend to become rich in this way; and I may also act exactly according to my intentions and yet go bankrupt instead of becoming rich. We have seen before that the aim is largely independent of my intentions and that this fact is very important for our grasping of internal reality,[1] and we shall see later why it is important to transform their difference into a clear opposition. For the time being it is sufficient to understand their difference.

(2) The example also shows that we cannot remain satisfied with the scale of values which express the relationship between means and ends,

[1] See pp. 43-5.

## THE INTERNAL OPPOSITES

but have to introduce other values as well—an extension which gradually forces us to include more and more of internal reality. For we have to make the following value-judgments:

(*a*) We have to value the means according to their suitability for the end.

(*b*) We must choose the ends as well and therefore value them according to their ability to conform to our intentions.

(*c*) Different intentions can lead to the same aim, and thus we have to decide which intention is the best.

(*d*) We have to choose between different aims, which needs a scale of values which applies to them.

(*e*) Different scales of values may be applicable to the same endeavour and we have, therefore, to value these scales themselves. We have to decide which of the different standards we want to accept.

(3) We have to refer to feeling, for the reasons why the four men made different choices cannot be explained by thinking alone. They may well believe that they can justify their decisions intellectually, but obviously they must have been influenced by feeling.

It would be useful if we could add here a definition of the concept 'value'. Unfortunately, it belongs to those basic concepts which cannot be defined, but we hope that we are gradually elucidating it by our investigation.

Let us now consider, in the light of what we have just said, the necessity of creating more scales of values.

If our interest is mainly concentrated on external reality, we may try to stick to the scale of values determined by the opposition between means and ends. We are attracted by things and practical achievements; ideas and beliefs seem rather vague to us, and so we try to value everything according to its usefulness. But even so we cannot restrict our valuation to the means; we have to choose ends as well. They are not simply given, for we have to decide what we want to be achieved; they have to be imposed upon external reality. Then, however, the question arises: what do we consider as useful? A wireless set is certainly a most ingenious means which serves its end with astonishing efficiency, but is the end itself useful? And if so, which of the uses we make of it constitutes its usefulness—transmitting news or entertainment? And if entertainment, then which kind, and why is such pleasure useful? Whether we want to or not, we have to apply further scales of values to be able to decide what we consider as useful. We are driven onwards to value the ends according to our intentions.

Now we could try to say that we have this or that intention and that this arbitrary decision finally determines our concept of usefulness. But we cannot really stop there. The four men want to become rich and so they could consider as useful what makes them rich. But there are several ways open of becoming rich. They can try to work hard, or they can try their hand on the stock-exchange or rely on betting, or they can marry a rich woman, or they can steal and murder, and so on. These different possibilities can no longer be judged in terms of mere usefulness; one man may work hard and remain poor all his life, and the other may become rich by a stroke of luck. Each of them may defend his decision as logically the most useful one, but we shall be aware all the time that he is, in fact, following his inclinations or, if he is working despite different inclinations, that he is following certain conventions or standards. Feeling will play its part in determining his scale of values and moral decisions can hardly be avoided; even if he himself disregards morals, we shall be unable to do so.

A similar process takes place when we include the aims in our consideration. The four men want to become rich in order to achieve something else; even the first wants to get pleasure with the help of his money. Again, their ways of reaching these aims are not the only ones. The first, when he has become rich, may recognize that he has become a slave to his money; to live a simple life might have served his purpose better; he ought to have recognized what is really pleasurable and what not. The second tries to become an industrialist, but he might have had better opportunities as a manager of a big firm; his desire for personal freedom misled him. The third will perhaps never feel able to retire and could have achieved his purpose better by leading a different life altogether; his standards of an aesthetically pleasing or dignified life have been wrong. The fourth may find it increasingly doubtful whether it is possible to reconcile business methods with his moral intentions; he might have helped others better by developing his personality, by becoming a doctor, by devoting himself to a religious task. All of them may find that selfishness has played too large a part in their decisions and that they ought to have considered the true meaning of life. The scale of values based on usefulness will be left far behind. We have to add to the many scales of values based on the relationships between means and ends a great number of quite different scales which are far more abstract.

These further scales no longer refer to qualities of external things which can be tested by experiments, but to abstract principles. It is true that judgments as to what is dignified or good can also be due to impressions or sudden impulses, but if we want to base upon them intentions and aims which help us decide how to live, we have to develop general principles so as to derive from them scales of values which we can always apply. Even usefulness does not simply represent the concrete relationship between special means and the definite end which they serve, but an abstraction from this relationship, transformed into a principle. Beauty, which perhaps represents the other extreme, is most dependent on actual impressions, but the artist has to be conscious of

## THE INTERNAL OPPOSITES

principles to be able to embody it, and the philosophers, too, have throughout the ages exerted themselves to establish aesthetic principles.

Principles represent another attempt to make clear what values mean. In this case, we do not bestow the values upon something which can represent them, but try to develop their abstract side; we try to discover what kind of relationships, actions and results the meaning of these concepts implies. By stating what the value demands from us and from that upon which it is bestowed, we hope to find laws, such as moral laws, which can guide us in our endeavour to make the values real. We shall return to these principles in a moment; the fact that we use them is certainly obvious without further investigation.

These principles are bound to drive the process of valuing further onwards. As they are based on the meaning of the values, they must have a close relationship to internal reality, and as they represent an attempt to establish laws, they must make it conscious. We are led to seek a firm basis for our valuations within internal reality. Thus, however, we shall no longer be able to stop before we have definitely reached those basic values which we have already touched, namely, truth, goodness and beauty—that is, the values which are called absolute because they are the only ones which can give us absolute certainty and because, while the other values depend on them, they do not depend on any further ones.

That this cannot be avoided can be seen when we imagine that one man has to choose between the aims which, up to now, we have ascribed to four different people. There are no longer any external elements to help him make up his mind, nor can he establish any further aim by which to judge these aims. If he does not want to hover in the air, he will have to find and to apply principles, and he will also have to consider absolute values. He may try to keep his feet firmly on the earth and want everything to be of advantage to him; but what is his advantage? He wants to be happy. But what is happiness, what kind of happiness does he want? Does he want to be able to use things and men just as he likes, in order to fulfil every wish which happens to occur to him? But this means selfishness as a principle and the rejection of moral standards. Does he want to be happy with his wife and children? But this implies human relationships and certain standards which go with such relationships. It needs at least mutual trust, and complete trust between people is hardly possible without the absolute values. As other people confront us with their independent will-power, we can only fully trust them if they are subject to the same unconditional standards as we are.[1] The man himself may be aware neither of the principles nor of these values, but they still pervade his way of valuing all the same, and we have to be aware of them if we want to understand his behaviour.

[1] See H. H. Farmer, *The World and God*, pp. 19–21.

## THE EXTERNAL AND INTERNAL OPPOSITES

In fact he cannot avoid valuing different scales of values and deciding which to apply. He may be very much attracted by merely following his whims, but his conscience, or respect for generally accepted rules, or fear of behaving unconventionally, oppose this wish. His decision—a decision which hardly anybody can avoid—will imply further valuing; so long as he merely follows his whims he values everything in accordance with them, but the whims themselves are not being valued; when he decides that he will rather follow his whims than subordinate himself to another principle, he values them and his selfishness more highly than anything else. He will see the different scales of values which different ways of behaviour presuppose. He may act against his better knowledge and follow his whims although he feels that he ought to behave better, but then he obviously knows that there are higher standards than his. Nor will it be possible to make this decision once for all; his better knowledge will make itself felt again, and so his activity of valuing will be further increased and refined. He will even become conscious of the absolute values.

As the same aims, moreover, can spring from different intentions, they also force us to test whether our valuation has been correct. The wish of the first man to become rich can be purely selfish, or he may not want to become a burden to others; the fourth man may wish to do good for its own sake, or he may wish in this way to acquire a good reputation or a better social position. These contradictory motives may also struggle against each other in his mind; we are rarely able, even if we want to do good for its own sake, to overlook the practical advantages which this may produce for us. There are what Dostoevsky has called the 'double motives'.[1] We have, therefore, to confront our aims with our intentions, for only if we discover our real intentions are we able to value our aims correctly. That is one of the reasons why we have to establish an opposition between intentions and aims; we shall see further reasons later. This test ensures that we do not interrupt the progress of our valuation.

It is true that intentions and aims can also agree completely, but even then the 'double motives' will make themselves felt. They work both ways. It is hardly possible that, on our way to achieve purely selfish aims, we shall never experience moral impulses or be confronted with moral principles, nor that we remain entirely untouched by beauty and truth, and it is even less probable that a moral endeavour, even if it is really unselfish, will never have to struggle against selfishness. We shall experience internal opposites which contradict each other, which will make us conscious of the principles underlying them, and if we have to choose between contradictory principles, we shall require some reference to absolute values. The valuation of the different scales of values,

[1] *The Idiot*, Everyman Ed., p. 298.

## THE INTERNAL OPPOSITES

to which the decision between different principles leads, will have to be based on these values. The mere fact that selfishness is bad, whereas a proper regard for one's own person is not, is puzzling enough to give us no rest before we have tried to understand goodness.

There is no escape—unless our thinking takes a completely wrong turn. As soon as we enter upon valuation, which we are unable to avoid, we shall also be unable to stop the progress of valuation. We have to perform practical tasks, we have intentions and aims, and this makes it necessary for us to apply a constantly increasing number of scales of values, so that we are forced to pay greater and greater attention to internal reality. Finally we have even to include the absolute values which are, as we shall see, among the purest manifestations of this reality.

The last examples also show that we have to acknowledge the existence of internal reality, for the agreement or disagreement between our intentions and the principles can only be tested by feeling and inner experience. We can transform the principles into a set of rules or even laws; there are different codes of behaviour for soldiers and for businessmen; there are moral laws; artists and philosophers try to find æsthetic laws. We shall have to say more about this too. But even laws are not sufficient to throw into relief the discrepancy between intentions and principles; we may act in complete accordance with the moral laws and our motives may yet be quite immoral. We have to know our intentions from inside. The case can be rather complicated; we ourselves can be perfectly convinced that we act morally and yet discover afterwards hidden selfish motives. Any such discovery can only be made with the help of feeling and inner experiences. All this shows that internal reality has indeed an existence independent of ourselves and that our inner experiences, though they have to be ours, disclose an aspect of primary reality. Such a discovery can be very painful, we may very much hate to make it and try by all means to escape it, and yet we are forced to make it, because internal reality does not depend on our intentions or wishes.

All the different scales of values and all internal opposites help to make internal reality accessible. The net cast over external reality, of which we have spoken, is not destroyed by the more abstract values; on the contrary, these form, so to speak, more and narrower meshes which conform more and more closely to the fabric of internal reality. None of these further scales of values make the others superfluous; if we apply moral standards, for instance, the scale which helped us in lighting our rooms remains completely untouched; earning our living, if it does not infringe these principles, also remains outside; we still have to judge usefulness in its own terms and pleasure and pain need not have anything to do with morals. The difficulties which always arise when we try to establish a definite relationship between morality and beauty or truth

## THE EXTERNAL AND INTERNAL OPPOSITES

show clearly that these values, too, are largely independent of each other. The different scales may clash and then we have to decide which value is the more important, but there are vast regions where they cannot clash. All the internal opposites develop the wealth of different feelings which make internal reality real for us—so real that we can no longer doubt its existence.

When we finally have to value the different scales of values, we can, it is true, establish a certain order and derive from this valuation a hierarchy of values. This is a very important basis for making the right decisions; since different scales of values exist, we cannot dispense with this hierarchy. Our lives are determined by the order of values which we accept. But even such a hierarchy does not fundamentally alter the situation so far as it concerns the wealth of feelings and the variety of different scales, for there is no single scale of values which could comprise all the others. Otherwise it would not be so difficult to define the relationship between morals and beauty or truth. When we discuss the dangers which beset valuation, we shall see that an artificial unity in this sphere is as dangerous as the unitary explanation of external reality. The hierarchy must not destroy the single scales, and no hierarchy can define the rank of all possible scales.

Thus, however, another problem arises, or rather recurs. The internal opposites, after all, should not only help us to grasp internal reality, but also to grasp it reliably. We have had to refer increasingly to feelings, but they can be very misleading, and we have said before that the internal opposites are needed to safeguard the right development of feeling. As we are carried towards the absolute values, we have to develop feeling as an organ of knowledge. Yet if the different scales of values remain independent of each other to such a degree that not even a hierarchy of values can be all-embracing, how can they help us to discover the right kind of valuation? To work out clear oppositions may help to apply the single scales more correctly; but how can we know that we are applying the right scale? Our claim, however, that internal reality has an existence independent of ourselves should certainly mean, too, that there are ways of recognizing whether or not we feel, think and act in accordance with the true nature of this reality.

But we have not yet covered the whole range of internal opposites.

### 3. THE CONSTRUCTIVE CONCEPTS

We have stated that there are several conditions which must be fulfilled if we want to grasp internal reality.

(1) We have a knowledge of the content which is fundamentally very definite, but we cannot seize it properly so long as it is entirely confined to internal reality. To bring out what we really know, we

## THE INTERNAL OPPOSITES

have to find an expression for it; we have to give it an external form which we can grasp. To understand goodness, for instance, we have to recognize that something or somebody is good.

(2) All such knowledge must be our own, so that internal reality can completely pervade the form and change it fully into the expression of our inner knowledge and experience. Only thus can we make sure that the form will not remain empty, but really contain a living content. We have said several times that abstract statements or mere rules are insufficient in this sphere.[1] We have said, too, that internal reality can only be made real for us if we constantly experience it anew, which also means that it must be our own experience.

(3) Despite this last condition, however, we have had to stress that there is a contradictory element of anticipation. Only if we know what to expect shall we recognize it when we meet it. Although, for instance, we realize the meaning of the good only when we experience it, we must, even if we meet it for the first time, have some knowledge of it, to be able to recognize it at all. We have also to anticipate the future, for this has to enable us to fulfil a further condition of the grasping of internal reality—that we must have a full experience of the present.[2]

These conditions are fulfilled by those internal opposites which are formed by the constructive concepts transferred from external reality. We shall again discuss first their fruitful application and return later to their possible distortions.

The first step in the application of the internal opposites is that of the constructive concepts 'means' and 'end'; they prepare external reality in such a way that the first condition just mentioned can be fulfilled and external reality used to express internal reality.

The first step is very significant, for it points to an important difference in the functioning of the constructive concepts in the two realities. In external reality, we start from the actual impressions which are gradually made intelligible by the simultaneous application of abstraction and the constructive concepts. In our consideration of internal opposites, we have had to apply these concepts right from the beginning; we have to start from them because we can never approach internal reality without using external elements and thus we have first to know how to transform them before they can disclose internal reality. These applications of the constructive concepts are therefore different. In external reality we are transferring concepts derived from our knowledge of internal reality and using them as such. In internal reality we are using the external elements as such, and the constructive concepts explain how we are using them. We apply them to external reality and

[1] See pp. 98–9, and also J. Oman, *The Natural and the Supernatural*, p. 316.
[2] See pp. 52–4.

## THE EXTERNAL AND INTERNAL OPPOSITES

then transfer, not the concepts themselves, but the external elements which have been transformed by them.

To give an example—the opposites 'means' and 'end' create, as we have seen, a relationship which is similar to that between cause and effect, but their application is completely different. The concepts 'cause' and 'effect', though they have to be applied to actual events, are also important in themselves for external reality, for they have, apart from their application, so much significance of their own that we can progress from them to the causal laws; we employ abstractions to exclude the real things more and more, in order to be able to deal in general with the relationships between causes and effects as such. In internal reality, no such abstraction would serve any important purpose; the concepts 'means' and 'end' have to be applied to external reality to acquire meaning. We can derive from them, it is true, the principle of usefulness, but its significance cannot be compared with that of causality; while causality is one of our main helps in grasping external reality, usefulness hovers in the air unless we confine it to a quite definite and limited practical sphere; otherwise it merely forces us to progress to other principles which, in their turn, show similar shortcomings. Cause and effect, moreover, though they are derived from internal reality, need no further reference to it and even exclude it; the constructive concepts 'means' and 'end' teach us how to transform external reality so as to be able to include it in internal reality, but they do not make it superfluous to add the external elements themselves. In this case we have had to discuss, not only the abstract concepts, but the particular means and ends as such.

The second main step in the application of internal opposites consisted in the creation of principles. These principles have a peculiar position within the realm of the constructive concepts, and so we have to consider them at greater length.

Most of the principles are concerned with our actions, and thus they borrow their form from external events. We explain the principle by creating a necessary relationship between cause and effect. It is true that principles cannot claim the general validity of natural laws, for we can choose between them; they do not say what will happen, but what we ought to do. Yet within the range of the principle itself, necessity is nevertheless established. We make the assumption which is needed to introduce the principle—if you want to be successful, if you want to be considered a 'gentleman', if you want to act morally—and then claim that, according to the principle, in such and such a situation this or that action must be performed. The principle represents the law, the situation the cause, and our action the necessary effect. We can also, as in external reality, gain a deeper knowledge which shifts the cause further back; as our actions are caused by intentions and as the principle

## THE INTERNAL OPPOSITES

is applied because we want to stick to it, the principle itself can be regarded as the true cause, just as the force of gravity and not the opening of our hand was the true cause of the falling of the stone. The principles, moreover, are endowed, when we accept them, with power over us, and can therefore also be considered in the same way as we consider external forces. Thus the forms of external events are well fitted to give a definite form to these principles.

The development of principles is important because it transforms internal reality into something more external which can be preserved, remembered and surveyed. A principle tells us what we have to consider as useful or useless, as good or bad, as noble or mean, and so on. If we did not transform these opposites into a set of connections between different causes and their effects and derive a law from them—in short, if we did not develop the principle, we should remain entirely dependent on our individual experiences and the feelings which they evoke; we should have to apply the basic internal opposites over and over again. The principle gives us a more or less complete picture of the valuation which such an attitude, or an aim chosen in accordance with it, implies; we need not wait for the actual experience, but can define, with the help of a few experiences, the value which any action will have in its relation to the principle. We can establish the whole scale of values, instead of remaining confined to the single opposites which apply to each separate experience. This will help us greatly in becoming conscious of the intrinsic knowledge of the values which we possess, and in our anticipation of the future which we need in order to have a full experience of the present. We gain a clear idea of what to expect and know how to relate the momentary impression or experience to the values which we want to make real.

To develop such scales of values is also important for another reason. Our experiences are rarely so extreme that we have to apply the basic opposition between good and evil or between similar positive and negative opposites; usually these opposites have to help us to recognize what is better or worse—that is, to recognize degrees.[1] The hierarchy of values of which we have spoken is, moreover, mainly built upon such differences of degrees. Each single degree of any scale has to be developed by using the opposites as such, but it is obvious that we have to fix them within a scale to be able to establish a correct relationship between the different degrees. Otherwise the actual experience would acquire a far higher significance than it has when we compare it with other experiences in retrospect.

There are certain difficulties involved in those principles which do

---

[1] 'Decisions between right and wrong... are rare and become rarer if rightly decided. What is continuous and what most determines the character is the absoluteness of the decision between higher and lower.' J. Oman, op. cit., pp. 317-18.

## THE EXTERNAL AND INTERNAL OPPOSITES

not refer to our actions, but to their results or to things and facts; yet these difficulties show once more that we take the form of the principles from external events. This is the reason, for instance, why we encounter so many obstacles when trying to formulate æsthetic laws; we have to apply such concepts as cause and effect and thus to presuppose certain actions, but beauty need not be the result of action and can be embodied in something static which does not change. The problem is easier for the artist who wants to explain his methods, for this refers to actions, yet even here the laws usually remain unsatisfactory, because results of the same value can be achieved by different methods, and it is the value which matters. The same difficulty may also partially explain why it hardly seems possible to define truth, for again we cannot apply a principle to what is usually a static result, though truthfulness, as it refers to our behaviour, can easily become a principle.

However, this failure of certain principles also shows that we cannot remain satisfied with them. To grasp internal reality, we have to seize upon the unrepeatable; but the principles, like natural laws, are concerned with what can be repeated.[1] Principles, despite their undeniable importance, are too abstract; they alone cannot enable us to find the form which we need to express internal reality. We have already mentioned that they can cover different intentions and thus do not allow us to distinguish between them; we have just had to mention, too, that they save us from having always to apply the opposites anew, which is right so long as we are concerned with the principle itself or with anticipation, but wrong when it comes to the point where internal reality has to be made real. Nor can principles really be our own. This is not because we mostly take over principles which are generally accepted; for even if we do not create the principles, we can adapt them to our needs and convictions and develop them further. We have to do the same with most values. But we are bound to accept principles as abstract laws, and our own contributions have to be included in these abstract laws, and this severs their connection with our personal experience.

The danger of the generalizations which principles attempt can be seen in the fact that we can apply the opposites 'good' and 'bad' to almost any scale of values so long as that scale rests only on principles. Something is good because it is of advantage, or because it shows our good upbringing, and it is bad for the opposite reasons. Thus, however, these opposites mean nothing but different degrees of value, without referring to any special value, and lose their distinctive moral quality. They become an abstract opposition which can be used in all kinds of contexts. To make sure that we are applying internal opposites, we should be on our guard and always find out whether it is possible to

[1] See pp. 49–51.

## THE INTERNAL OPPOSITES

say 'evil' instead of 'bad', or whether we actually need a quite different opposition. But principles influence us in the opposite direction.

This limitation of the principles is not, in fact, surprising, for we are not applying those constructive concepts which belong to internal reality. We are using such concepts as 'cause' and 'necessity', but these are concepts abstracted from internal reality and transferred to external reality; it is not surprising, therefore, that they prove to be purely abstract when we take them back into internal reality. They serve to make external reality accessible and so, with their help, we cannot adapt external elements to internal reality, but are in danger of making internal reality too much like external reality. The concept of necessity, for instance, is formed as the opposite of freedom, but the problem of freedom which opens the way towards internal reality cannot even be discussed with the help of these principles. It is true that they start from freedom by saying what we ought to do, but we have seen that this is only their presupposition which has to be taken for granted. Necessity reigns within the range of the principle itself.

The application of external constructive concepts explains the peculiar nature of the principles. Their great importance is due to the fact that, as we have seen, internal reality also consists of the processes going on within ourselves, of thinking, feeling and willing, and the principles, as they take their form from events, help us to transform these processes into clear actions which we can reliably anticipate and direct. As the principles refer to our actions, moreover, they can also be tested by these actions and thus give us a high degree of certainty. But they can neither explain the anticipation, nor can they alone make internal reality accessible. For this reality is embodied, not in the process, but in the result of our action, and this cannot be judged by principles alone, but must also be considered as such. Like the first step, this second step is quite indispensable as a preparation; this time internal reality itself is transformed so that we can reliably approach it. But to be able to grasp it we must return to those constructive concepts which belong to this reality.

Instead of proceeding in this direction, however, we sometimes try to make up for the abstract nature of the principles by trying to construct ideals with their help, to show in concrete terms what the abstract principle implies. This attempt could easily be mistaken for the form which embodies internal reality, but we must beware of this mistake.

The word 'ideal' has, apart from some others, three special meanings which could be mixed up in this context, and so we must first distinguish between them.

(1) We can draw, with the help of the principles, a picture of an ideal reality which would completely fulfil all their demands. We can try to construct an ideal state, an ideal society, a golden age, an ideal man.

## THE EXTERNAL AND INTERNAL OPPOSITES

(2) We sometimes talk of the ideal of the good or of beauty or of some other value. This means that we aim at the purest realization of the highest degree of the scale of values with which we are concerned. This meaning of the concept 'ideal' we shall dismiss altogether, because this attempt is better expressed by saying that we try to grasp and to make real the value as such, for it depends entirely on our understanding of the value whether or not such an ideal has any meaning at all. The 'ideal values' can also mean what we prefer to call the 'absolute values'. We prefer this term, because the first meaning of 'ideal' could suggest that these values do not belong to internal reality but to our imagination.

(3) We can make a personality, an historical or contemporary person, the embodiment of the ideal, seeing that he or she comes nearest to the complete fulfilment of our intentions, wishes and demands.

Here we are concerned with the first meaning. This kind of ideal can help to make details of the principles clearer, because it shows how they can be applied and where they lead. But it is not fundamentally different from the principles themselves; both remain abstract and cannot alone help us to grasp internal reality. The ideal must remain abstract too, because it endows certain external elements—society, man—with perfect qualities, and these, by their very perfection, can never occur in the imperfect reality which, owing to our limited abilities, we are bound to be or to create. The ideals, therefore, are helpful so long as we realize that they are merely a means of explaining abstractions; the ideal society cannot show us a possible real society, but it can help us to recognize what true human relationships mean. If we mistake ideals for external embodiments of internal reality, we only increase, as we shall see later, the dangers of the abstractions contained in the principles.

The difference between the ideals and the forms which make internal reality real can perhaps be most clearly seen when we compare the first and the third meaning of the concept. If we construct an 'ideal man', we shall soon discover that we cannot live up to this ideal, and if we still insist on trying to do so, we shall be forced to retire more and more from the world, to suppress the feelings which tell us that we are different, and to live in an abstract region where thought and imagination can replace all actual experience. If, on the other hand, we find our ideal embodied in a real man, and do not conceive him wrongly as an 'ideal man' but as the personality he really is, we shall have to try to understand him, to connect his deeds or works with his experiences and feelings, to be able to follow them with our own feeling and to translate them into the different experiences which we have in our own lives. We find internal reality embodied in a special form which expresses the content, and as our personality is different, we must try to discover

## THE INTERNAL OPPOSITES

the meaning of this form to be able to apply the knowledge we thus win. We shall be forced to approach internal reality.

This example shows once more that we have to include in internal reality external things or facts or events and to transform them by apprehending them from a different point of view. When trying to describe internal reality, we have seen again and again that the most important concepts for this purpose were the constructive concepts 'form' and 'content'. They alone can help us to make this transformation complete, and so their application represents the third main step in the application of the internal opposites.

The concepts 'form' and 'content' remain the same in both realities, but we have seen before that their meaning in external and internal reality is very different.[1] In external reality, the content is something unknown and hidden towards which we try to advance, but always when we think that we have reached it, it seems to retire once more and we have only discovered another external form. As all these forms remain abstract, the mere idea of a content without any further substance is sufficient to enable us to grasp them. In internal reality, on the contrary, we know the content and it is, therefore, concrete and has a substance; we have to find the form which will make it intelligible, and this also changes the form thoroughly. It is no longer abstract; we are unable to apply it, as we do in external reality, to many different things and events; we need the unique form which brings out completely one special experience of the content. We have found the principles insufficient just because they remain abstract forms which can be applied on many different occasions.

The requirements of such a form can be seen when we remember that the same aim can spring from different intentions and that the same intentions can lead to different results. Thus we cannot consider them as the forms of our striving. What we need is a special deed in which intentions and aims, our motives and the results we achieve, are blended in such a way that they leave no ambiguity, so that the value, or the set of values, which determines our deed and which we want to make real becomes visible and recognizable. Every single detail of the form, the connection between our motives and their execution, between our deed and the circumstances, the feelings involved in our action and the choices we make—every single detail must refer to the content and help to make it unmistakably clear. The form must be created by the content and we must be able to see in all the single particulars that the external form is the expression of that which led to its creation. All genuine works of art, which perhaps most distinctly represent such a form, are necessarily unique.

[1] In the following we take up again the differences between the two realities which we have stated on pp. 47–54. For form and content see also pp. 27–30 and 38–40.

## THE EXTERNAL AND INTERNAL OPPOSITES

This difference between external and internal forms and between their relationships with the content can also be seen from another point of view. If we get a few pieces of a broken stone, for instance, we are able to investigate certain qualities and to achieve results which apply to this kind of stone in general, but unless we find almost all the pieces we shall be unable to reconstruct the shape of the particular stone to which these pieces belonged. The situation is somewhat different with organisms; here the single parts say more about the whole to which they belong; but to reconstruct an unknown organism from its parts needs, again, a great number of them, and the reconstruction remains uncertain. The relationship between the parts and the whole is not quite definite. If we are confronted, however, with a form belonging to internal reality, with a deed, with a personality, a sudden insight can reveal to us the whole man, even if we know only a single reaction on a single occasion, or a single trait of his character. A few passages of a poem, a single sketch, a few remnants of an old civilization, may reveal to us a world which was previously hidden from us. The relationship between the parts and the whole is so definite that even a single part can disclose the whole; as the content is expressed in every detail of a unique form, each of the details can, by its uniqueness, disclose the content.

These three steps in the application of the internal opposites are, of course, only the main steps; we have seen before how many more different approaches and shades there are in the sphere of both ends and principles and in the transition from one to the other. This is also the case in the sphere of forms, and the consideration of some of these other steps may further help to give us a clear idea of the task of the constructive concepts in internal reality. There is, for instance, the transformation which the constructive concepts the One and the Many —again the same for both realities—undergo when applied to internal reality.

In external reality we try to eliminate the peculiarity of the single object or event and to make it an instance of many similar units, so as to be able to consider it as nothing but one unit among many of the same kind. We have to grasp the Many and therefore to reduce the One to abstractions which can be generally applied. Internal reality, on the contrary, can only be grasped if the experiences are our own, and we are confronted with the two facts—that we ourselves are unique persons and that our feelings which make the experiences our own cannot be repeated exactly. Thus the experience must have the character of a particular personality, and each experience, to create new feelings, must be in some ways new and unique. It is true that, as internal reality has an existence of its own, we must finally achieve a knowledge which is of general validity, but it is only when we give a unique form to our own experience and are obliged to understand

## THE INTERNAL OPPOSITES

those created by others that internal reality is brought into play and allows us to recognize the general validity of its special manifestation. Therefore, we have to isolate the One and to dissolve the Many into all its different components, so that the single unit can no longer be counted or discounted.

This explains, too, why we have to concentrate on the accidental as such when concerned with internal reality. When we eliminate it, we open the way for the establishment of external necessity which needs uniform units to lead to the general law valid for many instances. Freedom, however, belonging to internal reality, can only be grasped if the accidental, as an individual unit, transforms the external happening into our own fate.

All these necessities confirm once more that we have to establish a clear opposition between intentions and aims, for they also imply the transformation of the concept of time. We have seen that, in external reality, we try to build on the past and thus on what we reliably know; in the exact sciences time as such plays no essential part; as events can be repeated, we do not consider time as something which can never be made to regress and is irretrievably lost once it has gone; it remains an abstract and repeatable form, independent, as it were, of the real course of time. In internal reality, we have to start from the future, which we do by creating aims. But the aim, when we reach it, may have another meaning from the one we expected, and so we have to confront it with our original intentions to see whether there is harmony or discrepancy. We have to pay attention to the special historical process which cannot be repeated, and thus to use intentions and aims in a constructive opposition which enables us to see this special historical development.

These examples may be sufficient to show that the transformation of the constructive concepts follows very definite lines, and this supports our claim that the fact that internal experiences have to be ours does not make internal reality subjective in the usual sense of the word. The transferring of concepts from one reality to the other, though in one case they are used as concepts and in the other only teach us what to do, establishes, in internal reality too, a secure basis for the application of opposites, and as this basis is independent of the conscious working of our minds, it forms a barrier against arbitrary thinking. We can, of course, disregard or falsify this basis, but if we recognize it, it shows us how to apply the opposites and indicates whether we did so correctly or not.

How far we have advanced towards solving the problems connected with internal reality can be seen when we look back, in passing, on the problem of anticipation. This problem also crops up when we have to create the appropriate form, for to create it we must know what to

## THE EXTERNAL AND INTERNAL OPPOSITES

express, and how can we know this when only its form makes it known to us? But this anticipation no longer looks as puzzling as it did, for if internal reality has an existence of its own and if we ourselves are the bearers of this reality, the process of forming brings out parts of the reality which are in existence within us. We recognize at once that we are giving form to something which has always been part of our being, and this makes us able to control the creation of the form. The possibility of anticipation, therefore, even confirms that internal reality is largely independent of ourselves, for we can anticipate something of which we are hardly conscious, and our activities, because they belong to internal reality, make it real even though our conscious aims may have been quite different. The 'double motives' make us conscious of the good while we want only to seek our own advantage, and we recognize it, even if we meet it for the first time, because it is inherent in our being. The principles, though they could not explain anticipation, must, in this case, be a sufficient help in transforming this reality in such a way that it can be formed, for they can be developed from slight indications.

Nevertheless, in spite of this narrowing down of the sphere of arbitrariness, it has not completely disappeared, but we can see now which is the fundamental question. We can perhaps isolate it best when we compare external qualities with values, their equivalent in internal reality.

These concepts do not belong to the constructive concepts; they are names which we give to certain elements of the two realities and cannot be further explained. But they are clearly equivalents; both make us apply scales of degrees and both represent the essential elements by which we get to know the two realities. Their difference, however, shows exactly the point which is at the root of the difficulty of making the knowledge of internal reality reliable.

We apprehend external qualities by isolating certain elements of a reality which is presented to us; we apply the opposites to something which exists outside ourselves and can be tested in many ways. External reality stands over against us, so that thinking is opposed by something different to which it can be applied. Values, on the contrary, are based on judgments; they can also be applied to external reality, yet even then they do not refer to this reality as such, but to the activities of our minds. Thinking is only confronted with itself, for the feelings on which such judgments are based have to be translated into thought to make us conscious of a value. It is true that, in the end, as we have seen, we get down to the absolute values, but this does not fundamentally improve the situation. In a certain sense, these values also stand over against us, for we cannot alter them arbitrarily, but thinking is still confronted with itself, for they do not exist somewhere in space and

## THE INTERNAL OPPOSITES

time, but have to be established by our thinking. They are based on feelings, too, but this makes them very different from things we can see and touch, for though feeling is very definite and certain this time, it can affirm errors as absolutely as truth. While our knowledge of external reality seems firmly grounded in it, the absolute values seem to lack the necessary foundation; we obviously ought to base them on something more fundamental, but we cannot progress to further values or further internal opposites. The problem is how to test the absolute values; without such a test it seems impossible to make the knowledge of internal reality as reliable as that of external reality. The success of our investigation still depends on the solution of this problem.

But the comparison between qualities and values also increases our hope that there is a solution to it. In the last resort, the knowledge of both realities leads towards the absolute—that is, towards a direct experience of primary reality. In external reality we touch this sphere, as we have seen, where modern physics leaves the constructive concepts behind. But at this point our knowledge becomes entirely incomprehensible and meaningless and confirms that we cannot grasp the absolute in this way; we are confronted with numbers and mathematical formulae which can neither be translated into something which we could imagine nor convey any meaning whatever.[1] In internal reality, we meet the absolute in the absolute values. These are certainly not so exact as mathematics, but they are full of meaning and able to give content to our lives—a content of a richness and fullness which no knowledge of external reality could ever convey. Is it probable, then, that the certainty which we experience with the help of these values should leave us in a complete void?

Before discussing this question, however, let us first see the distortions with which a wrong development of feeling threatens the application of internal opposites. This will further narrow down the scope of possible errors.

---

[1] Max Planck describes the inexplicable elementary constant quantum of energy which he has discovered and which he thinks belongs to the absolute reality behind external reality as 'a new mysterious messenger from the real world' (*Das Weltbild der neuen Physik*, p. 19). This application of a personal term to a figure called 'q' shows most conspicuously how meaningless is this kind of absolute.

## Chapter VIII

## RIGHT AND WRONG DEVELOPMENT OF FEELING

### 1. THE INTRUSION OF FEELING INTO THE REALM OF THOUGHT

WE have seen that the application of internal opposites, starting from the simple opposition between means and ends, can lead us from stage to stage, thus disclosing more and more of internal reality, until we reach the absolute values. This development can be interrupted and each single stage can become final by that intrusion of feeling which we have discussed.[1] This interruption means, at the same time, that internal reality is either completely suppressed or dangerously distorted.

The intrusion of feeling can take place even if we only apply the simple opposites 'means' and 'end'. We can be obsessed by the wish for certain possessions or practical achievements, for instance by the desire for money as such or as a means of acquiring things or having comfort or security; we may be completely absorbed by some investigation which promises to lead to a particular invention or discovery. All such material aims can attract our feelings so strongly that we become almost blind to everything else. As they are dependent on the achievement of quite definite ends, this end will entirely dominate our valuations; all we experience or see and all that we or others do is only valued as a means to the end we have in mind; strong feelings force all our processes of thought to serve exclusively this particular obsession. We shall have, of course, some minor likes and dislikes too, as well as other impressions and other knowledge, but these are either valued in accordance with the dominating scale or not taken seriously. We are prevented from proceeding from this kind of valuation to any more fundamental values.

This kind of obsession, however, though it can be very strong, need

[1] See pp. 106–9.

## RIGHT AND WRONG DEVELOPMENT OF FEELING

not be considered as very dangerous, for its objects are so obviously limited that it may be comparatively easy to break their power. Some different and more serious experiences can easily show us how little such achievements mean, or we may also achieve what we so fervently wanted and thus become free and open-minded again. But the preoccupation with the purely material can take more dangerous forms too.

If we are so much interested in material things, we are apt to believe that material achievements are the only ones which matter. Instead of clinging to the single end, our feelings can be completely dominated by the idea of progress, especially in scientific and technical developments, or by that of creating the greatest material happiness for everybody. Here it becomes very clear indeed that further progress in valuation is cut off by feeling. Most of the forms of consistent materialism are based on further values; the wish to make life easier and healthier by scientific progress, the desire to secure the well-being of everybody presuppose love and a real appreciation of the human being; the wish for a better distribution of wealth springs from a sense of justice. But if feeling is mainly attracted by the material things as such, the question whether material things and technical progress really procure happiness or are in themselves sufficient to do so is not even asked; they are valued so highly that they are desired at any cost, even if, in fact, they destroy happiness or life or human freedom and dignity. Man merely has to accept this kind of happiness, and this shows that it is not happiness which determines the scale of values, but the material things. Although other values are involved, we are cut off from them; love and justice are not taken into account, but scorned. In order to suppress them, the mixture of external and internal negation which we have discussed is summoned up [1]—external negation to exclude them logically and internal negation to ascribe a negative value to them and to endow the negative with feeling. The more genuine the original motives, the stronger the negation; thinking is forced to work out the most elaborate systems to justify and to increase the strength of feeling. Here already the breaking down of these barriers has become extremely difficult.

Concentration on external reality can also have a different effect. If we recognize that material things are not significant enough, but still remain under the spell of external reality, we can turn to the different forms of society, such as the nation, the state or the race, which we seem able to grasp like any other part of that reality and which are yet human at the same time. They too, as we all know, can prove most attractive for that feeling which seeks satisfaction outside; it is even easier to charge them with feeling.

[1] See pp. 54-5, 94-6.

## THE EXTERNAL AND INTERNAL OPPOSITES

States and nations are no longer quite so real in the material sense; they depend on human conceptions and limitations. This can be seen when we try to define them; there is no completely satisfactory definition of any such concept. If we treat nations and states as purely external, we cannot account for the human bonds which keep them in being, nor for the fact that the definition itself can exercise an influence upon them and alter their external appearance. If we stress the human element, we do not account for the different historical forms which they have acquired and by which they have become material facts. It is this very uncertainty, however, which proves so dangerously attractive for feeling, for if feeling turns towards external reality and finds facts which are not completely self-sufficient, it can most easily influence thinking and transform the meaning of the facts in accordance with its own desires. As the concepts defy any clear definition, they can be considered as mysterious or mystical, which is most fascinating for feeling. The basic doubts which can never be entirely overcome stimulate feeling too, for it has to cover them up by stronger and stronger emotions. Every nation or state, moreover, is all too obviously only a small part of external reality; if it has to satisfy all our feelings, negation must once more be summoned up and, to fulfil its task, exaggerated and used in the most false way possible; the small part of reality with which we are obsessed has to represent all the good and everything else, which is the greater part of our world, has to be considered as more or less bad; some part of it has even to be seen as extremely evil or wicked, for otherwise our obsession could not be upheld. The subjugation of thinking by feeling will then most probably become complete.

Both materialism in all its forms and nationalism are naturally dangerous in many different ways. A combination of the two, in particular, frequently leads to the striving for power, and this age-old and yet necessarily futile aim shows perhaps even more clearly how the intrusion of feeling works.

If a man's interests remain directed towards external reality alone, he has to consider himself as a material being and his values must, therefore, coincide with the external opposites. He has to replace the human qualities, which he is unable to appreciate, by size in space and duration in time; a greatness which can be measured will represent the highest value for him. Hence he tends to seek power, conquest and fame; deprived of the non-material relations with his fellow-men, his ambition has to concentrate on enlarging himself at the expense of others, or he will at least admire those who do so. Owing to human smallness and frailty, however, such an endeavour cannot lead very far; even if a man could conquer the whole earth, he would still remain infinitesimally small when compared with the universe, and the length of his life is but a moment in the eternal flux of time. No future fame can lengthen his actual life. To be able to overlook such obvious limitations, he must believe that the next step, the next deed or conquest, will make up for the shortcomings which he is bound to feel whenever he reaches one of his aims. He must be incessantly driven onwards, for if he were allowed to rest the vanity of his endeavours would make itself felt. Feeling has to invade thinking again and again to enable him to restrict all his valuations to external opposites, for if thinking could proceed to internal opposites, it would clear a way through all his different emotions and show him both the correct external proportions and the real internal values, and power and glory could no longer be enjoyed nor overrated. It is the very insecurity of such obsessions which constantly increases the strength of feeling and makes it so difficult to loosen its hold on thought.

The more we advance towards the more abstract values, the less dangerous the effects of the intrusion of feeling appear, for there fanaticism is less likely to develop. But these effects are just as important, because they destroy positive elements which otherwise could be very valuable for the progress of valuation. The intrinsic value of the elements which give occasion for the intrusion of feeling, moreover, makes it more difficult to discover that the possibility of their further development has been destroyed, and so this progress is as definitely interrupted as before.

Principles, for instance, have to be transformed into clear laws, for our intentions are too easily misled and our feelings not always acute enough to allow us to rely on intuitions right from the beginning. But the laws must not be more than guides; finally they have to give way to spontaneous reactions, for only these will allow us to find that full personal expression which alone makes internal reality completely real. If the law as such, however, becomes the object of feeling, we shall pin it down by connecting it definitely with corresponding external actions; external rules will smother all spontaneity, but allow us instead to obey them for the wrong reasons.[1] Or, to give another example—the technique of art has its important rules which can help the artist to find his own expression and to make himself understood. Yet if these rules become the main interest, the external form seems more important than the content, and a perfect but empty form is preferred to the form which, perhaps by its very imperfection or by its boldness, really discloses the content. The intrusion of feeling transforms principles, laws and rules, all of which could be a great help, into a great obstacle.

This danger can be seen particularly clearly if we think of such

---

[1] The last temptation is the greatest treason:
To do the right deed for the wrong reason.
T. S. ELIOT, *Murder in the Cathedral*, p. 44.

concepts as, for instance, duty. If feeling concentrates on such a purely formal concept which establishes a necessity and formal laws which have no connection with the content, but only require discipline as such, almost everything can be used to give a content to this form and to enable us to do our duty. Again, the idea of duty can be an important help; who can say that he will always want to do the good for its own sake without any compulsion? But if we forget that it is a mere form which has to have a good content to be good, not only the routine of bureaucracy, but even the worst crimes in the service of any authority can be considered as sacred duties. Our obsession is the following of a law regardless of what it entails. We turn everything into its fulfilment, even if the very nature of the deed contradicts entirely the original intention which made us accept duty for moral reasons. The process is the same as with the empty artistic form, but infinitely more dangerous; the obsession with the mere form makes us overlook the fact that it remains senseless or is filled with a wrong or destructive content. As duty seems to justify them, even the worst crimes can no longer be morally attacked.

Something similar happens if ideals are used to support principles in the wrong way. We have seen that we need ideals too; we must aim at something which is better or more perfect than our present achievements, for otherwise we shall hardly be able to go on striving. Nor shall we be able to do so without a fairly clear notion of the aim to which this striving ought to lead, even if this aim in fact represents an ideal beyond our reach; indeed this is frequently necessary to make us strive at all.[1] But if the ideal attracts all our feelings, its effect is exactly the opposite.

The ideal embodies internal reality; it should be understood as an imaginative construction which acquires meaning only through its relationship with this reality. All the details of the ideal should help us to grasp possibilities and shades of feelings. The description of an ideal state, as we have said, does not depict an external aim, for no state can be perfect, but makes clear what love and justice and neighbourliness mean and demand.[2] In that way, the ideal can help us to bring about a better state. If feeling, however, concentrates on the ideal as such, no consideration is allowed to lessen its importance; all that represents inner meaning is accepted as externally possible and every detail matters, again not because of its meaning, but quite literally. We insist that nothing is to be altered or left out, and in this hopeless struggle for every detail the real task of the ideal is forgotten. Love will be turned into hatred or contempt for those who oppose us for very good reasons. We shall always believe that we know better and thus become unable to acquire knowledge. Every ideal, moreover, to fulfil its func-

[1] See J. Oman, *The Natural and the Supernatural*, p. 397.    [2] See p. 130.

tion of promoting clearer ideas, necessarily includes utopian elements which lift it above the level of everyday experience. If these are mistaken for real possibilities, they can even make us unable to cope with our actual experiences and opportunities. As we thus believe that an ideal perfection can be attained, we shall despise the necessary little steps and imperfect achievements which are within our reach. To mistake internal elements for external things and to invest them with feelings is as dangerous, therefore, as to attach feeling to the external aims themselves.

It is no help if the intrusion of feeling chooses instead elements or concepts which belong entirely to internal reality. We can also be completely dominated by the wish to enjoy our feelings, to have strong feelings at any cost, to feel that we are alive—that is, the intrusion of feeling can concentrate on itself. But if we look at our feelings in this way, we are not satisfied with the content which they, with the help of external objects, gradually disclose; the feeling as such has to be the content. We want either strong will and strong vitality, because they give rise to strong feeling, or experiences which strongly excite us. We forget that any inner activity can be of positive or negative value and that this depends on its inner content which cannot develop when we enjoy our feelings as such. We overrate the mere strength of feeling and underrate spiritual strength; without any scruples and any possibility of judging we merely accept as positive anything which can make us feel strongly, even if it be the worst adventure. Bombing can be more exciting than sitting in an office. Nor does it help to break the chain of external necessity by a complete concentration on the accidental, for if the accident is stressed as such and not as the unique form of internal reality, necessity is replaced by arbitrariness or licence which also cut us off from this reality. We follow every impulse, enjoy every impression or change, dramatize every situation, without knowing what they do or could mean or of what value they are, and without ever allowing any experience to bear its fruit. Here as elsewhere, the intrusion of feeling forces us to regress.[1]

Intensity of feeling obviously becomes less dangerous as we reach those constructive concepts which belong to internal reality; for as these secure the right relationship between feeling and thinking, it is an advantage if our feelings are strong enough to make full use of their opportunities. But if an intrusion of feeling occurs, even the right values can become a source of dangers and distortions.

---

[1] To avoid misunderstandings, it should perhaps be mentioned that this 'enjoying one's feeling' can also be very painful. Like any intrusion of feeling, this form, too, can be entirely independent of our will; we may be overwhelmed and haunted by our feelings and unable to combat them. Then, however, a new element enters—that of suffering—and this we shall discuss later.

## THE EXTERNAL AND INTERNAL OPPOSITES

This can best be seen when we consider the intrusion of feeling due to its too strong attachment to a hierarchy of values. As such a hierarchy represents, in this field, the most comprehensive order which we are able to achieve, this kind of intrusion also shows the fundamental and most dangerous motive which always contributes to the overwhelming of thinking by feeling—the longing for an all-embracing unity.

Our examples have already shown why such a hierarchy is important. As so many scales of values have to be applied, we always need some kind of hierarchy to find our way through this maze; all the different wrong consequences of the intrusion of feeling could also be described as attempts to establish wrong hierarchies. Nevertheless, a hierarchy can also become dangerous if feeling concentrates entirely on it. To safeguard its positive value, we have to make two restrictions; first, owing to the nature of the scales of values, no hierarchy can become all-embracing; second, it must remain dependent on the values themselves, for if it hardens into an external structure, it can become an empty form and filled with the wrong content. It is exactly these two restrictions, however, which are swept away by the intrusion of feeling.

The sweeping away of the first restriction shows that the desire to create an all-embracing unity is, in fact, the motive behind any intrusion of feeling. We have seen that even in external reality this attempt has to be supported by what we would call now an intrusion of feeling. In internal reality, the part played by feeling naturally becomes more obvious. As a feeling which is cut off from any further development can only become stronger, it must quite directly try—as again all we have discussed has shown—to create the all-embracing unity which justifies the complete concentration on this special feeling. The concentration on a hierarchy is only another attempt of this kind. It is less conspicuous, because any hierarchy has to include a great number of scales of values, but it is hardly less dangerous, as the sweeping away of the second restriction shows.

If our feelings are too subtle to succumb to the simpler temptations, a hierarchy can become their obsession, for it always represents a pattern of many degrees of positive and negative values which cannot be further reduced, as they can if we concentrate on a single scale, and thus passion need not become so obvious. Yet if a hierarchy has to embrace everything, it must also allot to any possible phenomenon its well defined rank. This task, however, cannot be fulfilled if the hierarchy remains dependent on the actual experience of the different values, for these always leave scope for unexpected changes; instead, the hierarchy hardens into a fixed external order, and such an order can all too easily degenerate into some kind of caste system which destroys all human value. But even if this does not happen and if we try to stick

## RIGHT AND WRONG DEVELOPMENT OF FEELING

to the right values, the intrusion of feeling can make it seem natural that the higher and the lower ranks have to accept different kinds of morality, and if this is allowed to pass, there can be no doubt that it is not morality but the external order which establishes our scale of values. Morality itself cannot help hardening into a formal law which keeps the hierarchy in being, and the chance of any further development of values is as thoroughly destroyed as in any other case.

The distortions which we have discussed are still only a few general examples of the dangers connected with the wrong development of feeling. But as they are taken from different levels, they are probably sufficient to show that not only the motive but also the result of any intrusion of feeling is always the same. A wrong conclusion is endowed with a strength of feeling which seems identical with that certainty which we experience with the help of the absolute values. The difficulty which made us ask before how to test these values could also be expressed by the question of how to distinguish between the intrusion of feeling and the right kind of absolute certainty.

It is true that it does not always need an intrusion of feeling to interrupt the development of valuation; weakness of feeling can also lead to many of the results which we have tried to describe, from the pursuit of an external aim which may appear as the easiest way of living or merely occupy all our available strength, to the acceptance of the nation, of laws and duty and the recognized hierarchy, in order to avoid conflicts and difficulties. In this case, feeling does not overwhelm thinking, but is usually separated from it, and it will never lead to any knowledge which can be considered as absolute. Yet this needs no special discussion, for we have seen that in both cases feeling is being distorted in a similar way.[1] The intrusion of feeling shows most clearly of all the dangerous consequences of any of its aberrations.

### 2. THE NECESSARY CONCENTRATION ON VALUES

The intrusion of feeling into the realm of thought, as shown in the preceding examples, becomes dangerous for the following reasons:

(1) External reality as such, not transformed into an expression of internal reality, calls into play too great a part of our feelings.

We start with the application of internal opposites, for as we have to perform practical tasks, we cannot avoid establishing the opposition between means and ends, and we may also proceed to principles and abstract values or even to the constructive concepts, yet at some stage the external fact which should be transformed into an expression of internal reality is accepted as such, simply as a part of external reality. The internal opposites, so far as they have been applied, are hardened

[1] See p. 104.

## THE EXTERNAL AND INTERNAL OPPOSITES

into external facts too, while the others are being suppressed. Feeling, attached to external reality, is forced to develop in the wrong direction; to preserve the external fact, it must not progress to any further knowledge conveyed by feeling, but instead become stronger. Thinking, instead of pursuing the internal opposites, returns to the external opposites. But these are now also distorted, for as feeling has become the determining factor they have to support whatever stage of knowledge feeling wants to preserve.

When nationality becomes our highest value, for instance, our thinking has usually been occupied before this with morality. But now the knowledge of our special national gifts is not used to enable us to grasp our own moral task better; on the contrary, moral development is arrested and our ideas of morality are further determined by those national characteristics which appeal to us. They determine our concepts of good and evil. This, however, also makes it impossible to apply the external opposites properly, for the subordination of morality makes the national characteristics appear the best and the most valuable.

(2) Internal knowledge is mistaken for an external fact.

We disclose the existence of internal facts by discovering the meaning of external ones. The duty of loving our neighbour, for instance, is an internal fact; it belongs to that reality which we experience within ourselves and yet as independent of ourselves; but, as we have seen, we understand it only if we learn to see the meaning of human relationships, if we love somebody or are loved by somebody, or if we experience what family, friendship, human society really mean. The existence of beauty is an internal fact, but we discover it when we understand this special kind of meaning of some external thing or event which is beautiful. The external fact does not represent the internal fact completely, for it remains necessarily limited and imperfect; our experiences allow us only occasionally to catch a glimpse of a greater perfection. But by understanding the meaning of these facts, we gradually get a clearer idea of what they imply and of the full scope of their meaning, and this enables us to grasp the internal fact better and better. We learn to imagine perfection, and it is thus that we grasp the internal fact more or less completely.

If, however, we mistake these experiences for external facts, we ascribe to these the perfection which we discovered with the help of their meaning, or we consider the ideal perfection which we can imagine as something which could have external existence. In both cases we transform the meaning into something external and, at the same time, deprive the external facts of their meaning. If we think that love means that the relationships in marriage, in family life, in society, must always be exactly like those which taught us love, or that beauty must

## RIGHT AND WRONG DEVELOPMENT OF FEELING

follow those laws which agree with our special experience, love and beauty will most probably vanish. To follow certain rules in married life can spring from love, but, if insisted upon or enforced, it rather shows indifference or covers discord or hatred; and forms, originally beautiful, can produce ugliness if they are applied mechanically. At the same time, as conforming to these rules alone seems important, we miss the meaning of our actual experiences. When we try to reach, in external reality, the ideal which we imagine, we can only succeed in certain particulars which we then naturally overrate, and this and the struggle for the impossible perfection make us overlook whatever meaning our real experiences have. If feeling clings to externals, we are bound to destroy internal reality, even if we start from the meaning of external reality and if the external facts had originally represented, or are meant to represent, this meaning.

(3) External and internal negation are mixed up and internal negation is used in a wrong way.

We have discussed several times the mixing up of the two kinds of negation, but there is also a special use of negation in internal reality which we have not mentioned so far. If the different scales of values are to remain independent of each other, we must, within internal reality itself, use not only internal, but also logical negation—that is, external negation—so as to separate the scales from one another. If we do not want to evaluate the lighting of our rooms by moral standards, which would obviously be wrong, we have to exclude it from the moral scale without creating a negative moral value;[1] therefore we must negate it purely logically and not use internal negation which creates negative values. This, however, is not done if an intrusion of feeling forces us to accept only a single scale of values. If we then recognize that something lies outside the special scale we cherish—which means that we ought to exclude it by using logical negation—we do not exclude it, but use internal negation to make it seem worthless or evil or wrong, so that it can remain within the scope of the scale and does not require a further scale to be dealt with. We do not merely exclude moral values when deciding such questions as the lighting of our rooms, but say that moral values are a nonsensical prejudice because they do not help us to get on with practical tasks. The two kinds of negation are identified; what ought to be mere exclusion is taken for condemnation. This mistake can easily be overlooked because it may seem natural that, in internal reality, we should only use internal negation. But internal negation should be used exclusively within the different scales of values and not to subordinate everything to a single scale. Otherwise, as we have seen, even such a limited part of external reality as the nation can become the basis of an all-inclusive scale.

[1] See pp. 123–4.

## THE EXTERNAL AND INTERNAL OPPOSITES

The process is very similar to that which we have described when discussing how external knowledge can claim to be the only knowledge we possess.[1] In both cases external negation is mistaken for, and mixed up with, internal negation. But this time the mistake is perhaps even more dangerous, because here we are concerned with values which always need internal negation. If we enslave people for the sake of their happiness or of ideal society, or if duty suppresses help and love and justifies hatred and murder, our whole ability to value is corrupted.

(4) Instead of separating external and internal reality, we try, by mixing up external and internal opposites, to create an all-embracing unity.

It is the subordination of everything to a single scale of values which, in internal reality, represents the attempt to create an all-embracing unity. We can also use instead an all-inclusive hierarchy, but this, as we have seen, is not fundamentally different. To establish such a unity requires not only the mixing up of the two kinds of negation, but also that of the two kinds of opposites.

The attempt to create such a unity with the help of values is different from that which we have discussed when considering the wrong application of external opposites. When we concentrate on external reality alone, we can represent it as the only one and deny the existence of opposites and of internal reality altogether. When we start from internal reality, opposites have to be used; as the internal opposites are dependent on each other, we have to apply both their parts. We cannot find a unitary explanation, but have to establish the unity by a very strong emphasis upon the positive and the negative; we have to declare our highest values as overwhelmingly important and to denounce everything which contradicts their importance so violently that it appears negligible. If materialism or nationalism become all-embracing for us, liberty or equality or fraternity or all of them have to become, in Marx's words, 'lip-service to modern mythological gods'.

This unity, however, must remain fundamentally unstable, for mere denunciation does not abolish the contradictory facts, and this is why external and internal opposites have also to be mixed up. Positive and negative values have to be seen as something with an external existence, as something as solid as external objects or natural laws, for then a comprehensive unitary order is established which cannot be shaken by any creation of further values or any further inner experiences. Supported by such a consolidated external order which does not admit different value-judgments, we can accept mere denunciation as definite negation and exclusion.

This order is very powerful because it is based on the splitting-up of all our feeling into violent acceptance and violent rejection, which

[1] See pp. 95–6.

## RIGHT AND WRONG DEVELOPMENT OF FEELING

we have described before [1] and because it inevitably makes this split final. If the values which help to bring this about are believed to have an unshakable external existence—they are usually embodied in 'the enemy' who, by his nature, is bound to be wicked—the split cannot be healed, for feelings are determined by their objects. But that this split results from the attempt to create a unity shows more clearly, too, why it is so disastrous, for it is feeling alone which can help us to experience unity.

We are easily able to experience different or even opposite emotions simultaneously. If the impact of a sudden joy is painful, or if sorrow reveals to us a new insight which makes us grateful and happy, the contradictory emotions are simply experienced as one. Awe is a feeling consisting of the two opposed emotions of admiration and fear. We have also seen that positive and negative feelings cannot develop independently of each other, and we can ask for the development of the wealth of feelings because, so long as their whole sphere is not split up, very different emotions, including negative ones, can grow together without finally destroying this unity of feeling. If we are frightened and shocked by ugliness or evil, we may, at the same time, feel more clearly the happiness conveyed by beauty and the redeeming power of goodness; it is on this quality of feeling that the poet relies when writing a tragedy. This power of reconciliation makes it possible for feeling to lead to the experience of unity. Love, as we shall see later, though we have to define it intellectually with the help of some such opposites as indifference or hate, can become independent of them and reconcile all opposites.

This power of reconciliation agrees with the fundamental fact which we have mentioned [2]—that each single emotion draws its strength from our undifferentiated power of feeling and thus takes part in it. As the source is the same, the different results are not necessarily altogether separated. But again we must beware of identifying this unity with mere strength of feeling. Whether or not we attain the unity depends entirely on the development of feeling; the right development can lead to unity, the wrong must lead to sentimentality or to a complete split in our personality.

This unity can never be adequately translated into thought, for when we start thinking we are also confronted with the opposition of external and internal reality, and we can think correctly only if we acknowledge their opposition and thus use all the other opposites as well. Owing to the nature of feeling, moreover, such a unity must always be experienced anew; it cannot be transformed into a lasting edifice; any knowledge of it is based on the knowledge that we have had, and therefore can have again, such an experience. But thinking

---

[1] See pp. 107-8.   [2] See p. 100.

can either block or open the way to it. All the effects of the intrusion of feeling force thinking to bar the way; if we avoid them, thinking can go on in the right direction and this, as we hope to show, will finally help us to experience this unity in the realm of feeling. It is the only one which we can attain.

To ensure that thinking moves in this direction, we must concentrate on the values as such. All the dangers which we have discussed show that this is the common point which has always been missed.

Any intrusion of feeling is bound to suppress some further values which have already come in sight. Materialism does not acknowledge that it is based on love and justice; nationalism subjugates morality; duty suppresses love; laws and hierarchies, if hardened into external facts, prevent the development of the values from which they originated. The progress of thinking is interrupted artificially. If we concentrate on the values themselves, we free thinking from these unnatural fetters and it can develop in the right direction. We are attracted by, and in search of, these further values; we are able to defy the great attraction exercised by external reality and by short cuts to definite statements, because values are dependent on continuous new experiences, and thus we always want to understand them better and to experience them more fully. When we succeed, for instance, in performing a good deed, we are inclined to make the special form of this deed the model or law for future behaviour, or to see it as being in accordance with an existing law, and thus we lose sight of the good. If, on the contrary, we stress the value, if we see that what matters is that the deed is done for the sake of the good and because of love and the urge to help, we shall remain aware of the content and of our shortcomings. This shows us that it needs better forms to express it more fully, and these new forms will, in their turn, help us to grasp the content more and more completely.

If we are willing, moreover, to continue in the application of the internal opposites, we cannot stop, as we have seen, until we reach the absolute values, and it is with them that we find the only reliable safeguard. The absolute values can definitely help us to make sure that we do not succumb to any dangerous temptation, for as they are absolute they guarantee a complete fulfilment of the conditions which we have come to regard as essential for making internal reality real for us.

All the values need external reality and our experience of it, but relative values, though they ought to be experienced always anew, can be identified with the special form of such an experience which has become the embodiment of the value. Like the other values, we experience and recognize the absolute values by embodying them in a special external form. Yet as all our actual experience and all our knowledge of external reality must needs remain relative and limited, we realize at the same time that this form cannot possibly contain the whole value. Values become absolute—to this we shall return in the next chapter—when, by our activity of valuing, we meet something which stands over against us, something which we are forced to acknowledge as transcending our powers and our relative world, not because of an actual failure to influence or assimilate it, but because of its very nature. It becomes quite clear, therefore, that these values cannot be experienced once for all and that we are unable to make any conclusive statements about them; as we have to embody them in something relative to become aware of them, we see at once that we have to embody them again and again. Each embodiment is only a step toward a fuller experience of something which is so much beyond our reach that its experience can never become complete. Thus feeling always remains expectant and capable of further development; it cannot be definitely attached to anything, for each success in grasping such an absolute value necessarily becomes a stimulus to us to make it more and more real by further attempts to grasp it.

Nor is it possible to establish an all-inclusive scale of values which would prevent further thought, for each experience of an absolute value strengthens the readiness for other and unexpected experiences. Truth implies open-mindedness, for we must respect any fact which we may still happen to recognize and pay attention to any knowledge which may still be acquired; goodness makes violent denunciation impossible, for we may still discover good motives behind evil deeds and though we have to call the deed evil, we must refrain from judging the person; beauty is never exhausted, but can be conveyed by any experience or impression. If all the three absolute values have been recognized, moreover, we also recognize that their relationships are most intricate—is it necessary that truth and beauty agree with morals? Can morality remain independent of truth and beauty?—and this also does not allow us to subordinate all the values to a single scale.

The power of the absolute values can be seen when we remember that it proved impossible to give a clear definition of such concepts as nation, race and state, whether we approached them from the external or the human point of view. Any such approach leaves us in an uncertainty which, in practice, represents a grave problem. This problem disappears once we reach the level of the absolute values. Friendship and love can overcome all the differences of nations, races and creeds; if we concentrate on the absolute values, especially on goodness, all these differences appear as minor and relative and we are also able to see the external facts in the right perspective. The grave difficulty is not that these problems are insoluble—they were solved the moment we really loved our neighbour and did the good which we usually profess

## THE EXTERNAL AND INTERNAL OPPOSITES

to believe—but that too few of us live on the level of the absolute values.[1]

It is the very importance of these values, however, which could support the claim that all valuation remains doubtful and that the investigation of the internal opposites leads to a result which is less satisfactory than that to which we were led by the external opposites. In external reality, we are able to proceed gradually towards the absolute, and even if we are unable to reach it, or if the few indications of an absolute knowledge which we reach remain completely meaningless, the knowledge acquired on the way remains valuable. It is true that it is purely external and so in many respects superficial, but for our dealing with external reality this is all we need. Yet in internal reality any reliable valuation presupposes the absolute values; only when we reach them can we know that all the other values—apart perhaps from the merely practical ones—are correct, that they are in accordance with internal reality and help to make it real. Otherwise all our values may be wrong and illusory.

We still have not solved the fundamental problem which we had to mention so often, though we have excluded many possible causes of error. How can we distinguish between the right certainty due to an experience of absolute values and the wrong certainty due to an intrusion of feeling? How can we recognize that we are not under the spell of an intrusion of feeling? To deal with these questions, we must consider the absolute values themselves.

[1] See J. Macmurray, *Reason and Emotion*, pp. 103–4.

# Part Three
ABSOLUTE VALUES AND THE
INTERCONNECTED OPPOSITES

# Chapter IX

## THE ABSOLUTE VALUES

### 1. TRUTH, GOODNESS AND BEAUTY

THE difficult problem of the absolute values cannot be adequately dealt with in a few pages. We shall not try, therefore, to find out their full meaning, but confine ourselves to those aspects of them which have a bearing upon thinking in opposites.

Truth, goodness and beauty are quite generally accepted as the only three absolute values. Let us consider these concepts first, to clear away some of the ambiguities connected with their common usage.

Age-old wisdom has counted truth among the absolute values. We seem still to be doing the same, but actually are rarely conscious of what this implies and hardly believe in it any longer. Truth, for us, is not a value like goodness and beauty, but rather a statement of indubitable facts; it is more or less identified with a correct statement about external reality. If we think of truth, we most probably think first of the results of scientific investigation which can be tested experimentally. Even with regard to man we seek truth in those statements which, according to our definition, include man in external reality. From all we have said, however, it has become quite clear that no knowledge of external reality can ever lead to that comprehensive, fundamental and unshakable truth which has been considered as an absolute value and which we certainly still mean when we use the word in any important context. We shall distinguish, therefore, between correct statements and truth. Correct statements are those which can be tested within the realm of external reality and which any deviation from the known facts requires us to alter, as, for instance, 'this is a table' or 'the earth revolves round the sun'. Truth we shall use to mean that comprehensive and fundamental truth which has been considered as an absolute value. The statement that it is better to suffer wrong than to do wrong, for instance, belongs to this category.[1] But before

[1] For a very good example of this distinction, though the author speaks in terms of different kinds of truth, see K. Jaspers, *The Perennial Scope of Philosophy*, p. 9.

we can accept this distinction, we have to ask whether it is right to consider truth as a value.

That the search for truth leads us in the direction of value can be seen even within the realm of external reality.[1] There, the nearest approach to truth is not scientific theories which, as we have seen, must not exclude possible future changes, but mathematical laws. These seem to be fundamentally true because they are not dependent on any knowledge of external facts; on the contrary, if we want to understand the facts, we have to bring them into agreement with these laws which are developed solely in accordance with their own inner consistency. All mathematics, however, is based on axioms which cannot be further proved; they have to be accepted because they are self-evident, because 'they shine in their own light'. Thus even here truth can only be established by statements which appeal to our sense of truth; we have to accept them as true because we cannot help believing them. But—and this also is important—such a statement will convince us of its truth only when we consider it in its proper context; unless we think in mathematical terms, any such truth will remain meaningless and have no conviction for us. Yet mathematics, though unshakable, is obviously not the right context for finding any comprehensive truth, for these abstract statements leave out the whole of our lives and of our actual experience of reality. We therefore have to look for truth in internal reality.

We are entitled to do this, for truth shows all the important characteristics of internal reality.

(1) As soon as we leave behind mathematical or logical knowledge which, being purely formal, is clearly insufficient, it becomes obvious that the necessary appeal to our sense of truth means an appeal to our feelings. Only the impact of an experience or knowledge on our feeling can give us the certainty that we have met truth. Thus, however, it has also to be our own experience and insight, for only then can its impact upon us make it shine in its own light. To be self-evident, truth has to convince us. A whole encyclopædia of correct statements is not truth, nor does the Bible convey truth unless we believe it.[2] Our own participation is essential; we ourselves must see that the claim is true, otherwise we neither know nor experience truth.[3]

(2) Our participation which helps to constitute truth is only the

[1] I am following here H. H. Farmer's discussion of truth in *God and Men*, pp. 18 ff.

[2] See J. Oman, *Grace and Personality*, 4th ed., pp. 4, 257–8, and *The Natural and the Supernatural*, p. 208.

[3] This necessity for our own participation becomes obvious even in the simplest use of language. If somebody has stolen something, we shall say that he has done so; only if our statement is doubted so that our own belief or honesty is involved, shall we say that it is true that he has done so.

necessary method which enables us to discover it and is not in itself sufficient to guarantee that we have recognized truth. As in internal reality, our own experience must, at the same time, be the experience of something which stands over against us and which cannot be influenced by our wills or intentions. We reach truth when we have to acknowledge that it has an existence independent of our own and that the personal approach has been merely the necessary way of grasping something which transcends our persons.

The mistake of considering scientific discoveries representing a mixture of correct statements and theories as truth may be partially due to the fact that, in the beginning, these discoveries and the conclusions based on them transformed the whole conception of our world; thus they were of the greatest importance, were charged with feelings, and attracted an intense attention and personal participation. In the meantime, the development of science has shown that all such conclusions must remain theories because they have to be altered or replaced. It has become clear, therefore, that it is wrong to greet every new discovery as a further approach to truth, even if the person who does so is the scientist who has taken part in them and to whose feelings, therefore, they strongly appeal.

(3) Truth must be embodied in external reality. For the very reason that it has to become true for us, it cannot remain an abstract statement which we are not truly able to experience and can, at best, accompany with some vague feelings; we must meet truth embodied in a unique and compelling form which brings it to life for us. The truth, for instance, that love reveals our highest potentialities does not mean anything unless we experience love; the statement that God exists remains empty and meaningless unless we experience Him by an impact of external reality upon us, or within our personal relationships and with the help of feelings which are closely connected with our real lives. Some vague general feelings as well as abstract statements may help us to have such experiences or to discover the meaning of our experiences, but they can never replace the unique and definite form.

(4) This implies that no such external form can ever become a final embodiment of truth; it must always be experienced anew. Again, the knowledge of the forms in which we or others have experienced truth can help us greatly to experience it again or to experience it at all, but unless the form comes to a new life it is transformed into an abstract statement or an empty ceremony which no longer conveys truth. Our belief in God becomes meaningless if we do not live in face of God. As truth represents knowledge, it can be better preserved than the feelings themselves, for it can be embodied and stated, but the statements convey truth only when they awaken the right feelings and lead to the right experience.

(5) The nature of truth is also similar to that of feeling in so far as the single forms convey single truths; but to become true, each such special truth must participate in the whole truth. As truth has to be fundamental and comprehensive, nothing can be true in this sense unless it gives us some idea of the whole truth. It must appeal to our sense of truth, which means that we must recognize that we have at least touched the fundamental facts which underlie our existence. Correct statements can refer to details alone; true statements which refer to details must, at the same time, indicate their place in a comprehensive order. If we consider as true that love develops our highest potentialities, we imply that it is the highest expression of the nature of man and that it must play an important part in the order of the universe.

All this shows that truth has to be considered as an absolute value. It is a value because it has to convince us, and an absolute value because it has to convince us absolutely; only complete certainty can prove that we have met truth. As it has to be absolute, however, it can never be completely known in our actual experience; we have to meet it again and again to understand it better and more fully. Each single experience has to take part in the absolute, but naturally it can only take part in it and neither represent it once for all nor entirely.

As we are not concerned with the absolute values as such, we can accept the concept of goodness, as it is generally understood, as sufficiently clear to be used here without further definition. Whether we base our judgment on humanism or Christianity or another ethical or religious conviction, we know what we mean when we say that something is good. There is hardly any need to show that goodness, too, has all the characteristics of internal reality; most of the examples we have mentioned apply to goodness as well.

That beauty also is a value is hardly ever doubted; it is usually considered to-day as a matter of taste which makes it a value and dependent on our feelings. But this interpretation would exclude it from the absolute values; it is, in fact, no longer understandable why it should still be counted among them. The difficulty here is to see why we have to consider it as absolute.

We have already said that beauty cannot be merely a matter of taste; if someone denies that the poetry of Shakespeare is beautiful we shall be convinced he is wrong.[1] This claim can only be understood when we remember the original meaning of the concept. It was hardly ever confined to a beauty which pleases our senses, but meant that a content had found a perfect expression. In this sense, the sculpture of an ugly man can be beautiful because the contrast can help to express his spiritual beauty, and thus ugliness may become its perfect form. But even the representation of a real monster can help us by its impact

[1] See p. 36.

## THE ABSOLUTE VALUES

to deepen our appreciation of beauty and thus belong in this realm. The strong impression of the sculptures in Gothic cathedrals is frequently due to such contrasts, and the Greeks as well as the artists of the Renaissance knew their power. Nor does the beauty of Shakespeare's tragedies or even comedies exclude the horrible. Any full realization of beauty transcends the merely pleasant impression; a pure beauty, too, appeals to deeper emotions. We shall use, therefore, the concept in its fuller original meaning. It is also this meaning alone which can adequately express the way in which the artist works.[1]

When beauty means this complete agreement between form and content, however, it must belong to the absolute values. Once more we are able to recognize this agreement only by our sense of beauty—that is, by its appeal to our feelings, and we shall recognize it by its compelling force, when we feel that there is no escape, that every detail of the form has grown out of the content and belongs to it, and that the content necessarily requires this special form. As their agreement has to be freely reproduced by our feelings, the completeness which represents a full experience of beauty can only mean that this reproduction leads to complete satisfaction and certainty. Any experience of beauty is either based on, or at least touches upon, such a complete identity between form and content.

There is, however, an obvious difficulty. While truth and goodness are concerned with single results, beauty presupposes the understanding of both form and content, and although the experience of beauty is absolute, the understanding of these two elements which leads to it remains dependent on temporal and individual conditions. This explains the great fluctuations in the judgment of what is beautiful. It is probably also important, in this context, to remember that the name 'absolute values' may be misleading. It is never the actual embodiment of any such value which is absolute—goodness remains dependent on the motive of the action, truth on our appreciation of it—but if such an embodiment is experienced as absolute value, it produces a meeting with the absolute which is perceived through it. We feel that this experience is compelling, that it can be neither influenced nor altered arbitrarily, that we cannot help accepting it. This applies also to beauty, once both its conditions—form and content—have been understood.

That our feelings have to react in such a definite way shows the inadequacy of mere pleasantness as a criterion for another reason, too. The beautiful has to represent something which is of importance for us; otherwise its impact could not evoke those feelings which can give

---

[1] The difficult problem of beauty in nature will be discussed later (see p. 224). But obviously, if we are deeply moved by such an experience, we experience it at the same time as an expression of something which transcends what we actually see, though we do not always realize this.

us real certainty. There is undoubtedly a connection between the deterioration in the meaning of the concept and the fact that the later development of art and literature has tended to reach formal achievements independent of the importance of the subject.[1]

The nature of the absolute values explains why we have had to stress that we may be the only ones who recognize that something is true or good or beautiful and yet be right.[2] If these values have to appeal to our sense of truth or goodness or beauty, this sense must be of fundamental importance, and our sense can be more strongly developed than that of others, or the special embodiment of the absolute value can have some qualities which make it easily accessible to us because they agree with our particular gifts or sensitivity, and this can help us to see where others remain blind. It is usually such a coincidence between particular qualities of the values and the person experiencing them which opens the way towards a fuller knowledge of these values; the creative artist is entirely dependent on it.

These remarks may be sufficient to make clear what we mean when we talk about the absolute values, and so we can now proceed to discuss the relationship between them and the results of our investigation of the opposites.

## 2. THE MAJOR OPERATIONS OF THINKING

When we survey our investigation of the external and internal opposites, we recognize that, owing to the division into two realities, three operations of our thinking stand out as the fundamentally important ones.

The investigation of the external opposites has shown that thinking, when concerned with external reality, always moves in the same direction. We automatically try to find out what is behind the external forms which we apprehend first; we try to penetrate the surface so as to be able to grasp the content. Right from the beginning, we have to use abstractions which force us in this direction, and most of the constructive concepts which are applied simultaneously—form and content, cause and effect, accident and necessity—serve the same purpose. Eventually we even try to exclude these concepts, too, to get at the content directly. The constructive concepts the One and the Many are the only ones which do not lead this way, and this explains why they have proved such an obstacle to all these attempts. But although they show that we cannot succeed in finding the content within external reality, they do not alter the direction of our endeavours; on the contrary, the great importance of mathematical formulae for the explana-

---

[1] *'L'art pour l'art'* becomes an articulate doctrine only in the nineteenth century.
[2] See pp. 36–7.

tion of external reality encourages us more than anything else to continue in these efforts.

The investigation of the internal opposites has shown that thinking, when concerned with internal reality, also moves in one direction, but we could discern three distinct stages in this movement. These stages need not necessarily follow one upon the other, because the progress can be interrupted at any of them; we have, therefore, to consider them separately.

The first stage, the application of the opposites 'means' and 'end', is not of fundamental importance. We have seen that it makes external reality accessible for the application of internal opposites, but it does not disclose internal reality as such. It is true that we need these opposites to deal with external reality in a practical way as well as to enter into internal reality, but they still hover, so to speak, undecided between the two realities; we can either turn back to external reality or proceed to internal reality, and in both cases we must leave them behind if we want to understand either. So we need not take them into account here.

The second stage, that of the principles, is indispensable because it helps us to deal with those parts of internal reality which are embodied in the activities of our mind. We have seen that internal reality is first experienced as a continuous process; we think, feel and will, and it is by these actions and reactions that the existence of internal reality makes itself felt. But we cannot grasp it so long as it remains submerged in a continuous and elusive flux of thoughts, feelings and impulses; we have to establish some framework on which we can rely to be able to grasp the constant reality behind. The task of the principles is to give us this support. They establish laws and a necessity which, contrary to external laws and external necessity, do not refer to the past but to the future; they thus disclose internal reality, because they do not restrict the inner processes, but help us to understand their meaning. Even if we misunderstand or misapply them, internal reality remains involved and we must become aware of it.

The third stage is the finding of the unique form which expresses internal reality distinctly and definitely. This we have discussed at great length, so that there is no need to explain it further. Only if we find such a form shall we be able to understand the content to which the principles refer.

We can say, therefore, that to grasp the divided reality our thinking has to perform three major operations.

First, we have to try to penetrate the surface in order to get hold of the content.

Second, we have to establish principles in order to deal with the inner processes of thinking, feeling and willing.

## ABSOLUTE VALUES AND INTERCONNECTED OPPOSITES

Third, we have to find the form which expresses internal reality as perfectly as possible.

It needs hardly any further explanation to show that these three operations of thinking form, at the same time, the basis of the three absolute values; the fact that thinking has to perform these operations explains why there are three such values and not more nor less. The absolute values are experienced when these operations have been so successful that we are left in no doubt that we have met with the absolute: truth, if we discover, behind and underneath the surface of reality, a content which shines in its own light; goodness, if we succeed in establishing a principle on which we can absolutely rely and which proves completely adequate to deal with our motives and actions; beauty, if a content has found its perfect form and expression.

This basis of the absolute values helps us to understand why we have had to stress that these values, though absolute, are not quite satisfactory. We experience them as final and inexhaustible when we actually succeed in experiencing them, but as they are absolute we also expect them to lead to a complete knowledge on which we could always rely, and this expectation is not fulfilled. The mere fact that there are three such different values, which makes it impossible to unify them, shows that they must be subject to certain limitations, and their basis in thinking explains the nature of these limitations.

First it shows why truth is the most difficult and perplexing of these concepts. Truth is based on that operation of thinking which leads to the knowledge of external reality, but we have seen that no knowledge of this reality can ever reach the absolute. Yet as we have to perform this operation of thinking, we expect truth to come within the definition of reliable external statements, and do not recognize it, or are not willing to acknowledge it, when it turns out to have all the characteristics of internal reality. Instead, we try desperately to find some truth of the nature of external reality—that is, we look for comprehensive metaphysical statements which, as we have shown, are bound to mislead or to disappoint us.[1] Truth can be found only in goodness or beauty or in those regions of belief which, though accessible to thinking, are not based on its discoveries. This we shall discuss later when we come to consider the final barrier which cuts us off from any absolute knowledge in external reality—the constructive concepts the One and the Many. For the time being it is sufficient to see the contradictory nature of truth which transforms it, against our original expectations, into a continuous search.[2] It is natural, even, that this searching should be more evident in our approach to truth than to the other values, for our search is constantly stimulated by the fact that we have to approach truth in the same way as external reality. We constantly go on, because

---

[1] See pp. 6–8.     [2] See p. 155.

## THE ABSOLUTE VALUES

we are looking for the unattainable—the definite truth which thinking alone cannot reach—and are not prepared to accept as final truth anything which we have always to experience anew.

It is this contradictory nature of truth which justifies Kant's saying that it is 'a device of nature' to combine the urge for metaphysical truth with the impossibility of finding it where we look for it, for thus this urge leads us away from external reality and into the realm of values.[1] It even forces us in the end to transcend this realm too, and this, as we shall see in a moment, is of the greatest importance.

Goodness is the only absolute embodiment of the principles, and this means again a very strict limitation. We should expect to find principles for all the different spheres of life; we are constantly looking for æsthetic principles, for instance, and it would also be a great help to know principles which would allow us to give a clear definition of usefulness or which would make the search for truth safer. Principles should regulate all the inner processes we experience. But it is the principles of morality alone which can lead to a meeting with the absolute; all the others have only a very relative value. Truth can contribute to them in so far as truthfulness belongs to the moral world, but this must not be mixed up with the search for truth itself. This limitation, however, is natural, for as principles borrow their form from external events their hold upon internal reality remains uncertain and they can be safely applied only to those human intentions and actions in which this reality is inevitably involved. The limitation also implies that we cannot definitely transform this absolute value into a code of laws, for the other spheres influence our motives too; we must always experience goodness anew to make sure that no relative principle disguises itself as absolute—that we do not, for instance, mistake mere obedience to the law for morality. It is very important to be conscious of this limitation, for the similarity with other principles could lead to some such extension of the sphere of goodness to make it seem self-sufficient and comprehensive; but if it loses its distinctive quality, it can no longer lead to a meeting with the absolute. If we consider every detail of correct behaviour or of a ritual as an essential part of goodness, we easily forget to love our neighbour.[2]

Beauty is perhaps the most satisfactory of the absolute values, for as it refers to single objects and experiences we need not become aware of its limitations. But they exist, too, and are of no less importance. The deterioration in the meaning of the concept is no mere accident; owing to its limitation beauty is in danger of remaining too vague. As we are mainly concerned with the finding or understanding of the appropriate form, beauty is not in itself sufficient to grasp the content; it does not necessarily enable us to get a firm hold on internal reality.

[1] See p. 78.     [2] Cf. pp. 128–9.

## ABSOLUTE VALUES AND INTERCONNECTED OPPOSITES

To find the right form, we must already know the content, and to understand the form fully, previous experiences must have at least enabled us to move towards the point from which the creator of the form started. Beauty alone does not enable us to understand beauty. Yet in spite of its limitation it remains of the utmost importance, for only the experience of the form can give us a full knowledge of the content. But it must be based on the right presuppositions; if it is, it can probably be considered as the highest of the three values; if it is not, it sinks to mere enjoyment.[1]

It is their very limitation, however, which makes the absolute values fruitful; though often disappointing or even painful, both the limitation and the uncertainty connected with them are, in fact, very positive elements. Being values, they belong to internal reality, and thus they cannot be the final embodiment of knowledge; the absolute cannot possibly belong to one part of the divided reality, but must belong to, or be identical with, primary reality. It would be a grave mistake to identify these values with the absolute itself, and this mistake is prevented by their limitations.

The three major operations of thinking include external and internal reality, and the absolute values, based on them, lead onwards from external to internal reality. Thus they stress, on the one hand, the existence of internal reality which we are in danger of overlooking; as the absolute values conform to the nature of this reality and yet lead to the meeting with the absolute, they confirm that we can trust our method of grasping this reality. On the other hand, the limitations of these values make it quite clear that the absolute, nevertheless, cannot be found in internal reality and that we merely meet with it there; we cannot doubt that it must be different and transcend both realities. Without their limitation and uncertainty, the absolute values would most probably mislead us; we could consider internal reality as the whole of reality and lose sight of everything else. By being absolute and limited at the same time, they leave room for external reality as well as for a further progress of thought and experience.

---

[1] The magnificence and glory of God, i.e. His beauty, are considered as the highest attributes of God. We shall see later that this reveals a deep insight. Cf. also the words of Christ, 'I am the way, the truth and the life.' The constant search for a comprehensive truth which we never finally reach is the way; goodness is the only truth which we are able to grasp with complete certainty, because it can be tested by our actions; but it comes to life only with the help of beauty, by being embodied in a perfect form. The 'I', at the same time, indicates that it is necessary to transcend the absolute values.

# THE ABSOLUTE VALUES

## 3. THE CORRECT APPLICATION OF THE ABSOLUTE VALUES

The problem whose solution we are still seeking is that of testing the absolute values. If we consider something as true, good or beautiful, we bestow a value upon it, but obviously it must also in fact be true, good or beautiful, so as not to mislead us but to be capable of representing this value. We must at least be able to distinguish between the real meeting with the absolute and the misleading intrusion of feeling, for the reaction of our feeling in both cases is almost identical. Yet if truth does not mean correct statements which can be tested experimentally, if goodness has always to be experienced anew so that we cannot rely on laws alone, and if beauty means something more important than is commonly assumed, then the possibility of testing these values has still to be found.

This problem seems to create insuperable difficulties. The only test of the absolute values would lie in their confrontation with the absolute itself, for only this would enable us to see whether they represent it correctly; but as we are unable to grasp the absolute in any more direct way, such a confrontation remains impossible. We possess no more immediate knowledge of the absolute; even revelation, as we have seen, remains dependent on belief.[1] When we look back on our explanation of the absolute values, however, we can see that this problem creates these difficulties because it is stated in a wrong way.

The absolute values belong to internal reality. This is the fundamental fact which we must never overlook. It has just helped us to explain some of the difficulties which beset the problem of these values, and it also helps us to see which is the real problem and thus contributes to its solution.

The fact that the absolute values belong to internal reality implies the following reservations.

(1) These values, although they are absolute, cannot lead to a comprehensive explanation of the whole of existence. We have seen that the abstract explanations of these values can perhaps help us to experience them, but that they remain meaningless without this experience; they can lead to it, but never replace it. Naturally, an explanation of such a limited significance must not be mistaken for an explanation which would apply to both realities; we must not mistake internal knowledge, moreover, for a statement about external reality. The universe is neither good nor true nor beautiful in any sense we are able to give to these concepts, for we are dependent on single experiences to disclose this meaning, and we cannot become entirely independent of these experiences, for they only disclose this meaning

---
[1] See p. 154.

## ABSOLUTE VALUES AND INTERCONNECTED OPPOSITES

gradually and never finally. We can believe, of course, in an absolute truth, goodness, and beauty, which transcend internal reality and apply to the whole universe, but then they must also transcend our understanding and so they do not explain anything. There is great wisdom in the teaching of religions that these qualities of God are not discovered by ourselves, but revealed to us; this we shall discuss later. In any case our knowledge of the absolute values must not be mistaken for a general knowledge of the universe which explains it.

(2) As the absolute values do not explain the universe, they cannot be tested by a confrontation with it. Whether the course of events seems to agree with, or to contradict, our mistaken generalizations derived from the absolute values is of no consequence. They belong to internal reality and can be tested only within this reality.

In external reality, the test of our correct apprehension consists, as we have shown, in its agreement with the laws of our thinking, and the test of these laws in the agreement of the results to which they lead with our actual apprehension.[1] In internal reality the main organ of knowledge is feeling, and thus the test can only be that we satisfy our feelings completely and that this satisfaction stands the test of further experiences. But as feelings have always to be experienced anew, this test cannot be the test for which we are looking, nor can we possibly find it so long as we have to rely on feeling alone.

(3) If the absolute values, however, are absolute only as values, they cannot represent the final embodiment of knowledge, for this would have to refer to both realities. Therefore the real problem is not whether we can test these values as such, but whether we can progress further. If we can, the problem would be solved, for by forcing our thinking to develop towards the absolute we could make sure that no short cut occurs in our thought at this stage and that these values are applied correctly. The right question to ask is whether we can get beyond them.

To be able to answer this question, we must look in the right direction. We can never hope to grasp primary reality directly, for the division into two realities remains the inescapable condition of all correct thinking. The nearest approach to primary reality is the establishing of the right opposition between external and internal reality. As the division is our only way of apprehending reality at all, the perfection of this division must represent the highest perfection we are able to achieve.

We have said already that such a progress is possible—that we can discover the interconnected opposites which refer directly to the division and thus enable us to find a more definite basis for all our thought. We shall discuss them presently. But to understand how they can help us,

---

[1] See pp. 20, note, and 92–3.

## THE ABSOLUTE VALUES

we must again know what help we can possibly expect from them and what we must not expect, and this we can recognize best when we ask how we can secure the right application of the absolute values.

The tests within external and internal reality which we have just mentioned give us certainty, because they show that the two realities fit together and agree with each other. In external reality, where we need only formal knowledge, the agreement is established between our apprehension and the constructive concepts transferred from internal reality, and this gives us certainty because it can be stated in abstract terms of general validity. In internal reality, where we grasp the content, the agreement is established with the help of external forms transferred and adapted to fit the content, and the certainty is felt when our experience confirms that the external form fits the content completely. Every single value becomes convincing only when we feel that that upon which we have bestowed the value really represents it. The absolute values give the highest certainty, but it is still of the same kind; in their case we feel that our single experience must be in accordance with the true nature of the universe.

Owing to the division into two realities, this kind of certainty is the only one which we can achieve. As there is no way of getting hold of the absolute or primary reality, we are only able to approach it by creating or experiencing an agreement between the two realities.

Both the agreements within the two realities show obvious shortcomings. In external reality, where we have only formal knowledge, the agreement remains purely formal, and so it lacks the compelling force which alone can give us the feeling of complete certainty. In internal reality, it is feeling which makes the content accessible, and so the certainty is compelling, but it is restricted to single personal experiences. It lacks, even in the case of the absolute values, that general validity which would lift it above the level of personal experience; it cannot be made generally compelling.[1]

We cannot hope to overcome these shortcomings completely. The agreement between the two realities can never become comprehensive and definite, for to fit them together entirely and once for all we would have to grasp both of them as a whole and simultaneously. This would mean that we would establish, at last, the all-inclusive unity; but there is hardly any need to explain that this escape from the division also is quite impossible. Our ways of apprehending the two realities are too different; the formal knowledge of external reality does not provide us with the form which we need to embody internal reality, nor does this form give us sufficient knowledge of external reality. We have to know the two realities separately; the agreement can only be established within single experiences and achievements.

[1] See pp. 45-6.

## ABSOLUTE VALUES AND INTERCONNECTED OPPOSITES

Nor can we hope to transcend the sphere of internal reality altogether. As it is there that we grasp the content, it must remain of greater importance for all those experiences whose meaning we want to understand, and so we have to experience them always anew. The absolute values can be neither overcome nor excluded; they remain the most important help in bringing about a meeting with the absolute.

This is also confirmed by the three major operations of thinking. They represent the three possibilities of reaching an agreement between the two realities. As our knowledge of external reality is confined to that of the form and our knowledge of internal reality to that of the content, the agreement between the two realities has to be between form and content. This we can reach either by starting from the form and by trying to discover the content, or by starting from the content and by trying to find its most adequate form. Both realities, moreover, consist of events, and thus we can also try to fit together external and internal events. If we aim at grasping the absolute, however, all these operations must aim at internal reality. To find the content behind the forms is the operation which originally serves the apprehension of external reality, but we have seen that it can lead to truth only in internal reality. Beauty, the fitting of the form to the content, naturally belongs to internal reality. The agreement between the events is established in external reality too, for we explain external events with the help of the laws of thinking, but the principles which lead to goodness have to apply external forms to internal reality, because it is there that we can understand the events and processes which we experience.

But we can hope for something different which is of no less importance—we can hope to establish a limited agreement between the two realities consciously and intentionally and thus to become independent of accidental experiences in reaching the absolute values. We can hope to be enabled to oppose external and internal reality to each other in such a way that we can control their agreement and thus make sure that their opposition leads to the absolute values.

The interconnected opposites represent further opposites which refer to the relationship between the two realities, and as they thus enable us to see how certainty can be found, we can confront the absolute values with them. Such a confrontation is of the utmost importance, for without it the absolute values, as they remain completely dependent on personal experiences which we are unable to control, hover indeed in the void. If experienced correctly, they prove that an agreement between the two realities has been achieved, but we cannot be sure that we have had the right experience. It is only the interconnected opposites which, by disclosing the conditions of a genuine agreement, allow us to recognize that the values have really been experienced correctly. These opposites thus prevent, on the one hand, any falsifica-

## THE ABSOLUTE VALUES

tion of the absolute values by misleading feelings: we can no longer mistake an intrusion of feeling for an experience of these values; on the other hand, they prevent our being misled by the absolute values themselves, for we are shown how to come into harmony with the absolute.

Without the interconnected opposites, we are always in danger of being led by the absolute values, so to speak, into a blind alley. We feel the absolute behind them, but as we are unable to approach it in any other way we are inclined to confine ourselves entirely to these values. Yet this, a frequent form of pure humanism, means a profound inconsistency, for thus we neglect or deny the more comprehensive absolute which transcends any value and which we have already met in them, and as we are not aware of this inconsistency the absolute values, too, can no longer be truly understood and experienced; they become more and more formal and empty. Only if we advance further and thus remain conscious of the absolute as such are the values themselves kept alive.

It is also true that these opposites—because they refer to the two realities—do not explain the universe or the absolute itself, but they represent abstract concepts of general validity, and though these can never replace our personal experience—which has to confirm that the interconnected opposites have really led to certainty—they provide the absolute values with a background which enables us to see to it that we interpret our experience reliably.

The importance of this further step can be seen in many ways. If we are able to create the absolute values with certainty, we can make them the basis of all our valuations, which we have found necessary, and thus become certain that we grasp internal reality correctly. We still cannot test them, for the interconnected opposites do not disclose the absolute, but the absolute values themselves can become an important test; when we know how they ought to come into being, our actual experience of them will confirm that we have applied all the opposites correctly, for the interconnected opposites presuppose the correct application of external and internal opposites. The interplay between the absolute values and interconnected opposites will, finally, help us to test belief, for though neither of them can tell us what to believe, a belief in the absolute can obviously only be correct if these values, based on the right agreement between the two realities, confirm that this agreement has in fact been reached.[1]

But we see once more what we must not expect from them—abstract solutions and definite results. They do not represent the

---

[1] We shall see later that all this confirms the statement that, on the one hand, 'morality, without religion, lacks a wide heaven to breathe in', while, on the other hand, 'religion, without morality, lacks a solid earth to walk on', J. Oman, *Grace and Personality*, p. 62.

## ABSOLUTE VALUES AND INTERCONNECTED OPPOSITES

absolute as such and, therefore, cannot overcome our dependence either on internal reality or on belief. They are a method of thinking; they transform it into a constant activity and force us to oppose again and again to each other the two realities, to experience their opposition always anew and to test it by the absolute values. They thus contribute to the constant and never-ending development of our experience of the absolute and help us, by making us gradually more and more aware of it, to control thinking even in these regions. We can make sure that our personal experiences and our feelings are developed in the right direction.

## Chapter X

### THE INTERCONNECTED OPPOSITES

#### 1. THEIR NATURE AND PURPOSE

THE interconnected opposites are different from the others in so far as they contain an element of personal achievement. A few of them can be discovered by investigation, yet even these need not appear from the beginning as clear opposites but have to be established as such. Most of these opposites, however, have to be created by thinking, and each such creation represents a particular achievement in the realm of thought. We are unable to create very many, nor can we calculate how many are in existence; there are always a few only which are accessible and understandable to us. But even one such opposition, if rightly understood and applied, may suffice to make a vast realm of thought and experience accessible and intelligible.[1]

The discovery or creation of these opposites must not be imagined as a continuous process; the establishing of any such opposition is a rare event, a flash of sudden illuminating insight which, by penetrating more deeply beneath the surface of life, makes it fuller and richer. The true moments of insight in the realm of philosophy and human wisdom are not so numerous, after all; they are only gradually accumulated and frequently lost sight of again. Many a system of philosophy does not reach this level at all, but, if it does, it is in these opposites and not in the system as such that its ultimate value consists.[2]

The peculiarity of these opposites follows from what we have just said. We can never hope to overcome all shortcomings, and in particular we cannot possibly succeed always in influencing our feelings by thinking, so as to be able to create the unitary feeling at will. The sphere of

---

[1] E.g. M. Buber's *I and Thou*.

[2] Though Plato's system of ideas, for instance, is clearly wrong, his philosophy remains important because his distinction between appearance and true reality is similar to that between external and internal reality, and because, in his investigation, he touches upon such interconnected opposites as space and time and necessity and freedom. But he could not have established his unitary system had he paid attention to the opposition between the One and the Many.

influence of our will-power remains especially small when feelings come into play. Quite apart from outside influences, we are dependent on intuitions, on our general disposition and special talents, on our past experiences and present sensitiveness, not to mention the difficult problem of the true nature of man, which obviously leads us beyond mere human consciousness. We shall hardly succeed if we try to force ourselves; we must rather wait. It is here that the Christian conception of grace can be most easily understood.

We have always to remember the limitations of thinking which we have emphasized in the preface. But we have had to emphasize there, too, that thinking cannot be avoided, and this implies that even those processes which spring from other sources or which transcend thinking are gradually lifted into consciousness and translated into thought. It remains essential, however, that this should be done in a most cautious and careful way, so that those experiences which we can express only with the greatest difficulty in words are not falsified by logical or abstract thoughts. Thinking must serve, not govern; above all, it must never destroy the secret and mystery which is at the bottom of all existence. Thinking, in other words, must not transcend the boundaries which are drawn, as we have seen, by its very nature; in particular it must not claim to possess that absolute knowledge which it cannot reach alone. We must beware equally of excluding thought where we need it and of relying on thinking alone where it has to be subordinated to different experiences—and it is exactly this need which is safeguarded by the interconnected opposites.

As we must try, in this investigation, to expound possible results, the description of these opposites may give the impression that we are now leading up to final results, but this would be a gross misunderstanding. We must not forget what we have stressed again and again—that thinking in opposites does not lead to definite results, but rather transforms thinking into a constant activity, securing its right development and direction; and that we can never completely transcend internal reality because these thoughts, to have real significance, have to refer to our own experiences. The positive results we are going to describe are undoubtedly possible; they can be achieved in moments of great spiritual strength, and the knowledge of thinking in opposites in general and of the interconnected opposites in particular can greatly assist us in achieving these results more reliably and more frequently, and in understanding better the meaning of similar achievements. But they can only become real as the result of our own activity, and they remain well-nigh meaningless if they are merely considered as an interesting line of thought. We are approaching those regions where clear experience and its interpretation are becoming most difficult and exacting, and the danger of misinterpretation greatest. The final results to be

## THE INTERCONNECTED OPPOSITES

striven for lie in feeling and not in thinking, and this is probably sufficient to indicate the need for caution. This has to be borne in mind throughout the description of these opposites, and we shall remember it more easily if we always try to follow, not only the line of thought, but the experience underlying it.

The task of the interconnected opposites is to drive thinking into those opposite extremes which we can neither avoid nor reconcile. They enable us to use to the full our capacity to think by allotting to these extremes—one of which we usually try to exclude for the sake of an artificial unity—their rightful place within our thoughts. In this way they enable us to approach those spheres of our being which can otherwise hardly be grasped by thinking without dangerous falsifications.

To give an example—if we accept morality, we have to presuppose the complete and utter independence of man, for unless we are free to act according to our intentions we cannot be expected to choose between good and evil. At the same time, morality makes us completely and utterly dependent, for we are absolutely bound by the moral laws. These are the two extreme conclusions at which thinking has to arrive, and though they form an irreconcilable contradiction, we must not suppress either of them. If we stress freedom alone, we easily forget the mysterious nature of the absolute values; we forget that in them we meet something absolute which stands over against us and which we can never fully grasp; instead, as we believe ourselves to be in absolute control, we harden them into strict rules, and this threatens to destroy the very freedom from which we started. If we stress our dependence alone, we easily overlook the necessity of choice and action and thus endanger the meaning of morality, even though we want to make it the sole determining factor. We have to be aware of both these extreme conclusions at the same time; it is their contradiction which helps us to understand that we are dealing here with a sphere which we cannot completely explain by thinking—for whence do the absolute values spring? The fact that these two conclusions cannot be reconciled and yet both have to be accepted will sharpen our feelings and we shall experience more fully what morality implies—that it does not merely mean obeying rules, but being active ourselves and yet relying on something outside our control; relying on the absolute which is beyond our reach and yet striving for it. Feeling will make us aware that no success whatever can offer a final explanation or represent a definite achievement; we shall have to try again and again and thus be forced constantly to renew our experience. This alone, however, can enable us to understand morality better and better, for it fulfils the main condition for making internal reality real for us.[1]

[1] Cf. J. Oman, *Grace and Personality*, which is an admirable elaboration of this opposition.

## ABSOLUTE VALUES AND INTERCONNECTED OPPOSITES

To give another example—Christian doctrine promises judgment and grace. If we want to understand Christianity, both these thoughts have to be accepted, though, again, they form a complete contradiction. If it is important that we are persons, as Christian teaching claims, our deeds have to be of real consequence and must, therefore, be judged. The grace of God, however, cannot possibly be limited; the loss of a single soul would mean a defeat of God's love, and this cannot be reconciled with the Christian conception of God. These thoughts represent once more the last boundaries to which our logical thinking is able to advance, and we have to think both of them at the same time in spite of their contradiction; for if we stress judgment alone, God will no longer remain the God of Love, and if we stress grace alone, we may forget to try to become worthy of this love. But if we remain aware of both these thoughts, feeling will gradually disclose to us that judgment of our sins can be redeeming grace, and that the recognition of the nature of grace can be the severest punishment. We are no longer in danger of reducing the concept of God to a mere abstract notion, but experience the mystery which is at the core of all living religion.

We shall discuss these and other examples more fully later. But what has just been said is probably sufficient to show why it is so important to know the interconnected opposites, though such statements can be made and have been made without any conscious knowledge of these opposites.

The demand that we should drive our thought into the last extremes might suggest the way of abstraction; but this is exactly the way which has to be avoided. Abstraction always helps the simplification and unification of our experience; we try with its help to become able to deal with reality and to manipulate it. Obviously it cannot convey the experiences we have in mind, for it leads away from feeling into the purest regions of thought.

That abstraction has to be dropped at this point can be clearly seen when we consider the possible answers to the question 'Why?' We seem to be able to answer it when we rely on some abstract conception of general laws or of a force or a First Cause; these answers seem sufficient to allow us to turn away from anything mysterious and to proceed with thinking alone. As a matter of fact, however, answers to this question are only useful in some definite, concrete context and so far as practical achievements are concerned; we can say why a stone falls or why a means serves its end. But we must remain aware of the fact that this question can never be answered in any fundamental or comprehensive way. Why has the earth become the dwelling place of man? Why are we born in this or that country, into this or that family, and with such and such endowments and not with others, with better ones? Why is there so much misery and suffering, and why do promising people die

## THE INTERCONNECTED OPPOSITES

young and people afflicted with disabling diseases old? We cannot hope to answer such questions and must not even try; in such contexts it is no longer right to manipulate reality; to understand it at all, we have to accept it and to submit to it. We shall only begin to understand our lives when we renounce the attempt to escape into abstract regions.

The knowledge of thinking in opposites can prevent us, as we have seen, from using abstraction in the wrong way, but to be able to cope with these fundamental contradictions we must also know those opposite extremes which are at the bottom of all our experience. We have pointed out that external and internal opposites, when mixed up, seem to lead to definite answers which narrow down our field of vision and understanding, and the danger of falling into this trap is great, for the urge to ask the question 'Why?' is very strong indeed. We have to proceed, therefore, to the interconnected opposites, for they alone can make sure that we do not stop thinking before the last extremes are reached.

### 2. THEIR MAIN CHARACTERISTICS

There are, as we have just said, two kinds of interconnected opposites—those which can be discovered by investigation, and those which have to be created. In the following we shall discuss the first kind only, and afterwards deal separately with the second kind. It is true that the second kind is more important and that these opposites can be established without any reference to thinking in opposites. But the knowledge of the first kind will be of importance there, too, for as they are the clear outcome of a method of thinking, they enable us to test the others and prevent us from establishing wrong oppositions. Therefore we must first know those interconnected opposites which can be directly based on our knowledge of the laws of thinking.

To understand the following description, it is best to keep in mind the opposites which we are going to discuss—'space and time', 'necessity and freedom', and 'the One and the Many'. We have said that even the opposites belonging to this category are not simply presented to us as oppositions, but have to be discovered and recognized as such; they may not, therefore, appear as distinct opposites at first sight, especially in the case of 'space and time'. But the following general description will help us to see why they are to be considered as opposites, and they will then be discussed in greater detail.

The interconnected opposites combine the characteristics of external and internal opposites.[1]

Like the external opposites, they seem to be derived directly from external facts; they refer to something which exists, or to laws which

---
[1] Cf. pp. 81 and 110–11.

## ABSOLUTE VALUES AND INTERCONNECTED OPPOSITES

work, independently of ourselves. They could appear as a mere selection of facts which we apprehend in external reality. Their independence of the observer finds expression in their being highly independent of each other; each of the two parts of the opposites can be used by itself and seems to exist separately. If one part is taken away, the other remains unimpaired. We can consider either space or time; necessity and freedom seem to exclude each other so that we have to consider either the one or the other; we can concentrate on one unit alone, without paying attention to any other, or on quantity alone, without paying attention to particular units.

At the same time, however, the interconnected opposites also show the characteristics of internal opposites. Looked upon from external reality, they seem to consist of purely abstract concepts, but this does not necessarily distinguish them from external opposites, for we have to use abstractions there too. Yet unlike those which belong to external reality, such as logical or mathematical concepts or laws, these concepts have a definite meaning for us; they are abstract when applied to external reality, but not at all abstract in internal reality, for here they represent important elements in our actual experience. We are bodies in space and live through time; necessity and freedom determine our actions and are felt most intensely; we exist as single individuals in a society. All these concepts occur, moreover, not in one reality alone, but in both.

Their independence of each other, too, is paralleled by an equally strong dependence on each other; although we can separate them completely, we are unable to isolate them completely. They can be separated, but not disconnected. It is true that, in the case of external opposites, we have also to establish the opposites in our minds in order to form clear concepts; but these concepts, once formed, can be used in isolation. The night is dark and not light; the opposite 'light' serves only to form the concept 'dark'; the force of gravity is the cause of the falling of the stone and not its effect. Similarly, we can concentrate either on space or on time alone; on necessity or freedom; on a single unit or on many; yet we cannot succeed in excluding their opposites altogether, for everything which exists is related to both parts of these opposites. That spatial things do not disappear while we grasp them presupposes their lasting in time, and our measuring of time needs something which exists in space; it is no accident that, in the end, we have to measure space by light-years and that we usually measure time by the hands of a clock moving in space. Our understanding of absolute necessity, as we have seen, presupposes absolute freedom, but we cannot understand freedom as mere licence; we need moral laws or some definite attitude to make freedom a reality for us. The single unit we observe is dependent at least on a second unit, the observer (and this is

## THE INTERCONNECTED OPPOSITES

true, as we shall see, even if we observe ourselves, for even then we have to create such an opposition) and any quantity is made up of single units. No such statement as 'the night is dark and not light' is possible in the realm of the interconnected opposites; their two parts are both needed, even if we deal with them as existing separately.

They can be looked upon, therefore, both as dependent and as independent opposites—that is, as external and internal. If one part is taken away, the other remains unimpaired, but the separation does not exclude the other part. It not only remains present in our minds, as is the case with external opposites, but actually present, even if we pay no attention to it.

It is this puzzling combination of external and internal characteristics which explains why these concepts have remained stumbling blocks throughout the history of philosophy. To consider them as external facts has clearly become impossible, but it has been tried again and again, because most of those philosophers who included them in the laws of thinking did not account for their peculiar nature. Kant did so in respect of space and time, but we must break up his lists of categories.

The interdependence of these opposites also becomes obvious when we try to discuss the question which we had to answer when considering both external and internal opposites—namely, whether we can alter the relationship between the two parts of the opposites; for this question has become entirely meaningless. There is neither such a relationship which cannot be reversed as that between a light and a dark object or between cause and effect, nor such a dependence as that between good and evil or between beautiful and ugly, where the one concept simply vanishes if we deny the other; nor is there such an order as that of the scales of values where the same opposites can take different places in different scales. The interconnected opposites can be separated and yet not isolated; they are interlocked in such a way that their relationship can only be described as a simple opposition which cannot be altered in any way. No sequence or order qualifies their direct opposition; it is based on a complete equality of the two parts, in respect of their existence as well as of their value.

Instead, they show some of the characteristics of the constructive concepts, for one of their parts always refers to external and the other to internal reality. Space, necessity and the Many are fundamental to our understanding of external reality, time, freedom and the One to that of internal reality. We have further seen that the constructive concepts are either different in the two realities or, if formed by the same concepts, acquire a different meaning in each of them. The interconnected opposites show great similarities to the second category.

There is, however, an important difference too—the interconnected

## ABSOLUTE VALUES AND INTERCONNECTED OPPOSITES

opposites being the basis and the constructive concepts the consequence of the division into two realities. The constructive concepts, such as form and content, cause and effect, means and ends, need not be applied and acquire meaning only if they are; otherwise they remain purely abstract and formal concepts. The interconnected opposites, to acquire meaning, have to be applied too, but we cannot help applying them, for there is no perception of reality without them. They are purely abstract, moreover, only when referring to external reality, but important facts within internal reality.

But here we come up against a special technical difficulty. As this investigation represents the very first attempt to describe thinking in opposites, we could not introduce the distinction between constructive concepts and interconnected opposites right from the beginning, but had to proceed gradually from the more obvious processes of thinking towards those which underlie them. Nevertheless, to be able to discuss the working of our minds at all, we were forced to mention the interconnected opposites which we are discussing here among the constructive concepts. The direction of our investigation cannot be reversed, for we shall be able to explain the difference between the two only when we know the interconnected opposites, and so we cannot yet fill this gap. But the difference will become clear after we have discussed them. Yet we can see already how these opposites may help us to make sure that thinking in opposites is developed as a reliable method.

That these opposites can be found in each reality and yet represent both of them once more satisfies the two fundamental demands that external and internal reality should be completely separated from each other and yet both taken into account. To understand the interconnected opposites, we have to separate their external and internal appearance completely; we shall not understand external reality unless we use space and time as purely formal concepts and neglect their meaning for our lives; we shall not understand internal reality unless we use the One and the Many, not as mathematical formulæ, but as representing human relationships. We have to apply these opposites in each reality in the form in which we find them there. But, on the other hand, we can only be certain that we have arrived at them when we discover the same concepts in both realities. As they refer to the division into two realities itself, we cannot have grasped that division so long as these concepts remain different, for then we are obviously not yet in sight of the two realities themselves.

At the same time, these opposites also make sure that we pass through all the stages of thinking in opposites which we found necessary. For to discover interconnected opposites at all the following operations of thinking must have been performed:

(1) We have to be aware that we are thinking in opposites and try

## THE INTERCONNECTED OPPOSITES

to develop this thinking intentionally, for only then shall we try to discover these extreme oppositions. Otherwise we shall always be tempted to find a unitary final solution or, if we cannot help seeing opposites, to establish a dualism which also prevents any further development of thinking.

(2) Both external and internal opposites must have been applied correctly and not mixed up, for any such confusion, as we have seen, represents a short cut to a unitary solution and thus prevents us from discovering further opposites.

(3) The constructive concepts must have been applied correctly to both realities; they have to limit the two realities clearly in their relationship with each other, so that we can penetrate deeper into each of them without referring to the other. We have also to know the different applications of these concepts to the two realities, (for instance 'cause and effect' and 'means and end'), to be able to see what in these concepts recurs in both of them (necessity and freedom).

(4) Negation must have been applied correctly, external negation for the sake of limitation, and internal negation to create those values which come into being with the help of negation. For both parts of the interconnected opposites, because they refer to the two realities, must always be positive. Necessity and freedom, for instance, could be most easily mistaken for mutual negations; but the opposite of necessity is neither mere lack of any compulsion nor licence nor arbitrariness, but a positive conception of freedom; and necessity is not merely absence of freedom, but something which we know and experience as something real. Negation, therefore, must have played its part, so that we can dispense with it completely.

The task of the interconnected opposites, as we have said, is to give expression to the most extreme oppositions which we can possibly arrive at in our thinking; they enable us to make the right use of the right extremes. We must not be satisfied with merely paradoxical statements which combine contradictory assertions at will in order to shake our certainty or to create surprise; nor with the mere opposition between 'Yes' and 'No', between affirmation and negation, which, though extreme, leads only to an intrusion of feeling into thinking. Both parts of these opposites have always to consist of positive facts or conclusions which we cannot possibly avoid and which, therefore, have for us an equal power of conviction.

In short, as these opposites always refer to the division into two realities, to know them makes it impossible ever to overlook the necessity for applying opposites. But the ability to decide whether they can be rightly considered as such opposites has to be derived from the comprehensive knowledge of thinking in opposites.

If we are successful, these opposites solve those problems whose

## ABSOLUTE VALUES AND INTERCONNECTED OPPOSITES

solution we still found necessary for making this way of thinking fruitful, thus confirming that it has led us in the right direction. But we repeat, to avoid misunderstandings—they solve them without giving final solutions. We must always bear in mind that this is a method of thinking which excludes metaphysical results. Opposites and contradictions, after all, are no final answers.

It is these opposites and contradictions, however, which lead to that synthesis in the realm of feeling which, as we have claimed, represents our only true approach to the unity of primary reality.[1] We shall describe this process at greater length later, but it may be useful to give an idea of it here, to conclude this general description.

It can be understood at once when we remember those insoluble contradictions from which we started, as for instance that between the 'starry heaven above' which annihilates our importance and 'the moral law within' which makes us, nevertheless, the centre of the universe.[2] The confrontation of these two facts does not produce a stable equilibrium; it remains a contradiction which we cannot help experiencing painfully time and again. But if we remain conscious of these two contradictory and yet inevitable conclusions and succeed in realizing them at the same time, we create a feeling of awe which, though it cannot be expressed in words, does greater justice to our position in the universe and to our moral experience than any explanation. A strong feeling will arise and make us aware that we have touched upon truth; we shall feel the meaning of our precarious position in this world and be prevented both from overrating the material world and forgetting it altogether; we shall feel that there is something behind the moral laws which implies a mysterious connection with the nature of the universe, without being tempted to translate this feeling into a unifying metaphysical statement. The underlying experience of beauty, moreover, will work against any abstract hardening of the moral laws.

[1] See pp. 17–18 and 147.
[2] For a fuller explanation of these words of Kant, see pp. 1–2.

## Chapter XI

### INTERCONNECTED OPPOSITES AND ABSOLUTE VALUES

#### 1. SPACE AND TIME

THE fact that those interconnected opposites which we are going to take as our examples—space and time, necessity and freedom, the One and the Many—belong, not to the reality which we apprehend, but to the working of our minds which apprehend it, has been proved by Kant so conclusively that there is no need to enter into this discussion again. It remains to be shown why we consider them as interconnected opposites. Kant's investigation, moreover, refers mainly to external reality, and so we also have to connect them with our distinction between the two realities.[1] We shall always investigate first how they appear to us in external reality and then proceed to internal reality, starting with the two concepts which Kant, too, considered as fundamental to all our knowledge—with 'space' and 'time'.

(a) *In external reality*

We have said that 'space' represents the fundamental concept by which we grasp external reality. This can be seen when we remember those concepts which can be derived directly from it, such as 'stone', 'tree', 'matter', because they refer only to space and not to time. It is true that, to understand external reality, we have to concentrate on events and to transform even objects into events; but we have shown that this is done with the help of constructive concepts transferred from internal reality.[2] For 'time' is the basic concept of this reality.

Nevertheless, both space and time are needed when we want to know external reality; though it appears to us first in the form of space, we could not apprehend it without the conception of time. In fact it is only abstractions and not real objects which we can think of as purely spatial. The concept 'tree' may be timeless, but no real tree is, nor any

[1] See p. 20, note.   [2] See pp. 49–50, 56.

stone, though it may withstand unchanged a very long span of time. Above all, however, there could be no knowledge of external reality at all without memory; we would live in a completely shapeless and impenetrable chaos if we were unable, after a lapse of time, to recognize the same objects again—if the sun, for instance, were something entirely new at every hour and every day. It is memory which introduces constancy as well as 'the repeatable' into external reality, thus enabling us to acquire reliable knowledge; therefore, although space represents the basic concept of this reality as it appears to us, we have to relate it to time in order to apprehend it. Space and time, while referring to the two different realities, are nevertheless indissolubly interconnected, and thus both are needed for the grasping of external reality. They can never be disconnected; to test this, we need only try to leave out one of them and then think of events or of measuring space or time.[1]

Their opposition becomes obvious when we try to define them. As they belong to those basic concepts which cannot be further explained, this attempt cannot altogether succeed, but we can make sure that we use the pure concepts. To do this, we have to consider them as opposites and to exclude one of them as completely as possible; we cannot but describe pure space as absolutely timeless, and pure time as absolutely spaceless. This shows that, without being aware of it, we really consider them as opposites, and our further investigation will show how fruitful it is to do so. At the same time, this attempt proves once more their indissoluble interconnection, for the very endeavour to concentrate entirely on one of these concepts automatically drags in the other.

The only way of overcoming their opposition is to look at them as infinite, for infinity in space and eternity in time can no longer be distinguished and thus they become identical. But this only confirms that we have to use them as opposites, for external reality simply disappears when we attempt this unification. We must remain in the realm of the finite and the temporal if we want to grasp this reality—that is, we cannot achieve their unity.

The idea of infinity in space and time throws more light on several particular points.

(1) It confirms Kant's teaching about these two concepts, for, though we have to remain in the sphere of the finite, we are bound to think of space and time as being infinite. This proves that they belong to the laws of thinking, for infinity cannot be found within the realm of our limited experience. Kant deduces from this that we must not base any metaphysical conclusions upon the nature of these concepts, because all laws of thinking acquire meaning only when they are applied. We shall show in a moment that they remain purely formal, which confirms this conclusion too. Their different appearance in internal

[1] See p. 174.

## INTERCONNECTED OPPOSITES AND ABSOLUTE VALUES

reality does not affect this, for it leads on into the realm of value and not into that of external fact.

(2) Modern physics more and more excludes infinity. But this does not enable us to eliminate it; as soon as we consider the universe as limited, we have to think of it, as modern astronomy shows, as one among many, or we have to apply the opposites in such a way that they lead to mathematical formulæ and not to understanding, which leaves our normal thinking unaffected.[1] That scientific results remain without influence upon these opposites can also be seen from the transformation of time into a fourth dimension; we have mentioned that thus, too, we transcend the realm of what can be understood and imagined without altering our experience of space and time.[2] The progress of physics only shows that the sphere of our knowledge of external reality does not embrace even the whole of this reality; we can discover that there is something absolute behind it, we can tear single shreds of knowledge out of this absolute background, but we cannot possibly grasp and understand it.[3] The renewed discussion of the nature of space and time in physics proves that we have to look for truth elsewhere, thus confirming the necessity for our inclusion of internal reality.

(3) The idea of infinity can help us to distinguish between constructive concepts and interconnected opposites. While the latter have always to be thought of as being infinite,[4] the constructive concepts—such as form and content, or cause and effect—either cannot be thought of as infinite or become completely senseless if they are. To see an infinite God in a pantheistic way as a general kind of content or in a logical way as First Cause destroys any clear conception of God; constructive concepts cannot help us in approaching ultimate questions. Nor can any form be infinite, and though we may agree that effects of the same cause can go on infinitely producing further effects, the single effect, to be understood, must not be taken as something infinite or eternal.

The difference between the constructive concepts and the interconnected opposites is also seen in the fact that we usually have to apply both of them in combination, and this, in its turn, confirms once more that we can never exclude either space or time. For if we identify one of these concepts with one of these opposites, the other concept inevitably brings in the other opposite.

We can consider something spatial as form, but then the content will inevitably appear as something temporal. We can start, for instance, from the object and look at it as a form whose content has to be found; in this case we shall discover that this form has been produced by the movements of the atoms and molecules inside the objects or the move-

---

[1] See pp. 86–7.   [2] See p. 88.   [3] See p. 135.
[4] This may sound surprising when we think of the One and the Many, but it is true even there. This will be explained later. See pp. 210 ff.

## ABSOLUTE VALUES AND INTERCONNECTED OPPOSITES

ments and influence of other objects; the content will be represented by the forces which cause these movements and which can only be recognized by such temporal events. But we can also consider these temporal happenings as the form and set out to find their content, and then the content will be spatial, namely, the producing of a certain object or some other transformation of matter. In both these cases the causes are temporal and the effects spatial. Yet if we see the cause in terms of space such as the distance between objects and their size, the temporal becomes the effect, for we thus explain the force of gravity and the resulting movements. Even when considering a state of rest, we have to talk of latent energy.

In spite of their being indispensable, however, both space and time remain purely formal in external reality. We cannot grasp them directly nor prove their external existence; we grasp space with the help of objects and space as such can be imagined only as absence of objects, as emptiness; similarly, time is bound up with events and time as such can be imagined again only as absence of events. But this becomes entirely different when we look at internal reality.

*(b) In internal reality*

We have seen that, though internal reality is not confined to man, we can best start from man in an effort to grasp it, and that we first find within ourselves a constant flux of thinking, feeling and willing, all of which are activities proceeding in time. We cannot turn our attention to man without immediately becoming aware that time is the fundamental concept by which we grasp internal reality. No human action could ever be thought of without time, and even the most passive succumbing to a strong impression or overwhelming emotion represents an action of our mind. We may succeed in suppressing our willing and consciousness; but so long as we are alive we remain unable to eliminate time.

This close relationship between internal reality and time is also made obvious by the fact that, though we live as bodies in space and time, yet time appears more real to us than space. The consideration of space depends, to a large extent, on our intention. There is no definite centre of space; the attempts to make the earth the centre of the universe were clearly based on a confusion of external and internal reality. Nor is there any necessity, if we are confronted with space alone and not with additional obstacles, to proceed in one direction only; we can go to and fro, in opposite directions if we like, repeat what we have done or alter it; according to the theory of relativity it is merely a matter of convenience to say that the earth moves round the sun rather than that the sun moves round the earth. But the course of time moves in one direction only and we can neither alter it nor make it regress; time past is irretrievably past. The growth and ageing of man, moreover, makes this direction of time so real to us that it is far more difficult to believe that time is a mere form of thinking than to accept space as such a form. Great maturity is needed to acknowledge that absolute eternity must be something different from our conception of time and thus, too, from the idea of endless or infinite time.[1] It is no accident that, in most European languages, infinity in space is expressed by a concept negating the finite, while eternity is expressed by an independent positive concept.

It is true that growth and decay belong to external reality, but the close relationship between time and internal reality can be seen there too, for the more time has to be considered the less do sciences become exact. This applies not only to biology and psychology, but even to astronomy; the history of the stars is almost as bewildering as the history of man. Science is only exact when we can reduce time to an abstract and repeatable measure, as in all the other branches of physics; but the necessity of paying attention to time as such and thus to its definite direction makes it impossible to exclude internal reality completely.

Infinity and eternity, on the other hand, show once more the greater reality of time for us. Neither can be grasped as such, but we can get some clearer idea of them by advancing in the opposite direction towards the infinitesimally small. But here the difference between space and time reappears. The constellations of the cosmos and the atom are probably very similar; yet to discover this, we have to translate our observations into the most complete abstractions, using geometrical design and mathematical formulæ. Eternity, too, can only be experienced with the help of the smallest unit, the moment, as a flash of insight, but we experience eternity only if the moment becomes completely real to us, if it is lived to the full, so that this shortest span of time which, in theory, barely seems to exist, confutes all theories by its overwhelming content.[2]

Nevertheless, we could not possibly grasp internal reality without the help of space. We can neither divorce the existence of any inner process from that of our bodies, nor understand our feelings without objects, nor our willing without aims. We have had to stress again and again that internal reality needs an external form to find an intelligible expression, and this form is either spatial or dependent on space. No language would have developed in a world without objects and other men. Even the most extreme inner experience, that of the mystic, needs

---

[1] Cf. also the very clear discussion of time in St. Augustine's *Confessions*, Book X.
[2] Cf. Dostoevsky, *The Idiot*, in which this experience is described in many ways. There we find also an explanation of Mohammed's vision which led him through all the heavens before the water from his jug, which he had overturned when falling, had had time to flow out.

## ABSOLUTE VALUES AND INTERCONNECTED OPPOSITES

at least emptiness as a symbol for what otherwise could not be expressed at all.

These formal considerations of the concepts of space and time, however, do little justice to their real significance in internal reality, for here they do not remain purely formal, but have a definite meaning for us.

Time, as the fundamental concept of internal reality, makes this particularly clear. We have just mentioned that it appears so real to us that it is difficult to realize that even time belongs to the laws of thinking. How little formal it is can be seen when we compare the measuring of time with our actual experience.

We measure time by seconds and hours, days and years, and though there are some difficulties in fixing these purely formal measures which do not occur in space—especially in fixing the length of the year— they work in practice like the others. Thanks to day and night, to growth and seasons, even these measures are something very real to us; but so are distances. Yet our actual experience of time is different. If we experience, for instance, something very interesting or important, or live through some kind of excitement, time passes quickly and we hardly notice the passing of hours, or even of days and weeks; but if we are bored, time seems to creep utterly slowly, a few minutes may appear like hours and no day ever seems to end. This impression, however, changes into its complete opposite when we look back, for those periods in which we have experienced nothing of interest or importance shrink or even simply disappear in our memory, while a few days or weeks which were of great importance to us or full of events may appear longer than many a year. The length of time can no longer be measured by equal formal units, but depends entirely on what we have done with it.

This surprising difference between the present experience of time and our looking back on it helps to make clear what time means to us. We can and do measure the length of our lives by years, but this does not account for the fact that time, nevertheless, is not a simple possession, but represents a part of our lives which has to be conquered. The years alone do not tell the whole story, for if we lose the opportunity of making use of time, long periods of our lives may be completely lost, while the time which we were able to fill with a real content makes our lives fuller and richer. Time, though obviously part of our lives, can yet disappear or be added to them. This transforms it into a constant urge, closely related to conscience, for both its slow movement while we waste time and its later disappearance makes us painfully aware that we should treat it differently. Boredom can hardly be borne with equanimity. The popular phrase 'to kill time' is very apt, for if we are unable to make the right use of it, we have at least to kill it to get rid of its constant urge. Time is felt to be an enemy, and so we embark upon some senseless industry or activity so as not to be constantly reminded of its passing.

This urge can also, of course, be silenced by impressions or experiences forced upon us, and these may represent a full and right use of time. In this case, the urge does not lead to action, but it will, like responsibility, always reappear afterwards and make itself felt again as a stimulus demanding activity. Yet the urge is not silenced by the mere killing of time, for periods in which we have been senselessly busy disappear just as much as those of boredom, and this knowledge will never quite leave us while we are busy or killing time. It is not sufficient to make use of time; we have to make the right use of it. As this is not easy, however, indulging in senseless industry represents a strong temptation. It helps us at least to forget the passing of time; the feeling that we miss our opportunities drives us on and on, so as to enable us to avoid any moment of reflection in which we could no longer escape this underlying feeling and our ever-present knowledge of this waste. Satisfaction, however, can only be achieved when we conquer time in a way which gives it the right content.

The close relationship between time and conscience can also be seen when we remember that time appears to us as past, present and future. We have seen that it is essential for our making real of internal reality to experience the present, and that this is made possible by anticipating the future. This, however, presupposes that the present sinks back smoothly into the past, so that the past becomes the safe basis upon which to build our further lives, for so long as we are burdened with experiences or deeds which we cannot thus transform, we are unable to advance further; in this case the past constantly blocks the view towards the future. It is exactly this which happens when we make the wrong use of time, especially if we feel guilty; then the present does not sink into the past, but remains a constant burden which we have to carry with us through time. Our attention is directed towards past experiences which refuse to become 'the past', instead of being based upon the past and directed towards the future. Such burdens can only be discarded when we find the way to accept responsibility or to atone for them—that is, the natural course of time can only be re-established by following conscience.

The meaning of space is not quite so obvious, but, nevertheless, it is there. The merely formal conception of space has no centre, but we cannot help considering ourselves as the centre of our own world; even the greatest modesty will not abolish the need for relating the whole world to ourselves, for we have to transform ourselves into the centre of perception. It matters very much to us, moreover, whether we can establish some such central position, or whether we have to agree that 'the starry heaven above' annihilates our importance. Space appears to us as a very strong challenge; we cannot simply accept our infinitesimal smallness as final; we have to make up for it in one way or other.

This challenge can perhaps best be understood when we remember the temptation to which it leads and to which men throughout the ages have succumbed all too easily. Space, then, is experienced as an urge to become the master of space, to conquer and acquire it directly, for the simplest reaction against the overwhelming size even of the earth is the attempt to increase one's own size by conquering space, by subjugating people and by thus adding their strength and lands to one's own stature. The ideal of the great hero who, like Alexander or Napoleon, sets out to conquer the earth has always proved to be one of the most powerful and attractive ideals. Yet this does not show its true meaning, but only the existence and force of the challenge of space and the necessity of paying attention to it. For this way of answering it is quite obviously futile; even if a man conquered the whole earth, he would still remain infinitesimally small when compared with the universe. This urge, therefore, drives man onwards until he destroys himself; as no success whatever can really answer the underlying challenge, he is driven from deed to deed, always seeking the greater one which finally proves his greatness, until he meets the task which he can master no longer. Very much of this urge is also at work in modern technical development, one of whose most important aims is the overcoming of space by greater and greater speed.

We cannot possibly hope to become equal to space in spatial terms; this means only that we mix up external and internal reality and try to meet an inner challenge in an external way. The only hope of meeting it lies in finding one's right place in the universe, and this can only be done by fulfilling man's true task and destiny. We are unable to increase our size or power so as to become conspicuous entities in the infinity of space, but we can, to a higher or lower degree, achieve harmony with the universe. Just as the centre of a sphere or the focus of an orbit stands in a clear relationship to all points of the circumference and as its idea embraces them all, while other points remain unrelated, so we must find out what can put us in the central position which establishes a clear relationship to the whole of existence. We can neither hope to become the whole sphere ourselves, nor to create a universe of our own; we can only embrace it by being clearly related to it. Again, however, this metaphor must not be misunderstood in an external way; it is only the making real of internal reality which can enable us to establish the right relationship between the two realities and put us in the centre. Thus, however, 'the starry heaven above' really points to 'the moral law within'; we have to rely on values when we want to answer the challenge of space.

## INTERCONNECTED OPPOSITES AND ABSOLUTE VALUES

That space points to the moral world also becomes clear when we pay attention to the two forms in which space appears to us—as single objects or bodies and as infinity. The concentration on the single body means, in internal reality, self-centredness and egoism, and in this way we can never hope to find the right relation to the universe, for we then remain unrelated entities within space and cannot possibly stand up to its challenge. The concentration on infinity, on the other hand, threatens us with the predominance of the infinite within us, with vague feelings and impossible longings, with aimless intentions and misleading ideals, and in this way we lose ourselves without any hope of finding ourselves again.[1] The only possibility of doing justice to both these forms of space is to establish the right relationship between the different bodies within infinity and this clearly points to love. It is by love that the distance between the bodies which seems to isolate us is transformed into a relationship and connection, and only in love do we lose ourselves in such a way that we ourselves are enhanced as well. To this we shall return when discussing the opposition between the One and the Many.

Both the temptations—the killing of time and the conquest of space—show, moreover, the importance of the opposition between space and time. Nothing in time as such points to the right use of it, nor does space open up the realm of value; it is true that we shall recognize, while doing something or after we have done it, whether we have succeeded in satisfying these urges, but we cannot find our way with the help of time alone or space alone. However, the attempt to find satisfaction in mere industry presupposes that we forget the challenge of space; when the urge to make use of time is constantly confronted with this challenge, we remain aware of the fact that only something of importance and significance which establishes a relationship to the universe can satisfy this urge. On the other hand, to believe that we can become equal to the vastness of space implies that we forget or deny the reality of death; but when the challenge of space is constantly confronted with the passing of time, we cannot forget that we are unable to preserve ourselves as spatial beings and that only something absolute which is not destroyed by death can meet this challenge. Therefore, if we use space and time as opposites, we gradually learn how to avoid these temptations. The ideals of the industrious man and the great conqueror will disappear as meaningless and what emerges will be the man who tries to discover and to fulfil what it means to be a man.

There are other temptations to which time and space can also lead, and these perhaps confirm the importance of their opposition even more clearly. Achievements which give content to time are lasting achievements—those which add something to our lives; they must last in time

[1] This applies even to mysticism. See M. Buber, *I and Thou*, pp. 86–7.

and guarantee duration. Time, therefore, can also direct our attention to objects, to material possessions, which seem to erect a barrier against the constant flux; as they can be passed on to children and grandchildren, they even seem to secure a kind of immortality. But no possession can ever mean anything when confronted with the challenge of space. The conquest of space, on the other hand, is usually connected with the striving for fame, which seems to imply a conquest of time and the securing of immortality. But when we think of real time as experienced in our lives, fame will be recognized as a shadowy reward, for who could predict the future with certainty, and what does fame avail the dead? Nor can it possibly give a content to our lives which could satisfy the urge of time.

Thus the opposition between space and time always forces upon us, in one way or other, the recognition of the world of values and of morality. This can also be seen when we start directly from these. We have emphasized that the dangers here lie mainly in considering the values as external facts and in reducing morality to a set of fixed rules. But how could values be external facts when we cannot discover them in space? And how could merely formal rules ever satisfy us when we know that we must give a content to the flux of time? When thinking of the challenge of space we can no longer be tempted to confine ourselves to some merely human conventions, but are forced to remain aware that we have to experience a meeting with the absolute. Nor can we be tempted, when thinking of the urge of time, to reduce the absolute to something which can be grasped once for all. Our experience of the absolute, even if it satisfies the urge of space, will be seen in its limitations when we remember time; on the other hand, the rules for actions, though they may satisfy the urge of time, will be seen as means —and not as ends—when we remember the challenge of space. Faced with the opposition between space and time and thus with infinity and eternity, morality is bound to become that constant renewing of our striving and experience which we found necessary.

The interconnected opposites therefore represent the basis of the absolute values which we expected to find. This is confirmed when we confront space and time with them. We can proceed to this because there is no need, in this case, to enter into a discussion about the constructive concepts. As space and time represent completely real elements in internal reality, they cannot possibly be mixed up with purely formal concepts.

(c) *Truth*

In external reality, we are led to discover space and time by the same process which we have described as striving for truth. Wherever we succeed in breaking through the surface, whether advancing towards pure matter or pure energy, we are finally confronted by the concepts of space and time and unable to advance further. The prospect of excluding one of the two, which seems to promise further progress, is misleading. We can discover either the position or the speed of the electron, but to get to know it, we obviously would have to refer to both.

We have said, however, that truth cannot be found in external reality, because it has to convey a meaning important for our lives. Space and time, if rightly understood, make sure that we do not commit the mistake of looking for truth in the wrong direction, for their external aspects are not all we know of them. There are their internal aspects as well, and as it is these which convey meaning, we are referred to internal reality.

In internal reality, space and time can lead to the experience of truth. If we satisfy the urge of time, we are freed from the fear that our lives may be too short and thus remain senseless; we learn that, in the last resort, no factual achievement matters, but that even a moment can bring a full experience of eternity. If we meet the challenge of space, we are freed from the fear that the infinity of space can crush us; we see that we are able to find a harmony with the universe which cannot be destroyed by distance. This disappearance of fear is due to a feeling of certainty; it makes us aware that we face something absolute which we can trust unconditionally. We feel that we have touched upon truth.

Nevertheless, space and time only represent a beginning. Although they can lead to the experience of truth, they do not show us how to find truth. Their opposition prevents us from succumbing to misleading temptations, but does not say what we really have to do; both point in general towards actions and experiences of a certain kind, towards making internal reality real and to the values, but we still have to find out how to discover the right actions and values. Space and time provide a very important test, especially a negative test, excluding errors and wrong endeavours, but the experiences which can stand the test have to be brought about in a different way. We obviously need some further interconnected opposites.

We thus recognize a very important quality of truth—the search for truth alone is not sufficient to find truth. Just as space and time point to action, so the search for truth, by leading from external to internal reality, points to our making internal reality real for us, which also implies action. Now activity is certainly a most valuable means of finding truth, for we experience and understand more fully what we try to do, and we discover what cannot be influenced by us. But to know what we should do we still need, as space and time show, those values which are based on the absolute value of goodness and thus help us to understand morality and responsibility. Truth leads even further;

as it shows that we have to discover something which remains independent of ourselves, which stands over against us and can no longer be doubted, altered or transformed, it may not even need our actions, but reveal itself to us; we may meet it where we least expected it. Truth, that is, also points beyond goodness to beauty, which still needs understanding, but can force itself upon us most directly of all. We have seen that this, too, can be a way of satisfying the urge of space and time. In short, if we think that we can approach truth directly, we may, more probably than not, miss it; but we may experience it with the help of the other absolute values.

But truth remains indispensable. It does not allow us to forget that we have to arrive at something which appeals to our sense of truth by shining in its own light, and so we cannot remain satisfied with our own endeavours. We are made conscious of the fact that goodness as such cannot represent our last aim, especially not in the limited form in which alone we can make it real, but that it is a way of meeting the absolute. Nor shall we be tempted to look for a merely pleasurable experience of beauty; we shall understand the concept in its full significance. It is the experience of truth which, in any experience, confirms the meeting with the absolute; if we insist upon truth, therefore, we make sure that we are never cut off from the absolute.

We shall hardly be able to forget this when we remain aware of the challenge of space and the urge of time, especially when we remember that we find space and time in external as well as in internal reality. It is very important to pay attention to their double appearance. We have to find them in external reality, so as to see that this reality is finally built up upon something which we can experience and which thus points to internal reality. It is there that we can discover their meaning. Nevertheless, they do not lead away from external reality, but point back to it, for their meaning for us remains closely bound up with their external appearance; we could feel fully neither the challenge of space nor the urge of time without facing the universe and the passing away of measurable time and of men. We have to be aware that space and time, quite apart from their meaning for us, confront us as external forms, for this makes clear that it is primary reality which matters in the end, and that this absolute reality also transcends internal reality. This, however, is exactly how truth should work. It has to lead us first from external to internal reality, but finally also to point back to external reality, for though we have to experience it ourselves, it must, at the same time, be independent of us, firmly rooted in the unchangeable nature of the universe. It must belong to primary reality and thus determine both external and internal reality.

In the sphere of absolute reality, space and time become infinity and eternity. These we can experience in rare moments of grace, but we can

## INTERCONNECTED OPPOSITES AND ABSOLUTE VALUES

never fully know them; we have to accept something which is given to us. We have seen that the search for truth cannot succeed directly; as we are unable to achieve absolute knowledge, truth, too, must in the end be given to us and accepted. But even the mere concepts of space and time imply infinity and eternity; we must, therefore, never lose sight of them; and so we must never lose sight of truth which alone of the three values cannot be thought of without the absolute. We must not be satisfied by any of our endeavours unless the experience of truth is added to them.

Let us now consider the next step to which space, time and truth point—human action. To understand it, we have to consider those interconnected opposites without which no activity could be discussed—necessity and freedom.

### 2. NECESSITY AND FREEDOM

The many implications of the opposition between necessity and freedom would require, for a full elaboration, a separate study; what can be said about them here, therefore, has to be even more in the nature of indications than what we have said about space and time.

*(a) In external reality*

Once more, we need not discuss the fact that these concepts belong to our laws of thinking. Hume has proved that the concept of necessity cannot be derived from our actual experience, which only leads to probability, and Kant has shown that it is founded upon the opposite of freedom and thus established by our thinking.

The case of these interconnected opposites, however, is in a certain respect a special case. Necessity is based on events, and the knowledge of events, as we have seen, is based on concepts transferred from internal reality, quite apart from the fact that they are much more closely connected with time than with space. This makes this aspect of external reality rather similar to internal reality, and as necessity is thus based on internal reality in any case, we can easily overlook that it is interconnected with freedom. The opposition to freedom, which it still implies, can appear as a mere matter of definition. This inevitable and yet hidden participation of internal reality makes it understandable that it was possible to develop a purely mechanical view of the whole of existence and to deny freedom and internal reality altogether. But the mere fact that necessity is so closely linked with time should make us think, and we have seen that it is usually wrong to consider opposites as mere means of definition. In fact, the interconnection between necessity and freedom can be discovered easily when we approach them without prejudice, especially if we become aware of the distortions of our knowledge to which any overlooking of freedom has led and inevitably must lead.

Necessity, as we have seen, represents the fundamental concept of external reality. We could never deal satisfactorily with this reality if we could not rely on the same causes necessarily producing, in the same circumstances, the same effects—if, for instance, we had to be prepared for our tables jumping into the air at any moment, whenever they pleased. All such thoughts about the absence of necessity are, in fact, nothing but abstract speculations; our actual apprehension of, or dealing with, external reality is firmly based on the concept of necessity. It is true that we do not always succeed in establishing this basis, but this is always felt as a serious defect, and the resulting uncertainty and insecurity show that we can understand external reality only so far as the knowledge of it can be based on necessity. It is impossible to imagine this reality without the concept of necessity, for this would dissolve everything into a complete chaos which, as our daily experience with our tables shows, external reality is not.

This is confirmed when we consider those events which we are unable to recognize as necessary. There are undoubtedly inexplicable accidents, but we cannot help thinking that we only see them as accidents because we are unable to discover their real causes. We presuppose that we should recognize their necessity. Many modern physicists claim that there are regions in which we are definitely unable to exclude the accidental; but this only shows that necessity belongs to our thinking and not to reality as such; it does not contradict what we have said, for our understanding ends where necessity can no longer be discovered. There is also man's ability to choose; but if we think about it in purely external terms, we cannot account for it and are always led to deny it, claiming that man's activities, if only correctly understood, would appear just as mechanical as all other events. When using external terms, we never discover freedom, but only necessity.

Certainly, we have to deal with these accidental phenomena, too; we cannot simply wait until, in some distant future, necessity may have been discovered. But, in external reality, our ways of dealing with them are highly unsatisfactory. We are forced, for instance, to use the calculus of probability and this, as we have shown, helps us in the world of atoms and electrons where the individuality of the single unit does not matter, or when we are concerned with the purely material.[1] But it is of very little avail in our own lives, for, in spite of an overwhelming probability, the one improbable case may still happen or even recur and confute all our calculations. The possibility of choice, on the other hand, seems only to account for the chaos into which human society has been plunged time and again.

[1] See pp. 33–4.

## INTERCONNECTED OPPOSITES AND ABSOLUTE VALUES

Necessity thus seems to determine external reality far more exclusively than space. We can discover certain gaps, but not, as is the case of time, any definite external appearance of freedom. Nevertheless, the concept of freedom is needed if we want to grasp this reality fully.

We are inclined, owing to the enormous successes of modern science and the obvious failure to reduce the concept of God to a convincing 'First Cause', to forget that we really cannot think of necessity without a beginning, for any process must have started somehow. A beginning, however, cannot be further determined, and so necessity must have started from its opposite, freedom. Nor can we ever account for our grasping of external reality unless we consider ourselves as completely different—that is, free—agents.[1] If we deny this, we accept external reality as primary reality, as is done in all comprehensive mechanical explanations. But this means that we do not understand this reality at all; we are overwhelmed by it and submit to it completely, not only when this can help us to apprehend it but also when we should use it for making internal reality real. The accidental and man's ability to choose must not be regarded as mere shortcomings which can be entirely overcome if we accumulate a little more of the same kind of external knowledge; if we rely on this, we only blind ourselves to the fact that there are forces at work which we can neither explain nor subdue, and thus we destroy man together with his ability to choose. The use of the probable mechanical effects of propaganda for the directing of human affairs, to which the mechanical view is bound to lead, is only one of many examples of the inevitable disastrous consequences. These apparent shortcomings must be understood as definite signs of the essential limitations of external reality and as pointing beyond it. We have to relate them to freedom which, by revealing the existence of internal reality, is just as necessary for the correct grasping of external reality as necessity itself, for unless we see this distinction, we include in external reality absolute elements which make it impossible to remain 'objective'.

That necessity and freedom are indissolubly interconnected can be seen when we compare them with the constructive concepts. As necessity contains internal elements, the distinction between them is again more difficult than in the case of space and time, but this makes it even more imperative to remain aware of the difference between them.

Necessity is based on the opposition between cause and effect, for it refers to the sequence of events. At present, this opposition is overcome by deriving from it the law of causality, and this law is then identified with necessity. This identification, however, is quite wrong; causality refers only to a necessary and explicable connection between cause and effect, while necessity can also be imagined in different ways. It has been connected with such concepts as 'fate' and 'providence', with concepts,

[1] See p. 21.

## ABSOLUTE VALUES AND INTERCONNECTED OPPOSITES

that is, which make the participation of freedom even more obvious than the idea of a first cause, for fate stood above the gods and providence is the work of God; neither can be divorced from some such further concepts which represent inexplicable and free agents. To reduce the conception of necessity to that of causality is an arbitrary restriction of our knowledge, which leaves us completely bewildered when the physicists happen to disown the general validity of the causal law. We should recognize that necessity belongs to the interconnected opposites and thus points beyond external reality by its interconnection with freedom, while cause and effect are merely constructive concepts, indispensable if we want to grasp external reality as such, but purely formal and without further implications. Then both the impoverishment of our knowledge and our bewilderment when we discover it could be avoided.

This is confirmed by the constructive concepts 'form' and 'content'. Causality is a form of events, and necessity, as it is based on abstractions from internal reality, can also be only a form, and so both make us seek the content. Causality is made up of cause and effect and therefore makes us look for elements which we can find in external reality; we can be satisfied with the discovery of forces detected with the help of their effects, which, as we have seen, only push the content further back.[1] But we have to remember that the concept of necessity is comprehensive, so that we cannot push the content beyond it. It thus requires a completely different content which is itself not subject to necessity, but creates it. No purely external energy, even if we spell it Energy, can ever satisfy this demand.

As we could not make clear distinctions right from the beginning, we have had to mention necessity and freedom among the constructive concepts, but when describing the difference between the two realities, we have replaced the concept 'freedom' by that of 'the accidental'.[2] It would help, in fact, to introduce such concepts as 'the determined' and 'the accidental', to distinguish the constructive concepts from the interconnected opposites. Each single happening appears to us in either of these two forms; we either recognize its determination by a definite cause or not. But what appears determined to us may still take place within an accidental context—when we are wounded by a falling stone, the wound is determined by it, but the falling of the stone just at the moment when we happened to pass the spot seems still accidental—and what appears accidental to us may still be determined by an underlying necessity, as in this case, for instance, by fate. If we use these concepts systematically, we are not misled by the tendency, inevitably connected with the apprehension of external reality, to eliminate the accidental, but discover that the opposition between the determined and the accidental cannot be completely transcended any more than that between

[1] See p. 48.  [2] See pp. 51–2.

the other constructive concepts. This means that causality can never cover the whole field of necessity, and that therefore even the most comprehensive reign of necessity does not abolish freedom.

Whenever we drive our questioning far enough, we are inevitably confronted with the accidental. We have had to stress that the question 'Why?' can never be answered in any fundamental or comprehensive way.[1] But we could fully explain external reality only if we knew why everything is as it is. It is utterly superficial to think that we have explained external reality as soon as we seem to understand the motions and perhaps even the origin of the stars. Only the knowledge why stars have come into being at all, why there is a world of stars and the earth which we inhabit among them, and why there are forces which work in this and no other way, could lead to a full explanation. That is, we are bound to meet sooner or later what appears to us accidental, and thus prevented from forgetting freedom. Even the determined reminds us of freedom, for it shows that the accidental cannot be the final explanation; something more positive must be behind it, because it is unbelievable that mere accident could ever produce order. We may shuffle the single letters of the alphabet for ever without producing sense.

The constructive concepts and the interconnected opposites can again be distinguished by applying the test of infinity, for the latter have to be thought of as infinite, while the former are only distorted by it, as the mixing up of causality and necessity has shown. Infinity would also represent the only way of overcoming the opposition between necessity and freedom; if our understanding of necessity were complete, without leaving any gaps, we could also understand the free agency behind it, and if we knew freedom completely, we could completely translate it into unchangeable laws. But this thought only confirms our inability to unite them.

Even the full awareness of these opposites cannot transcend the barriers which cut us off from absolute knowledge in external reality, for both necessity and freedom remain here again purely formal. Necessity, though pointing to some positive power behind it, is grasped as the form of a connection or relationship; whether causal or not, it always indicates that the sequence of events cannot be altered nor influenced from outside; it is the expression of underlying laws. Freedom, on the other hand, whether it appears in accidents or choices, here means no more than something negative, than the absence of necessity. But this changes once more when we consider what these two concepts mean in internal reality.

(b) *In internal reality.*

The fact that even external necessity is closely connected with

[1] See pp. 172–3.

internal reality makes it all the more difficult to exclude the external forms of necessity and freedom from this reality. We have seen, moreover, that the principles, which are of great inner importance, borrow their forms from external events,[1] and so we must not even exclude the external forms of necessity and freedom. As these concepts refer to our actions, and as our actions interfere with external reality, we obviously have to pay greater attention to it than in the case of space and time which underlie our apprehension. We have to consider, therefore, both the meaning of their external appearance for internal reality and their purely internal forms. It is their double rôle which helps us to clear up many of the apparent contradictions which are contained in the conception of freedom.

The fundamental concept of internal reality is freedom. Just as no practical action would be possible unless the same cause necessarily produced the same effect, no value would be possible without freedom. The moral values, because they refer to actions, show this most clearly, for they are based on our ability to choose the right or wrong action; but, also, the search for truth and the appreciation of beauty would not make sense without our ability to act in freedom. If none but mechanical effects could be produced within us, the concept 'truth' would lose its meaning, for even the mechanistic theory would then be nothing but the necessary consequence of physiological causes,[2] and these effects would give rise to pleasant or unpleasant emotions, but nothing could be called beautiful. The idea that inner experiences are of any importance would have to be discarded altogether.

Freedom, however, appears to us in two forms. On the one hand, it means freedom of choice, and this means the making real of internal reality in the framework of external reality. It is true that we cannot discover this freedom with the help of external terms; we have just said that the external approach can always lead only to the discovery of necessity. Nevertheless, we could not possibly understand the position of man without presupposing his freedom; the most convincing proofs will never convince us that, for instance, we cannot raise our hand whenever we please; if we are unable to, we shall rightly come to the conclusion that something is wrong with us. We can neither prove man's freedom of choice externally nor discard it; we have to start from it if we want to arrive at any understanding at all. Yet this kind of freedom does not exhaust the meaning of this concept, for, on the other hand, it is only when we make the right choice that we really become free. Our choice can either enslave us or set us free; if we choose to follow our ambition or even a misinterpreted ideal, for instance, we become the slaves of this aim; we have to choose the right values in the right context to experience freedom. Thus freedom also means the realm of

[1] See pp. 126–7.    [2] See H. H. Farmer, *God and Men*, p. 40.

## INTERCONNECTED OPPOSITES AND ABSOLUTE VALUES

these values; we become free when we discover and choose the realm of freedom. The choice as such is the external form, but freedom has to be recognized and experienced as an inner content for it to come to life fully.

Both these forms of freedom are interconnected with necessity which therefore also acquires two forms.

External necessity plays a great part in our lives. We could not achieve anything practical if we did not act in accordance with external necessity, and there are vast regions in our minds which we have had to describe as impersonal and where external influences tend to produce mechanical effects. To counteract these compulsions, freedom has to be translated into compulsory laws too, such as moral laws or laws of honour, or into a convention of decent behaviour or the duties of a citizen. We have to confront external necessity by a necessity based on the presupposition of freedom, for we could not grasp the realm of freedom without expressing it in terms of necessity. If we consider freedom as mere arbitrariness or licence, we remain uncertain about what it means, and are never able to discover whether what appears to us as freedom is due to conforming to external necessity, of which we are unaware, or to our choice of the right path. We cannot clearly differentiate without applying the laws of thinking; we only know what freedom really implies when it is expressed by a binding necessity. So long as it is a question of choosing, therefore, we must have laws to tell us what is right and what wrong.

But this, once more, is a merely formal expression of necessity which cannot do justice to freedom as such. Freedom also needs another necessity; we should be so bound by freedom that we cannot do otherwise but act upon it; it has to be experienced as an inner necessity. 'By their fruits ye shall know them'—the effects of freedom should come forth necessarily and yet without any external compulsion, for even moral laws can falsify it; it should make itself felt at any moment directly. The full realization of freedom needs no laws; it produces, at any moment, an immediate inner necessity of its own.

This can be seen in several ways. External laws are based on the past, internal laws on the future; they do not explain what exists, but what we should do, thus leaving room for freedom. Yet we have shown that, though this including of the future is most important for our understanding of the present when we reach the goal, the present as such may have quite a different meaning when we actually experience it, and that we are in danger of missing this meaning if we still remain bound by our preconceptions.[1] We do not grasp freedom so long as we only see the laws which tell us how it should be made real; we must also have a fuller idea of it to be able to judge the result independently from the

[1] See pp. 52-3.

laws producing it. Moreover, as these laws refer to the future, they are based, not on cause and effect, but on intentions and aims. These cannot be dispensed with; we are bound to have intentions and this implies aims. We believe in a cause, however, only if we discover its effect, and we are inclined to believe the same of intentions. But this is a mistake, for intentions may not have any external effect whatever and still exist and even be genuine, and they may or may not produce unnoticeable, but important, internal effects. We simply cannot judge them in terms of external laws. The fruits by which we should know people may not spring from any intentions at all, but be the necessary consequence of a full realization of inner freedom. Necessity, therefore, though it has to be based on the relationship between intentions and aims and expressed by laws, must also transcend them.

The moral laws themselves confirm this conclusion. Any moral demand can perhaps best be described as an 'inescapable claim'.[1] Though necessary in its own context, it pays attention to our freedom by establishing, not a compulsion by a definite order, but a claim which leaves us free to accept or to reject it. But it has to be inescapable, and it becomes so when we recognize its justification, so that we are unable to reject it without knowing, at the same time, that we ought to accept it. To be understood, it has to be expressed by moral laws referring to external actions or relationships—'Thou shalt love thy neighbour as thyself'. But it can become inescapable only by the knowledge of that inner necessity within us which is freedom.

This need for purely internal forms of necessity and freedom, however, never allows us to dismiss their external forms altogether, because the tension between these two forms is also essential. So long as we consider the external forms of necessity and freedom alone, their relationship remains a complete mystery. As we recognize necessity and have to assume freedom, we can never succeed in drawing definite boundaries between their spheres. We could say, for instance, that necessity determines the external course of events and that freedom lies in their interpretation, for many events, though they cannot be altered, can be seen by us either as blessing or as disaster, and we may be able to transform even disaster into a fruitful stimulus. This is probably the nearest we can get to such a limitation and there is undoubtedly much truth in it, but it is insufficient. The exercise of freedom in the interpretation of events will gradually transform us; we then enter into the course of events as a different cause; and thus we shall be able to influence them in accordance with freedom. On the other hand, to insist on the possibility of our positive interpretation of events in all circumstances rather overtaxes our strength. We can only test the relationship between neces-

---

[1] I am following here H. H. Farmer. Cf., for example, *The Servant of the Word*, pp. 41-3; *The World and God*, pp. 70-2.

sity and freedom by our actions, and we have to test them again and again to find out in each particular case how we can assert our freedom. This, however, is not to be regretted as something inevitable to which we must resign ourselves. On the contrary, it is most important that the mystery should be preserved, for it is the constant attempt to find out by our actions where freedom can be exercised and where not that transforms necessity into an inner compulsion which can be experienced and which therefore makes it internally real. It is only when we experience necessity in this way that we can understand its opposite, freedom. If we could act as we liked, we could rely on our whims and intuitions and accept, if any, the standards we liked; the experience of compulsion and the disappointments due to it are necessary to make us transcend arbitrariness and to awaken our desire to find true freedom.

Any attempt to behave in accordance with moral laws shows the importance of this tension. If, for instance, we try to help our neighbour, we may succeed or fail, and we may fail either because we do not achieve what we intended or because our success which we considered as a help turns out to have no effect or the opposite one. The more we try to help, the more we see how little effective help depends upon us; our success is dependent on external circumstances and its effect on the character and circumstances of the other person, and we cannot count upon understanding his personal situation fully. This does not in the least affect our duty to help, but we have to strive for both, for helping and for taking our powerlessness into account. This will gradually make us see that it is most important to base our help on the right values and convictions, for our actions, even if they fail, can still help by embodying and expressing an attitude which helps. Our neighbour may not be helped if we get him the position he desires, for this may strengthen his wrong ambitions, but he may be helped, whether we succeed or not, if he experiences love. This we could not achieve if we insisted on external success alone, for this would, at the same time, transmit wrong and damaging convictions, nor if, recognizing our limitations, we took them all too easily for granted or gave up helping altogether, for this would inevitably harden us against our neighbour, nor if we restricted our help to purely spiritual help, for no intention can be believed unless it is seen to drive us towards action. Yet no theory can tell us how long we have to insist on external action and when we may give in; we simply have to try, and even if we try hard, we may still fail by giving in just a little too soon or too late. But if we experience each such failure fully and painfully, we feel and recognize the compulsion of necessity together with the urgent claims of freedom; by each such step, therefore, the true realm of freedom will become more clearly visible; and thus, in the end, we shall have helped by our example.

As the realm of freedom has to be made real in internal reality, the

## ABSOLUTE VALUES AND INTERCONNECTED OPPOSITES

personal example is the final embodiment of help. We shall see later that it is also the clearest embodiment of the 'inescapable claim', for it is both a claim only and yet inescapable if it makes the right appeal. Force and violence, compared with it, are nothing but weakness, for if we are led to use them to impose moral rules we betray our inability to make the right appeal.[1] It is here that we come to the roots of our responsibility. We should be an example, and it is within the powers of almost any one of us to become one, for the right striving, even if unsuccessful, can be sufficient to establish it. But who has not spoilt it by a wrong action or an action undone, by indifference or concern for himself, all of which he could have avoided? 'Understand that you too are guilty, for you might have been a light to the evildoers . . . and you were not a light to them.' [2] This responsibility we can no longer decline. But we also need for its full realization to be aware of the mystery of the relationship between necessity and freedom, for only because we never know how far the consequences of our actions reach can we never claim that this responsibility is limited and that we need not always pay attention to it. We have become accustomed, mainly under the influence of the natural sciences, to consider the relationship between cause and effect as something which can be easily recognized, but this does not apply to the human sphere; here it is bound to transcend our knowledge and we can never fully recognize what causes an effect. A word or action which we hardly notice may exercise a strong influence upon the development of a child; a forgotten book may suddenly influence the course of historical events; we may help or hurt where we least expect it. We have to accept unlimited responsibility because, even if we seem to decline it for very good reasons, we may still overlook some possible effects of our actions, and we may want to overlook them.[3]

That we must not destroy the tension between the two forms of both necessity and freedom also becomes clear when we look at the personal example from another point of view. Personality develops with the help of actions, for we cannot understand the principles of action embodied in the moral laws without trying to act according to them. We are hardly able to dispense with the law without obeying it first. But the accomplished example, too, though it no longer needs the law, cannot become obvious and believable without the attempt to translate it into action; even the most abstract striving for a mystical union with God, for instance, is not convincing unless it is accompanied by the renuncia-

---

[1] 'Loving humility is marvellously strong, the strongest of all things, and there is nothing else like it.' Dostoevsky, *The Brothers Karamazov*, vol. 1, p. 302 (Everyman Ed.).

[2] Ibid., p. 334.

[3] For a fuller treatment of this problem see my book, *The Misinterpretation of Man*, pp. 254 ff.

tion of worldly fame, possessions and power. How can we distinguish between these different kinds of action? [1]

It is true that there seem to be exceptions. There are great personalities, such as saints or geniuses, who have been given that for which we have to strive, and who seem to embody freedom perfectly, either by their nature or in consequence of one great experience or sudden illumination. No law or action has made them what they are, and freedom moulds and permeates their being so completely that they radiate it directly, again without the help of any action or any of the external forms of necessity and freedom. But these apparent exceptions only further elucidate what we have said.

On the one hand, we must not forget that actions due to laws, though embodying our freedom of choice, do not give expression to the realm of freedom. The true success of our free choice is to reach this realm, but no accomplishment here can ever be due to our efforts alone; it opens the gates to the realm of freedom and the effects of our endeavours thus infinitely transcend the cause. To consider it as merely our own merit would exclude everything besides the connection between cause and effect and thus destroy freedom. This is more than a purely logical conclusion; so long as we look for success, we think that everything depends on our intentions and overlook the independent existence of internal reality, and this will most probably find expression in our remaining enslaved by vanity or selfishness or ambition. We have to strive hard, and yet any result achieved must not be regarded as directly due to our striving; we can only understand freedom by opposing it to necessity. The mere thought that we can bring it about ourselves destroys it by excluding the very realm of freedom on which it is based. We have to strive for external aims and yet hope that the innermost core of internal reality will be touched and reveal the futility of all our striving. Here again we can see, from the human side, the meaning of the Christian concept of grace. As this means, however, that the results which matter have to be given to us, the exceptional personality only shows more clearly what we all have to experience.

On the other hand, no great personality concerned with the right values can be imagined without suffering, and this suffering, to establish the right kind of example, has to be of the right kind—that is, it must not be selfish, but due to the full experience of the suffering of others. Can such suffering arise without the desire to help others and see them saved? Its highest realization is certainly based on love, and there is no love of one's neighbour or of God which would not force man to include external reality again, and then the tension between the external

---

[1] How important this problem is can be seen in the age-old theological controversy about the true relationship between grace or faith and works. We shall return to it; see pp. 233 ff.

and internal forms of necessity and freedom reappears. Love for one's neighbour requires concern for him and help; love of God, if divorced from the Christian conception, can perhaps also be divorced from the love of one's neighbour, but even then, as all religions show, some other external discipline has to be introduced. Even those personalities, therefore, who simply radiate freedom and are examples by their very being show once more what is generally valid—that their being is based on the urge to be active. The internal forms of necessity and freedom also imply action.

The distinction between the two kinds of action may still be difficult to make, because they can be—and frequently are—very similar or even, seen from outside, identical. We can strive to help somebody, or we can help him because our nature forces us to do so, but the resulting action may be exactly the same. Yet we shall be greatly helped in making this distinction if we realize that both necessity and freedom have external and internal forms within internal reality, and if we always confront them anew.[1]

It remains difficult, however, to attain a clear knowledge of inner freedom as such. It is an inner necessity from which nothing but the right fruits can emanate, so that they come forth necessarily and yet freely. But what is this realm of freedom from which they thus come forth? We have just said that love is its fullest embodiment, for love sets us free by binding us; we never feel more completely ourselves and therefore free than when love makes us surrender completely. Then we solve the mystery of the relationship between necessity and freedom by transforming it into a clear experience. But this, though probably self-evident, can no longer be understood in terms of necessity and freedom; their opposition can help us to discover the right forms of love, but love must be there before these distinctions can be of any use. Necessity and freedom can no longer help us, because they refer to events and actions, while the realm of freedom, from which love springs, must be something existing and static. Once more, therefore, though they are of the greatest importance themselves, these interconnected opposites lead on to further such opposites; the more so as, in this case, we cannot separate external and internal reality as completely as they should be separated.

This is confirmed by the temptations to which necessity and freedom can make us succumb. The temptation of necessity is fatalism, the complete giving in to necessity and the renunciation of any attempt to break through it by actions of our own. Thus, however, necessity also destroys man, for nobody can live fully without at least trying to exercise his powers. It is true that fatalism is only a distortion of the trust and con-

[1] Particularly because of the interconnection between action and suffering. See pp. 235 ff.

fidence which we should possess, but it is a fundamental distortion, for we cannot have this trust and confidence without faith, and faith cannot be directed towards events alone, but must be directed towards their source. This can also be seen if such a faith in the events alone takes the opposite, optimistic form. We make necessity the basis of a belief in progress, but this only represents the same temptation in a different disguise. If we believe that everything which happens creates something good necessarily and automatically, we also rob man's freedom of its meaning and destroy it, for if the events themselves are bound to guarantee progress, we cannot feel justified in interfering with them for the sake of something we believe to be good. Any moral exertion on our part would only hinder the automatic working of progress. Just as in the case of fatalism, we have to submit passively to necessity.[1]

The temptation of freedom is licence and arbitrariness which, as we have seen before, are a dangerous distortion of freedom. They must, in the end, lead to pessimism, for if we believe that we can always do whatever we like, we are bound to be disappointed and finally to doubt the existence of any intelligible order. This, however, either leads back to necessity, for this kind of freedom becomes an unbearable burden which must be shaken off as completely as possible; or else man is again faced with destruction, for nobody can believe in the complete senselessness of existence without destroying internal reality and thus himself.

The temptations show, too, that necessity and freedom represent very important and real facts in our lives, and this distinguishes them again from the constructive concepts. At first, owing to the rather ambiguous nature of necessity and freedom, it may seem difficult to distinguish them from the constructive concepts; intentions and aims or means and ends seem just as real to us as moral or similar laws and the freedom to choose. This similarity disappears, however, when we are aware of inner necessity and the realm of freedom. If we know an inner necessity, this inescapable urge supersedes all intentions, ends and aims, which all depend on our will; if we know, not only the possibility of choice, but the realm of freedom, it becomes identical with internal reality itself and thus transcends all its single elements. By embracing the whole of internal reality, however, it points once more beyond this opposition and shows the need for opposites which refer to the basis of all such events.

*(c) Goodness*

As we have always had to refer to morality to explain the application of necessity and freedom, no further explanation is needed to show that they form the basis of the absolute value of goodness. It is the one of

[1] For a fuller treatment of the relationship between the belief in progress and morality see my book, *The Misinterpretation of Man*, pp. 147 ff.

these values, after all, which is concerned with our actions. But necessity and freedom help us to see goodness in the right perspective, for this value has a double aspect too. It is, at one and the same time, in some respects the most and in other respects the least important of the absolute values.

Goodness, by referring to our actions, is the only one of the absolute values which provides a test of its truth. Truth as such must shine in its own light, and beauty, too, cannot be further determined; but goodness, as we have to act upon it, is tested by the results we achieve. We have seen that these results can be quite different from what we expected, and that this contradiction helps us to recognize what goodness really means.[1] It is true that the appearance of goodness can hide very different —even immoral—intentions and motives, but this will hardly suffice to mislead us constantly in our own case or to disguise the truth in the actions of others for ever. As always, we must not expect perfection and the complete avoidance of error, but—in this case and not in others— we can learn to test, by their application and the results to which they lead, the laws and principles in which we believe. If we really and honestly want goodness, and when the patient testing of the boundaries between necessity and freedom has taught us the meaning of true freedom, there will be little mistake, in the end, in judging the fruits by which we shall know ourselves and others.

That we find truth in goodness can also be seen when we want to judge abstract convictions and ideas, for there is no other test than goodness. Neither belief in a necessary evolution leading to constant progress by a cruel life and death struggle nor totalitarianism could have exercised the disastrous attraction which they had if this fact had not been forgotten or despised, nor could natural science have led us astray to such an extent. Truth and beauty alone will never enable us to find our way through the wilderness of fascinating abstract ideas; and this, too, makes goodness so very important.

Nevertheless, it is also dangerous to concentrate on goodness alone and to divorce it from the other absolute values. This danger exists because goodness seems self-sufficient. Truth, as we have seen, always points beyond itself; beauty, as we shall see, can never be confined to the impressions or embodiments which we already know; only goodness, because it demands constant activity, can appear as a final principle which is sufficient to give content to the whole of our lives, especially when it is translated into moral laws. Though morality, even logically, needs some source from which to spring, we see that it has been divorced from religion or any other basis and accepted as the sole absolute guide in life. But in this case we are either easily forced into rigidity, into upholding the laws and their external aims at all costs, and this rigidity

[1] See pp. 44–5 and 120 ff.

## INTERCONNECTED OPPOSITES AND ABSOLUTE VALUES

hardens us and destroys goodness; or we may become sentimental, revel in our feelings and cherish them, so as to overlook the shortcomings of mere morality. We are then in danger of either becoming severe judges or of being unable to make any clear distinctions at all.

The source of this danger can be recognized when we remember that the absolute values are values—that is, that they have to be thought of as positive and negative. This, once more, is more important for goodness than for the other two. Falsehood and ugliness are certainly very real in our world, but we shall try to avoid falsehood and consider it as purely negative unless we want to make use of it for evil purposes, and the same applies to ugliness. Both acquire a positively dangerous aspect only by being related to the moral sphere; the negative value with which we have to concern ourselves, therefore, is evil. Evil, however, remains a stumbling block so long as we do not succeed in transcending the level of values.

We have seen that good and evil are dependent opposites and that no conception of good is possible if we remove the concept of evil; this concept as such, therefore, does not contradict the existence of the good. But values are more than mere concepts; they become real in human life and society; and there evil appears no longer as a mere opposite to goodness, but can become so strong that it destroys the good and makes us despair of its possibility and power. We only need to look at ourselves without prejudice to recognize that, at any moment, evil threatens to become much more real than good, and this is even more obvious in the society created by us. To make a value real, moreover, we have to bestow it upon objects or events, and as negation, in the moral sphere, is far more definite than the positive which we have to experience always anew, evil can also be more easily discovered than good. It is true that we have, nevertheless, a feeling that evil is somehow less real than good, for we know that it can help us to become more sensitive and that it may become a strong stimulus to make us strive for the better, and what appears to us as the unjust cruelty of fate can lead to fruitful suffering and atonement. Could we ever arrive at the good without suffering evil? Yet all this can hardly be upheld when we look at the world around us; there evil seems definitely the stronger force, and it appears as sentimentality or unforgivable naïveté to deny its power—a power so great that it seems able to destroy the very meaning of life. We have to agree that evil as such exists and works and leads to the gravest possible consequences; and our efforts to stick to the good may well appear as hopeless illusions.

There seem to be two solutions to this conflict. The one we have just discussed; we concentrate entirely on the moral laws which say how to overcome evil, and then it is our fault if we do not accept or follow these laws, but evil can be overcome. This is bound to force us eventu-

## ABSOLUTE VALUES AND INTERCONNECTED OPPOSITES

ally into rigidity or sentimentality, because, as we must denounce evil as mere failure, we remain unable to do justice to its external appearance. The other solution is dualism; we regard good and evil as the two fundamental forces which constitute primary reality. But this, too, is unsatisfactory, because values, as we have seen, do not belong to primary reality. It is when we conceive goodness in such ways as these that truth and beauty appear as far more significant and goodness as the least inspiring of the absolute values.

Goodness can be seen in its true perspective, however, without forcing us to deny the great power of evil, when we base this value on the opposition between necessity and freedom. For their different forms help us to grasp the two aspects of this value correctly.

First, there are the two forms of necessity. We need the laws, but must transcend them too, which means that the laws are absolute but not the aims. The laws are absolute, because they have to be compelling and must not be broken; yet this absoluteness does not contradict the need finally to overcome them, for by developing our moral nature, they can make themselves superfluous.[1] Only if external aims were absolute should we never be able to dispense with the laws which tend to make us rigid. But the aims are not absolute because we can, and should, progress from external to internal reality.

Second, there are the two forms of freedom. The values are the equivalent of the freedom of choice, for it is this freedom which implies the freedom to do wrong. But there is the realm of freedom, too, to which goodness has to conform as well; goodness, therefore, must lead beyond choice and value. This realm of freedom is purely positive and thus, though evil is real outside this realm, it is less real than goodness, for goodness applies both outside and inside this realm. Good and evil must be experienced with equal strength, for only thus can our experience of the good become complete, yet the realm of freedom cannot be conceived in a negative way; the negative value, therefore, must have helped us to experience the positive fully and must be left behind. We have to progress from the freedom of choice to the realm of freedom; this shows that goodness is more than a mere opposite of evil and that we must achieve more with it than a formal morality.

Third, there is the mystery of the interaction between necessity and freedom. The realm of freedom is not simply given, but we have to make it real by a constantly renewed testing of the boundaries between necessity and freedom—that is, we have to live the dualism between good and evil to discover the true nature and the power of the good. In other words, we must include evil in our responsibility, but cannot

[1] 'The deepest of all moral requirements . . . is not to act conscientiously, but to seek an ever more penetrating conscientiousness.' J. Oman, *Grace and Personality*, p. 63.

overcome it directly, for freedom and goodness, though they have to be made real by us, must not be included in the relationship of cause and effect. Evil must be wiped out by atonement and forgiveness, and we cannot achieve forgiveness, but must be forgiven.[1] The direct connection between morality and its effects is broken down and we can adhere to goodness without denying the reality of evil.

We see, therefore, that goodness cannot be regarded as self-sufficient, but that it points—as any absolute value should—to the absolute. For we could not make the good the expression of an inner necessity unless our conception of it were firmly grounded in the experience of the absolute which safeguards freedom.

This dependence of goodness on a more comprehensive absolute can also be recognized when we consider the possibility of failure in relation to the absolute values. We could say, for instance, that the obvious power of evil in our world destroys these values. But can they be destroyed? They do not exist as such somewhere in space and time; they become real only when we meet the absolute by applying them. To apply them means to bestow the value on objects or events, and so we cannot even discover them unless we look for their positive effects or try to bring them about. It is we who may fail to become good or to do the good and thus to meet the absolute, but the absolute values are not touched by this, for then we do not touch their sphere. Even if we only relate our failure to them, it is immediately changed into success, for this helps us to get a clearer knowledge of the absolute values. But if we remain powerless to make them real, they do not come into being at all; the idea of failure can always refer only to our power, never to that of the absolute values. This shows once more that the opposition between good and evil is different from that absolute which we meet in goodness as such and which must needs transcend it, for failure is only possible on the level of good and evil, but there remains a region in goodness itself which is not touched by it.

Necessity and freedom thus ensure that we get a clear idea of goodness. We have to see it also in two forms. As a pure value which, appearing as good and evil, provides us with the only test of truth, it is the most important of the absolute values. Nevertheless, we must not rely on goodness alone, for it also transcends evil and is dependent on a more fundamental absolute; it merges into a sphere which is beyond action. As this absolute cannot be grasped as the effect of a cause, as the result of our own efforts, we have, when we want to approach it more directly, to leave the striving for goodness behind. The absolute has to

---

[1] These terms may to many sound purely religious, but J. Macmurray remarks correctly: 'To describe the everyday experience of two people sharing a common life we have to use such words as fellowship, communion, enmity, estrangement, guilt, forgiveness, reconciliation.' *The Structure of Religious Experience*, p. 53.

confront us, we have to be forgiven, we have to be presented with it—that is, we are led beyond the sphere of action towards the absolute value of beauty.

### 3. THE ONE AND THE MANY

The names of these opposites are rather clumsy, and it would be useful to find other names for them to distinguish them more easily from the constructive concepts. This seems hardly possible, however, because their appearances in external and internal reality are so different that different names would be required, and it is only the concepts of the One and the Many which, in both realities, as we shall see, stress some of the essential points clearly. Their comparison with the constructive concepts will help sufficiently for us to get a distinct idea of them, despite their rather technical names.

*(a) In external reality*

We have said that we need repetitions to grasp external reality. These repetitions enable us, with the help of the constructive concepts the One and the Many, to apply numbers to this reality, and these, by forming the basis of mathematics, prove one of the most important means of getting a reliable hold of it. The constructive concepts are able to form the basis of numbers because they remain purely formal; we have to leave out all the particular aspects and characteristics of the single unit to make it one among many and thus to be able to count. We have seen that this is the process which enables us to apply the number 'five' to apples as well as to days.[1] The Many, too, must then remain purely formal to be able to indicate quantity and nothing else. Mere numbers, however, are obviously not the basis of our apprehension of external reality, for they give us no idea of its nature (as space and time or necessity and freedom do); the interconnected opposites, therefore, must have a different meaning.

As our knowledge of external reality is dependent on repetitions and numbers, its fundamental concept is the Many. We apprehend this reality as a multitude of objects and events, and it is only because there is this multitude that we can grasp external reality at all. We describe objects by qualities, but no quality could be isolated and defined without comparing different objects; we understand events with the help of laws, but no law could be discovered and stated if there were not many events. This shows, too, that this multitude must not be considered as complete diversity; we have to see in it these similarities and repetitions—that is, the term the Many means both diversity and uniformity. It shows us the nature of external reality

[1] See p. 58.

## INTERCONNECTED OPPOSITES AND ABSOLUTE VALUES

because it indicates a multitude which can never simply be summed up (even the number of electrons does not abolish the differences between houses and trees and animals and men) nor ever divided into completely disconnected units (there are common characteristics of everything external). Thus it also confirms that our knowledge is not simply derived from external reality, but that we have to apply the laws of thinking. We have seen before that the actual first impression we receive from this reality is 'the unrepeatable' and thus mere multitude and diversity; the idea of the Many, which allows us to grasp this reality, has to be introduced by us.[1]

The concept the One represents, as we shall see, the fundamental concept of internal reality, but nevertheless remains indispensable for our grasping of external reality too. The very nature of the idea of the Many shows that we cannot sever the interconnection between these two concepts. By pure logic, the Many consists of many single units, but this formal connection belongs once more to the constructive concepts; their interconnection is more than merely logical.

The transformation of a shapeless diversity into a multitude of definite similarities and repetitions can only be achieved if we gain a clear conception of the single unit. Things have to be perceived as limited units in space and events as limited single happenings in time; otherwise we could neither compare nor explain them. It is no accident that the other constructive concepts presuppose such units; there is no form without it and no content without form; cause and effect must be limited units too, and they must divide the constant flux of events to enable us to deal with it. Such a unit, however, must be more than a simple number; it must have certain qualities and characteristics, for only thus are the similarities and differences thrown into relief and the multitude made accessible to apprehension, organization and understanding. The Many consists, not of abstractions, but of units which we can recognize when we describe them; they have a one-ness distinguishing them from each other—that is, our thinking has also to supply the idea of that inner coherence of the form which we know only in internal reality. Even the electron, which represents both the nearest approach to pure mathematics and the attempt to overcome diversity completely, has particular qualities, special characteristics and this oneness, and we could not have discovered it without starting from an external reality seen as a multitude of more individual units with more distinct and complex forms which require the idea of inner coherence. How inescapable this demand of our thinking is can be recognized when the individuality of which we try to deprive the different objects, in order to arrive at a common denominator, reappears as a mysterious quality of the electron itself.

[1] See pp. 49–50.

## ABSOLUTE VALUES AND INTERCONNECTED OPPOSITES

The difference between the constructive concepts and the interconnected opposites can also be seen when we apply the test of infinity. It is true that we can go on counting infinitely and also introduce infinity into mathematical calculations, but even the largest number is still a single number and infinity remains a single item; this infinity is not the all-embracing infinity which this concept really suggests. But the interconnected opposites can be imagined as infinite; we are even forced to think of an all-inclusive unit representing the whole of the universe as the complete sphere of everything which exists; and as soon as we think, not of numbers, but of the different individual units, the sum total of the Many must produce the same wholeness and unity. Again, however, infinity remains beyond our reach and only shows that this opposition, too, cannot be overcome. We have seen that all attempts to establish such a comprehensive unity must fail; nor can we hope to sum up the Many. Modern physics, having discovered the individuality of the electron, may succeed in finding some such sum totals for our universe; but, as we have mentioned, this only transforms 'the' universe into 'a' universe among many, in spite of all the necessary simplifications which distort external reality beyond recognition.

As external reality is grasped with the help of abstractions, the impossibility of excluding these opposites and of including infinity can be hidden in many ways. We use such concepts as quantity, quality, energy in a very general way which seems to establish an infinite unity, and forget that, if these concepts are applied, their dependence on the One and the Many must become obvious, and that they have no meaning apart from their application. It is this possibility of abstraction which accounts for the constant recurrence of futile attempts to create the all-embracing unity. There is one sphere, however, in which no such abstractions will ever be convincing, and it is this sphere which represents for us, at the same time, the most important embodiment of these opposites. We can never get away from the fact that we are single human beings among many such beings.

This sphere raises some special difficulties which we always encounter when approaching the human realm in external reality; we have met them before when discussing nationalism.[1] We cannot satisfactorily describe it as pure external reality, because, with man, neither the unrepeatable nor internal reality can be completely eliminated; but neither can we concentrate solely on internal reality, because society obviously represents a most important external factor. Yet just as the problems of nationalism could be solved once we reached the level of the absolute values,[2] so these difficulties cease to be obstacles once we turn to the internal meaning of the One and the Many.

All this shows that these interconnected opposites belong to the

[1] See pp. 137-8.   [2] See pp. 149-50.

## INTERCONNECTED OPPOSITES AND ABSOLUTE VALUES

most important concepts for the task of grasping external reality, but that in this reality they are, at least outside the human sphere, at the same time very clear and simple. Like the other opposites which we have discussed, however, and despite their apparently purely formal names, the One and the Many also represent essential and very real basic elements in internal reality, and their nature and meaning there are more complex.

*(b) In internal reality*

The fundamental concept of internal reality is the One, for we could neither grasp external reality nor give form to the constant flux of thoughts, feelings and urges within us without being a definite and clearly circumscribed centre of a different kind.[1] Any development of personality always leads to the clearer awareness of being such a centre and of feeling and experiencing oneself as an 'Ego'. The ability to say 'I' is the condition of clear apprehension, knowledge, feeling and willing.

At the same time, we are once more unable to separate the One from the Many. No necessity for becoming such a centre would arise if man was not surrounded by objects and other men, and no development of personality could ever be thought of in complete isolation.[2] The One enables us to grasp the Many, but multitude and diversity have to be introduced from external reality, for without this opposition man and the world surrounding him would remain an undifferentiated and indefinable mass.

In internal reality, however, we approach and experience these concepts from inside, and so we can no longer be satisfied with this external description of their indispensability. We have to see how they come into being, what creates and constitutes them, and by what meaning they become real to us. We shall see once more that this transforms them into facts which are of the greatest importance for us.

The One can no longer be simply described as a unit characterized by certain qualities and boundaries; the emphasis shifts entirely to its one-ness; it is a unit by representing in itself an independent and indivisible, self-contained and self-sufficient whole.

The nature of this transformation can perhaps be best understood when we compare the nearest approach to such a unit in external reality —an organism—with other external units and with ourselves. Let us assume that a piece of wood, a house and an organism were smashed to pieces. The destruction of the piece of wood is not of much signifi-

---

[1] See pp. 20-1.
[2] See H. H. Farmer, *Towards Belief in God*, p. 246. Cf. also the many reports about people growing up in complete isolation without developing a clear consciousness and language.

cance; the result is other and more pieces of different size and shape, but still of the same kind. It may mean destruction if we wanted to use the particular piece for a definite purpose; but this refers only to our concern with the wood; even as sawdust the wood itself remains wood. The house is destroyed as such because our purpose was, in this case, the main determining factor; but the material of the house also may not be fundamentally changed by being smashed; the 'wholeness' of the house is only a kind of external addition to it. The organism, however, is quite definitely destroyed and ceases to be an organism; its parts are completely transformed and become inanimate matter. There the 'wholeness' was something essential and could not be separated from the conception of the particular unit. But even this organic unity still does not give the full impression of the unity which we experience within ourselves, for there it is no external knowledge, but inner experience. We do not see ourselves as a combination of different limbs, organs, and other parts of the body, held together by serving a common purpose and by being directed from a centre which seems to evade definition; on the contrary, the centre and the unity represent our actual experience, and all divisions remain later artificial additions. There the 'wholeness' is the basic reality. We may, of course, suffer by inner conflicts and the struggle of opposite tendencies within us, but the fact that this causes suffering confirms that the unity and the wholeness are fundamental and that their being threatened is a danger to our very existence. We may also accept modern psychological or old eastern doctrines and consider personality as a bunch of different and divergent tendencies or souls, but if our personality is really deeply split we become insane. The unity has to be felt underneath and beyond all conflicts and splits within us. It is this complete wholeness and unity which is the meaning of the One in internal reality.

How can we achieve this wholeness? The most obvious element which makes us recognizable as distinct separate units, different from others, is our individuality or our peculiarity. No person is ever exactly like any other, and it is this fact which divides humanity most conspicuously into different and unrepeatable units—which agrees with our previous statement that it is 'the unrepeatable' that allows us to grasp internal reality. On the other hand, this peculiarity can be only part of the truth, for we are human beings; to describe our unity correctly, we have also to see that which we have in common with others and which makes us human. We have to discover both what is peculiar to us and what is our share in the general nature of mankind and to establish the right relationship between the two.

The task of making the One real thus points in the same direction as the transformation of the form in internal reality. There we have to see what creates the form, so as to understand it as the expression of

## INTERCONNECTED OPPOSITES AND ABSOLUTE VALUES

the content.[1] Similarly, we achieve wholeness by making the particular the expression of the generally valid. We have to know both what we can consider as belonging to humanity within ourselves and what is our deviation from it, but we have to make the latter the expression of humanity, for a concentration on individuality alone would cut us off from the roots of our being and thus from achieving wholeness. It is true that the unrepeatable is the means of making internal reality real, but this it is only because the general basis is self-evident and existing and because it becomes clearer by constant new experiences; otherwise the unrepeatable would dissolve internal reality into innumerable disconnected particulars. To work out our own peculiarities is just as important, for this throws into relief what is of general validity within us; but it does so only if it is used for this purpose, for otherwise the stressing of the particular is bound to split our feelings and to make us eccentric. We have to use both our special individuality and the humanity within us to achieve personality—that is, to create that whole in which our person becomes the particular form and expression of humanity, so that the fact that no person is like any other makes clear all the facets of, and approaches to, this common humanity.

The conception of the Many undergoes a similar transformation. Number and quantity as such cannot be grasped in internal reality; the unrepeatable individualities and inner experiences are far too different to allow us to add them together; if we try this, we only destroy internal reality. There is, for instance, very much pain in the world, but we can never say that there is such and such an amount of pain; the different experiences of different persons can hardly be compared with each other and no quantity can ever be ascertained. The Many, therefore, can only be understood as pointing towards the individual and the unrepeatable. It stresses that there are great similarities between the units and that they have much in common, even in such a case as that of pain, but it remains a multitude which cannot be counted; it shows again that, to understand anything at all, we have to deal with the single case. Nevertheless, the Many remains the opposite of the One, for it does not allow us to forget that, despite all our experiences of one-ness and wholeness, we are still confronted with diversity.

This can also be seen when we approach diversity from inside, trying to base our knowledge, not on the external fact, but on the feeling it arouses, for our first experience is not one of differentiation, but of the internal reality which all of us have in common. It may be very painful to realize how different people are, but it is painful because we feel very strongly that the underlying unity should be the main experience. Clear differentiation is an effort because we first experience

[1] See pp. 131–2.

## ABSOLUTE VALUES AND INTERCONNECTED OPPOSITES

wholeness.[1] This approach is so natural that even a clearly felt realization of the multitude of things and beings on earth and in the universe awakens this feeling for wholeness. But this feeling remains vague and is disturbed by the irreconcilable peculiarities of the individual men and things which we are bound to discover, and so it is the task of the Many to make it necessary for us both to understand individuality in order to clarify our feelings and to relate the individuals to the whole.

This transformation of the One and the Many could make it seem advisable to replace these words, in internal reality, by such opposites as 'the particular' and 'the general' or 'the part' and 'the whole'. Yet the One and the Many prove to be once more the better names, because they not only include these different oppositions but also state the real opposition more clearly, pointing at the same time to some further relevant facts.

(1) The opposition between 'the particular' and 'the general' has the disadvantage that it is not an inevitable opposition which forces itself upon us, but a distinction which we have to make. We cannot help seeing many single units, but, unless we are successful, we shall be unable to consider the particular as an instance of the general. Thus we stress too much our own endeavours and achievements. It is true that these are needed; the possibility of external impressions depends on our understanding; we have to strive for knowledge and to develop our personality. But, as always in the sphere of internal reality, which is the realm of freedom, success must not be seen as the simple effect, nor our striving as the determining cause. We understand the result only if we leave intact the mystery of the interaction between necessity and freedom.

That this also applies in this case at once becomes obvious when we think of such simple experiences as the understanding of a poem or a picture or a piece of music. We may understand them immediately, or hear or see them many times without ever understanding them, or suddenly understand them after we have seen or heard them many times without appreciating them. We cannot enforce this understanding; our greatest endeavours, even if they make us see the particular work as an embodiment of general ideas, may not help in the least to produce a real understanding. It is probable that the right kind of endeavour and interest will help us to find the right approach and make us accessible to such an experience, but it will be the right endeavour only if it is combined with patience, with the readiness to accept. We must not rely on the will to succeed, for to understand that a form entirely and unambiguously expresses a content we have to have the complete inner experience of a whole and this wholeness cannot be

[1] This can be seen in many reports about primitive peoples and the development of children.

## INTERCONNECTED OPPOSITES AND ABSOLUTE VALUES

achieved or disclosed by analysis or by preconceived ideas, but must disclose itself to us. The real enrichment of our experience, however it may come about, is in any case not due to our endeavour but to the poem or picture or music; it has to be given to us. Works of art, moreover, though they are fruits of conscious striving, are essentially based on mystery—on the mystery of special talents and intuitions, on the inscrutable mystery of genius.

Or, to give another example—impressions made by nature, such as a beautiful sunset, may or may not awaken a strong response within us, and our sensitivity will not be the result of our striving. We cannot say to ourselves, 'Now I must enjoy the beauty of this sunset'; explanations will only destroy the experience of beauty; and is not the mystery behind such impressions even greater than that underlying works of art?[1]

Our striving never does more than make us accessible and susceptible to these influences, and it does so only if we remain aware that it cannot enforce them in that way in which a cause produces an effect. Internal reality becomes real because the inner meaning of the given facts impresses itself upon us; the final illumination must come from reality itself; the meeting with the absolute comes about when the absolute suddenly confronts us. Thus we need such opposites as 'the particular' and 'the general' to direct our striving and to interpret our experience, but it is important that they should remain subordinated to the less abstract and less logical opposition between the One and the Many, which, by representing both external and internal facts, makes us see that these experiences are fundamentally independent of ourselves.

(2) But does not 'the general', nevertheless, point more directly to that all-inclusive whole to which any final illumination and any meeting with the absolute lead? The opposites the One and the Many, though they make this unity accessible, also seem to hide it. So long as we are confronted with diversity and multitude, with the Many as such, internal reality has not become real, nor does its unity lie in the One which is one among the single units constituting the Many. The whole has to include everything, and thus also the One and the Many.

Yet even here it seems better to say that we pass, with the help of the Many, from the units which constitute it to a different, all-inclusive unit, and to describe this new unit once more with the help of the opposition between the One and the Many. For this new experience which transcends the Many is not that of some general principle or common quality, of a feeling or a value, but definitely that of another unit; it becomes a full and significant experience only if we find ourselves confronted with another single unit which, by its compelling

[1] See H. H. Farmer, *Things Not Seen*, p. 49.

wholeness, obliges us to believe. Whenever external impressions or works of art or personalities become transparent and reveal to us the bond between ourselves and the whole of existence, they do so by their wholeness which makes us feel ourselves to be a complete whole; it is always essential that their unity should be felt. Certainly, they may embody a principle or a value, but these become convincing because they are embodied, because we feel that they can create such a unity. Thus the opposition between the One and the Many, by stressing and clarifying the nature of the One, once more emphasizes a fact which is of fundamental importance and which would be blurred by such terms as 'the general', for we experience, not something which has been abstracted from many units and which can be generally applied, but the inner unity of the One, made accessible by the experience of the Many.

This double aspect of the One is in accordance with a characteristic of internal reality which we have met before. Feeling, though it works in many different ways, always springs from the same source. Single forms embody different contents, but to be 'content' in our meaning of the word, they have to partake of internal reality—that is, of one common content. Freedom, though the opposite of necessity, is at the same time identical with the whole of internal reality. Single truths remain part of one and the same truth. Similarly, we grasp single units, but their wholeness is the expression of the all-inclusive unit which, in its turn, has again to be grasped as a single unit. This double aspect is always characteristic of those concepts which represent internal reality.

Nor is it therefore quite true, as the term 'the general' suggests, that the all-inclusive whole completely replaces the Many. We are bound to have many such experiences, for any all-inclusive unity which we can experience is still opposed by ourselves—that is, by the single unit which remains interconnected with the Many. This, however, is of great significance too, for it reminds us that we can never achieve perfection or a full knowledge of infinity or grasp the absolute once for all, but that internal reality has to be made real by the constant renewing of many such experiences.

(3) We have had to use again the term 'wholeness'; would not, therefore, the opposition between 'the part' and 'the whole' save us from underlining this rather complicated double aspect of the One? But these terms again are only useful so far as we try to direct our own striving; we have to describe the accomplished inner form, for instance, by saying that each single part has become a necessary expression of the content, and we have to experience in this form what is most easily described as 'wholeness'. Yet these concepts, too, do not do justice to the fundamental facts underlying them; they suggest too mechanical a division. The single unit, though part of the all-inclusive whole, is

## INTERCONNECTED OPPOSITES AND ABSOLUTE VALUES

not a part, but itself represents a whole; we can distinguish parts of an accomplished form, but only as the result of a more or less artificial division; they cannot really be separated from the whole.[1] The confrontation with the all-inclusive whole, moreover, increases our own 'wholeness'; we feel ourselves in unity and harmony with it and thus far more complete than before; the opposite 'the part' gives a quite wrong idea. We can use it, therefore, as a means of understanding and explaining the conception of a whole, but not to replace the One, whose double aspect truly expresses our experience.

(4) The names 'the One' and 'the Many' show best that these concepts are of the same order as 'space' and 'time', and this fact makes it impossible to discard them. But it also reveals a difference between these two pairs of opposites which will later help us to explain the difference between truth and beauty. Space and time are discovered with some difficulty as the fundamental concepts in external reality; they appear as the result of a search similar to that for truth, yet, at the same time, they confront us directly as powerful demands in internal reality. The One and the Many are the most obvious and simple facts in external reality, so much so that we all too easily forget them when looking for further explanations, even in mathematics which is based on them. But their meaning in internal reality is not at all obvious; we have to discover what they mean; but, once discovered, they prove to be the most essential of all these concepts. While space and time, because they are discovered in external reality and lead on to internal demands, introduce a never ending search and spur us to constant activity, the One and the Many, when they are finally discovered and fully understood, indicate the goal of this search.

(5) These opposites are the most essential, because they alone are applicable to that opposition which is the most important for us—to the fact that we are single human beings among many such beings. They prevent us from disregarding this fact and help us to understand it better.

We see here, first of all, a further implication of the Many. We are one among many human beings, but so long as we think of them as many, we miss the human in the single man. Each single unit is, in this case, an embodiment of internal reality, and we miss this content unless we confront it directly; general conclusions based on many experiences are necessarily logical and external and do not enable us to gain a knowledge of internal reality. Hence the danger of loving mankind, which so easily leads to the neglect of the single individual; we are driven by it to the belief in some abstract external ideal which makes us

[1] The whole is always the first impression and the parts have to be discovered afterwards; we first hear the tune, not the single sounds; we first see the wood and not the single trees. Cf. Köhler's *Gestaltpsychologie*.

hate the men who seem to hinder its realization, and thus it destroys true love.[1] To do justice to our relationship to humanity, therefore, we have to see the opposition between two single units; the Many has to be replaced once more by another embodiment of the One. This time, however, it is not the all-inclusive whole, but a unit which, by being similar to ourselves, can be better understood. Thus this relationship provides us with a transition to the final experience of the absolute, which helps to make it accessible. But even there the concept of the Many as such does not disappear, for we remain one among many men, and we must not lose sight of this either, for it indicates, as we shall see, an essential gap in this relationship.

The opposition between two such units proves the utmost importance of these interconnected opposites, because it is here that the conditions for making internal reality real can be fulfilled. To understand this, however, it is good to remember that this opposition has been called the 'I-Thou relationship', for the meeting between persons which we are now going to discuss has to be understood in that sense which is indicated by stressing the 'I and Thou'. The other person must not be seen merely from outside, which makes him similar to a thing, to an 'It', but we have to meet a person to whom we can appeal and who can appeal and respond to us.[2] Everyone knows the great satisfaction of friendship, or that sharp feeling of disappointment which we experience when another person does not respond or wants to abuse our response; the meeting has to be so real as to be capable of evoking this particular positive or negative reaction. Or, in other words—the One has to be experienced as the internal opposite of the Many, as a single, indivisible and self-sufficient whole. It is when we see the meeting with the Thou in this light that we recognize why these opposites are so essential.

We have mentioned, for instance, that to make this reality real we have to concentrate entirely on the present.[3] This demand can be fulfilled, on the one hand, by any strong impression, experience or preoccupation, or, on the other hand, by the meeting with another person. If this meeting is a personal meeting in the sense just stated, the concentration on the present is so inescapable and complete that this demand is met far more fully than in the other cases.

An impression produced by nature, by a work of art or literature, or brought about by our own activity, attracts our attention so far as we understand it; it leaves us free, so to speak, to make our own choice and to react to it in the way we are wont to react. It may evoke some

[1] Dostoevsky remarks how much easier it is to love mankind than to share a room for two days with a stranger whom one does not like.
[2] The following is largely based on Martin Buber, *I and Thou*.
[3] See pp. 52-3.

feelings or thoughts which are very much against our wishes, or touch unknown layers of our personality or even develop it further, but reactions are forced upon us only so far as our sensitivity has been developed beforehand; we are able to escape the impact or some of its elements and thus the concentration on the present may remain incomplete. So long as we alone remain active, we also remain the determining force; moreover, as we are always concerned with the future, we are inclined to neglect the present, and all such impressions more or less allow us to do so. An external event which concerns us probably impresses us more forcefully, but no such event ever entirely hides the passing of time, and the present is only experienced as a fleeting and passing moment.

When we meet a person, he confronts us as an 'inescapable claim'; the mere existence of other persons has moral implications and means that we are confronted with claims which transcend our self-sufficient selves, and these claims become inescapable once we experience such a personal meeting fully. For we also meet another free will, which forces us to respond to his being, utterances and actions; we can no longer make our own choices nor escape whenever we like; our reactions are determined by what is confronting us. Fundamental demands, even if they have been deeply buried within us, are forced into the open, for as we experience the Thou as an undivided whole, we cannot help but react with our whole personality. The famous question, 'How do I know that other minds exist?' is completely meaningless, for I would hardly know that my mind exists unless I meet other minds. In any such meeting it is the other mind which is experienced with overwhelming certainty, and my immediate awareness of the other mind allows me no choice, but develops my mind by forcing me to react at once to his approach. I probably react first in my ordinary way, but if this reaction is inadequate I am hardly able to avoid noticing it for long. If I accept the claim which I undoubtedly feel, the presence of the other person does not allow me to wait or to retire, and if I do, I definitely feel that I am wrong.

To understand that this means a full experience of the present we need only remember that we can hardly avoid talking. If we speak to another person and listen to him, we must entirely concentrate on the present; as soon as our thoughts begin to float away we either cease talking or cease talking sense and no longer hear what the other person is saying. The language and the thoughts expressed by it have certainly been developed over a long period, and we can speak of past and future, but we can only speak in the present; this is so self-evident that to say so almost sounds like an absurd tautology. Thus, however, we are also kept within the present while we talk. If we follow a long conversation or explanation, our participation, to be real, has to force it to a point where we can react immediately, for otherwise we do not experience the meeting with a person. Listening to a lecture, for instance, is not sufficient to establish such a meeting; though the personality of the speaker makes itself felt, the lack of our own participation makes it rather similar to an external impression. Response, to be response at all, must be as immediate as talking to one another.

Even more important perhaps is the significance of such a meeting for the relationship between form and content.

We have said that, in internal reality, we first experience the content and have then to find the external form which expresses it.[1] All impressions and experiences, with the sole exception of the meeting with a person, acquire content by making us aware of our own being, feeling and inner activities—that is, of our own content, and this enables us to understand them as the forms of a content or to create forms which express a content. When meeting another person, however, we experience first the content within him and learn to understand our own individuality as the necessary form of the content within us. It is the only time when external reality is excluded, when the content is presented to us from outside, and when our own being becomes understandable as the necessary form of internal reality.

We understand the other person in such a fully personal meeting so far as we stand on common ground—that is, when we experience humanity within him. His person is different from ours, but because we understand it as embodying humanity, we have also to see what our different individuality means in its relation to this humanity. We are forced to make ourselves understood, to develop language and means of awakening response, which once more means that we have to relate our particular being to the common ground. If we succeed in this, the response must further clarify this common ground, either by strengthening our experience by agreement or by correcting it by disagreement, and so again we have a clearer experience of the content and recognize some more of our peculiarities—which we have perhaps identified with the content—as deviations which have to be related to it. Any such reaction makes us see better both how far our own individuality deviates from the generally valid and how far it expresses common humanity. The fact that the content is given from outside gives us, therefore, a far deeper knowledge of the form than we could acquire otherwise, and this knowledge, in its turn, gives us the fullest possible grasp of the content.

The One which we experience in the Thou thus also helps us to understand the all-inclusive unity to which the Many points. We can meet the other person because there is something common which we feel in ourselves, and because this common humanity transcends both

[1] See pp. 38–9.

of us and provides a ground on which we can move. Humanity, however, is still too abstract a name for it and one which does not do justice to our actual experience; as we experience a meeting, that which unites us must still be capable of being met and cannot be properly described by generalizations. A meeting with a person, though its fullness also depends on our attitude, on our willingness to accept the inescapable claim and to act according to it, is again not the result of our endeavours, for it becomes a meeting only if the other addresses us. We experience a claim because we are being addressed—by the other and by something through him—and because something within us, whether we want it or not, responds to thus being addressed. But we cannot be addressed by a principle or by humanity or by some quality of general validity; even if a person makes himself the mouthpiece of such an abstract conviction, we respond more than abstractly if something personal is touched within us. It is one-ness and not a general principle which is confronting us.

The meeting both makes us aware of the limitations of our individuality and frees us from them. Our unity is not dissolved, but we feel free because we feel that we—and the other person meeting us—are partaking of a unity which is distinct from ourselves and which, by transcending both of us, makes us conscious of itself. The single unit has met with that comprehensive 'One' which we have described.

It is true that we rarely come to this conclusion to-day; mainly accustomed to abstract thinking, we seem to be satisfied if a meeting with other men enables us to see some abstract common quality which we can endow with a vague feeling. We have to make a reservation because of this fact; the fully personal meeting is not an everyday experience, but has become a rare event. But once this event really happens, we see that the conclusions just arrived at are not merely logical, which would be no proof in this sphere; any unprejudiced approach will confirm that this meeting with persons implies the meeting with a unity which, though mysterious in its infinity, can only be grasped as an indivisible whole, complete in itself.

But here the Many, indissolubly interconnected with the One, interferes again. Not in its external form; the difficulties of society disappear in any such personal meeting. But we do not understand the mystery of the many different individualities which we inevitably meet; and because of these, each meeting makes us see a different aspect of our own person and of the unity transcending it, but none can clarify all aspects of both. To understand the meeting fully, we have to experience the present, but we cannot remain in the present for long; we have to live, to be active, to be practical, and so the present must pass away. We can never transcend internal reality completely, and so we need these ever renewed experiences, none of which leads to a comprehensive knowledge. Any response awakened within us touches upon another aspect of the infinite absolute, and any such response, even the strongest, is bound to become paler and weaker and finally to die away. We ourselves may be transformed by it, but even then we need further such experiences to give meaning to this transformation, and we remain unable simply to preserve or collect them by translating them completely into thought. We can never by our own efforts overcome the barrier of the Many; drawn by the all-inclusive One, we are left groping in the dark, lit up from time to time—rarely for some, frequently for others—by mysterious illuminations.

Thus, however, the Many has also a further implication. If we want, not only the certainty of the moment, but final certainty, if we want to find a definite way through the maze of the many new experiences which, though continually disclosing new aspects, never discloses an all-inclusive order and the fundamental relationship between these aspects—in short, if we want full knowledge, we have not only to be addressed, we have to be told. We need revelation.

There is an element of revelation in all the experiences which we have discussed. We are enriched by the impression, by the poem, by the work of art itself; the beautiful sunset speaks to us; the other person reveals himself to us; the experiences have to be given, and we destroy this gift if we insist on discovering everything by our own efforts alone. But even in the meeting with another person, the revelation is never complete. We are confronted with the content, but do not fully understand the individuality and situation of the other person; he helps us to understand our own individuality, not his; this is one reason why we must not judge. What is revealed within us, on the other hand, still mysteriously transcends us; even our own individuality, though it helps us as a form to understand the content, remains a strange gift which we cannot quite understand. A full knowledge can only be founded on a self-revelation of the ultimate unity which is addressing us—that is, it can only be grounded on a religion based on revelation. As we can transcend neither the division into external and internal reality nor the interconnected opposites, we cannot know primary reality by our own power.

It is love—*agape*—which gives us the greatest strength to overcome all such obstacles and to have a full and unweakened experience of all that matters. But love is the most spontaneous feeling; if we try to demand it from another person or to force ourselves to love, we most certainly destroy it. We may discover it as the most valuable principle and demand it in the name of a principle or value or law, but this can hardly make us love or be loved in the right way, for we then love not our neighbour, but our knowledge and conviction. Nevertheless, love is demanded from us. Yet love can be created only by love; it can be demanded only while love is addressing us and, by awakening the right response, is making the demand a spontaneous experience. As no love of the right kind is kindled by generalities, we are led once more to the One; love can be transformed into a demand only if we are not left dependent on our own feelings, but if the nature and meaning of it is quite distinctly revealed to us.

The One and the Many thus lead to the boundaries of pure thought and of philosophy, but they show that there are facts in man on which religion is based. They also help us to recognize those requirements which any religious revelation has to satisfy if it is to transform us, for none of these experiences can be brought about by external metaphysical statements. As we can never transcend internal reality completely, we have to be addressed; we need to be told what can awake a response. There is no use in telling us why God has created so many different individualities; this would only destroy the challenge of the Many; but it is essential to be told that God is Love. To be fully understood, revelation has also to be expressed in those opposites which help us to find access to inner experiences; it has to make use of, and we have to apply to it, those interconnected opposites which we have discussed and those created by our thinking. We shall see, when discussing the latter, that this is a correct description of the Christian revelation and the right way of understanding it.[1]

*(c) Beauty*

We have defined beauty as the complete agreement between form and content; it arises when we feel absolutely certain that the form expresses the content completely.[2] That it is based on the interconnected opposites the One and the Many has probably become clear already by the examples which we have given.

Beauty cannot be based on the opposition between space and time which drives us into a never ending search, for a perfect form has to confront us as a final result. We can strive to increase our sensitivity and understanding; but once beauty confronts us we search no longer. We have also had to mention that the external forms of space and time, though they cannot be divorced from a beautiful object, are of no help if we want to understand its beauty.[3]

Nor can necessity and freedom help us to understand it, for we experience beauty only if we are not concerned with actions as such and not bent on any purpose. When we have lost our way and desperately want to find it, we are hardly able to notice the beauty of the landscape or sunset. It is true that a beautiful form, especially in works of art, acquires an inner necessity by being determined by the content; but this

---

[1] See A. N. Whitehead, *Religion in the Making*, pp. 71–2.
[2] See pp. 156–7.  [3] See pp. 35–6.

necessity, unlike that of freedom, does not find expression in actions. On the contrary, it gives us the certainty that no further action, no correction or improvement, is required. Even if actions in, for instance, a drama are the subject of representation, they have become a finished form which invites, not further actions, but contemplation.

It is the opposition between the One and the Many which helps us to get a clearer idea of beauty. It makes us understand why beauty is the absolute value which is most directly experienced and yet most difficult to describe.

The main factor which helps us here is the difference between the two manifestations of the One to which the Many gives rise, for beauty comes into being when the single unit, the One originally opposed to the Many, becomes an expression of the other One at which the Many points—of the all-inclusive unit. There is no impression of beauty—if it is clearly seen as such and not identified with a merely pleasant impression—which is not felt to be created by a form of this general content.

We experience beauty on several levels, and most difficult to understand, perhaps, is that experience which seems, at the same time, simplest—the beauty of nature. But this is not surprising, for it is here that we confront the mystery of all existence; we confront, most immediately and directly, the all-inclusive unity which we can never fully express. Moreover, we confront it from outside, which makes it most difficult to translate it into other terms. The beauty of nature, therefore, is bound to make the most immediate impression; it seems hardly believable that any one should not experience this beauty at all; we feel quite definitely that we have met the absolute; but, at the same time, it must be well-nigh impossible to give it a clear meaning. If we have a definite belief concerning the absolute, we are confirmed in it; if not, we are still strongly impressed, but it seems easy to dispose of this impression. If we thus dismiss the absolute in this experience, we cannot account for the fact that its absoluteness is probably clearer, and also more commonly felt, than that of any other experience; but even if we accept the absoluteness, the all-inclusive unity appears less defined than in other and perhaps weaker experiences of beauty.[1] The confrontation with the all-inclusive unity is so direct that, of all our faculties, feeling alone can fully respond to it.

This difficulty must not be mixed up with another one—that we cannot define which landscape is beautiful. What appears beautiful to us here and now may make quite a different impression upon people from other zones, or upon ourselves in different circumstances. But this only shows that beauty is a value. It is not simply in the landscape as such; our participation is an indispensable part of any value. We have men-

[1] Hence the dangers of pantheism.

## INTERCONNECTED OPPOSITES AND ABSOLUTE VALUES

tioned that the name 'absolute value' can be misleading—that 'absolute' refers, not to the embodiment of the value, but to the fact that it makes us experience a meeting with the absolute.[1]

Works of art and literature, because they are created by persons and intended to embody a content, are more easily seen as symbols of the all-inclusive whole, for they also transmit the personal experience which we can follow. But even here we should not try too hard to express the content in a different way, for it is the personal experience which discloses the absolute and creates its special form; beauty, therefore, is closely bound up with it and easily vanishes if we try to understand the meaning of the work in a more general way. We have to experience the single unit of the work to be able to have this experience. There are several particular characteristics of such works, however, which, when considered in the light of the opposition between the One and the Many, make it easier to see what beauty really means.

(1) There are times when art serves religion, and then the artist usually remains anonymous. The Many needs the opposition of the One; if the belief in the all-inclusive unit is firm and clear, this unit suffices to establish this opposition and the single unit loses its importance. As we know the One, we are no longer forced to follow the single individual to be able to understand at all; the Many appears as the many facets of the same unit, which is sufficient to give meaning to it.

(2) This anonymity seems also to contradict the demand for 'uniqueness' which is so much stressed when we consider works of art to-day. This uniqueness, however, has two meanings. On the one hand, it is a quality of both forms of the One, of the single individual and the all-inclusive unit which must needs be unique; if the knowledge of the latter uniqueness forms the basis, then once again we no longer need that of the single individual. On the other hand, as we ourselves are individuals and unable to grasp the whole as such, we still need the uniqueness of the single impression to make us aware that we have met the absolute. We cannot grasp it in a general way. This uniqueness, however, never disappears; it is there when we enter a mediæval cathedral, when we look at its sculptures created by anonymous artists, and also when Shakespeare transforms subjects used before; in fact it is only the originality of the artist which we value differently to-day. This shows again that we always need the One to transform the Many; if the all-inclusive unit no longer clearly transcends it, the uniqueness of all the single individuals has to be stressed to replace it and to give some idea of its wholeness. Yet in this way we can also see that it is the unity of the all-inclusive whole which serves beauty best, for if we have to add to our own individuality that of the artist to be able to experience the

[1] See also p. 157.

uniqueness of the work, we cannot possibly have as clear a vision as if the whole shines through the work directly.

(3) We should like the great individual artist to be also a great moral example, an embodiment of pure humanity; but often he is not. Once the firm basis of the revealed all-inclusive unity is lost, its wholeness can only be expressed by transforming all the particularities of the individual into its expression. The artist, not concerned with other values, but only with this task, has to transform everything he finds within himself into a form which fits the content completely, and so he has to allow all his urges to contribute to his work. But we meet in his work the absolute which implies for us all the absolute values; to understand the work, therefore, we have to apply truth and goodness besides beauty. This frequently creates that painful tension between our appreciation of the work and the impossibility of accepting the personality of the artist with just as few reservations.

(4) If these particular units and qualities play such an important part, how can we ever claim that an artist is a great artist? We need only think of such names as Shakespeare or Bach or Leonardo to see that this is possible; but how can it be possible? Does not the fact that both the artist's and our own individualities are involved make beauty dependent on our personal taste?

As the work of the 'great' artist is unique, it need not be understood at once; we have to learn to understand this particular kind of expression before the work can disclose its meaning. The genius knows naturally more than we do; he is a contemporary of later generations. The uniqueness of the work of art, however, can have two sources. On the one hand, it can become unique because it is mainly related to the all-inclusive whole; on the other hand, its uniqueness can be mainly due to the individuality of the artist. If the work has become a perfect and accomplished form of the absolute unity, it represents a result of general validity; its understanding, therefore, can gradually lead to its recognition as truly great, for this experience is open to everybody and does not change. If, on the contrary, the uniqueness of the work remains linked up mainly with the individual and its particular situation, it will be understood so long as similar individuals experience this situation, but it will not withstand its change. Very similar individuals may appreciate the artist even later, but then he will seem rather to be strange or interesting than great. Hence the importance of the passing of time for our judgment of the value of works of art. There remains, of course, a margin of uncertainty; the uniqueness of the artist's work may not yet have been understood, even after a long time, or the understanding may be lost and found again. This margin necessarily remains greatest with regard to contemporary art, for we can hardly free ourselves entirely from the present situation, and the artist may or may not have trans-

## INTERCONNECTED OPPOSITES AND ABSOLUTE VALUES

cended it. But the main body of reliable judgments is undoubtedly large, and it can be so because of the relationship between the work of art and the all-inclusive unity.

Yet the Many does not disappear, and so we must neither neglect it nor be misled by it. The single work of art remains a single unit among many, and what matters is its singleness. Our judgments, therefore, to be justified, have always to refer to our experience of these single units, and the appreciation of art has to be built up in this way; we can never derive general principles from many works, nor, as we have seen before, can we rely merely on the number of such judgments.[1] The adjective 'great', though it can be applied with considerable certainty, cannot be defined; it has to be confirmed, in each single case, by our actual experience.

We have almost forgotten to apply the term 'beauty' to the inner qualities of persons and personal relationships, but it is here that we come nearest to an understanding of its full meaning.

Every experience of beauty has much in common with the meeting between persons which we have described. It is a meeting with an individual unit which reveals itself to us by addressing us, and it can address us because it points to a greater whole which we have in common with it and which helps us to understand it. It forces us to experience the present, for only so long as we are confronted with it do we experience beauty; even to remember beauty we have to imagine that we live through that present again. The expression has to be unique, as every person is, and it becomes clearer the more personal it is, though, just as with persons, we must not stress the individuality as such but see it as the particular form of the all-inclusive unit. We experience beauty most definitely, moreover, if the impression is so strong that we are no longer able to make our own choice and to interpret it arbitrarily, but are forced, whether we like it or not, to acknowledge a meeting with the absolute. This is the fundamental difference between a merely pleasant impression and a true experience of beauty, and it is always fulfilled in the meeting with a person, in the sense in which we have discussed it.

At the same time, personal relationships, personalities and personal actions undoubtedly can lead to the experience which we have described as that of beauty. It has become customary to limit this concept to its purely æsthetic meaning and to forget this application, but in fact it ought to be included. A perfect friendship, an overwhelming love between man and woman, a mother's love for her children, any great and costly sacrifice—these and innumerable other examples confirm that we experience, above all, beauty. Captain Oates, on Scott's Antarctic expedition, knew that his weakness was endangering the lives of his companions who had to carry him, and so he walked out of the tent

[1] See pp. 36–7.

into the blizzard and disappeared, sacrificing his life to save the others—are we not made to see that such a man's character is just as beautiful as a sunset or a work of art, or even that it is more beautiful?[1] The epentant sinner, the father who welcomes the returning prodigal, the man who has done wrong to another person and who succeeds in making up for it, not in a merely logical way, by money or external help, but by a unique deed of love which expresses his person fully and re-establishes love between him and his victim—is there any other concept but beauty which can do justice to the particular quality of these deeds? Many of them seem to contradict logic and justice and yet they all convey a deeper knowledge of what is good. The impression of such a deed is strongest when, in one way or another, it is unique, for this alone throws the acting person fully into relief; uniqueness, however, is a requirement, not of truth or goodness, but of beauty.

It is true that a similar impression of beauty can also be created by a strong vitality or by what is sometimes called 'the great criminal', but this only confirms what we have said. The impression made by a very natural or vital person, or even by a criminal whose deeds reveal a great strength which has not yet been broken by any scruples, appeals to us because we feel an inner unity and directness of expression which have been more or less lost in our world. But unless his personality is related to the comprehensive whole by a certain greatness (we admire the *great* conqueror, the *great* criminal) we look at him rather as we look at a beautiful animal; the beauty is very much of our own choice, due to our overlooking other aspects of his personality which we are unable to accept. Even in the case of greatness, it is usually admiration at a distance (the great man is admired by his subordinates or followers, or we read about him) which also allows us to concentrate only on some aspects of his character. An impression of beauty which allows us to choose, however, cannot be compared in importance with that of the examples mentioned before which force all our being to respond; the personal element and its relation to the all-inclusive unity, therefore, is clearly most important for our experience of beauty.

This can perhaps be best seen when we compare all these examples with the impression of beauty created by the external appearance of a person. A beautiful face, a beautiful appearance have something in them which is particularly moving, more moving probably than the beauty of a sunset or a work of art, because the meeting with a person offers to us the most direct access to the absolute. We are led to expect that the beautiful body corresponds to a beautiful soul. If we discover that we are mistaken, the impression of the beautiful face will hardly be different from any other beauty in nature; unless we are able to see it as

[1] Cf. also the discussion of this event in H. H. Farmer, *Towards Belief in God*, pp. 115–17.

such, the beauty will be mixed up with, or give way to, regret or irritation. The personal element proves to be the finally determining one. We soon discover that a face is beautiful because it expresses a personality, and that a face which does so, even though it conflicts with all the conventional standards of beauty, may be the most beautiful of all. There are also exceptional cases; an extremely beautiful face may correspond to so evil a character that we are unable to forget the very contradiction. But we shall experience it as a painful contradiction, or even as a terrifying one, for the great beauty necessarily evokes the meeting with the absolute and thus makes us aware of its hidden depths from which evil also may arise. It makes us fear that evil has a significance which transcends the powers of the good as we know it.[1]

We are entitled to say, therefore, that there is no clearer revelation of beauty than that through meeting personalities to whom we can fully respond because they present to us that content which gives meaning to our own persons. Beauty confirms the fact that a form reveals a content to us completely and perfectly; and it is in such a meeting that beauty, as any perfect form has to be, is a final result, for this experience is one of wholeness and leaves no further choice, no loose ends, which any other experience of beauty—and any dogma and teaching—still leave. We experience that unitary feeling which alone can make us know that, despite all the opposites which we still need and which are once more embodied in the persons who meet, the division into two realities has been overcome.

That there are many persons and many such experiences confirms again that, to understand what happens in such a meeting, revelation has still to be added to it. Otherwise we can hardly see—except by doubtful analogies—why it is the personal expression which comes nearest to the all-inclusive unit. But the experience shows, too, that revelation itself, to fulfil its task, is in need of beauty. It is only when beauty is added to truth that truth really shines in its own light and that our search is ended, and goodness has to be beautiful to make us see the realm of freedom from which it springs—that is, the fullness of internal reality by which it transcends us. Revelation has to appeal to our personalities in such a way that we can fully respond, and thus it is beauty, and particularly beauty in persons, which makes sure that the meaning of revelation really reveals itself to us.

[1] Cf., for example, the description of some of the famous figures of the Renaissance. There is great significance in the original myth that the devil is not, as in the Middle Ages, an ugly creature, but a fallen angel of outstanding beauty.

## Chapter XII

### THE CREATION OF FURTHER INTERCONNECTED OPPOSITES

THE few examples of the interconnected opposites which we have discussed certainly suffice to make clear that the application of opposites transforms thinking into a constant activity. Space and time, by raising moral demands, have led us to necessity and freedom, which in their turn pointed to the One and the Many, for these alone can make sure that the absolute is embodied in such a way as the other opposites demand. Yet the final barrier of the Many has shown that, to be understood, even revelation must lead to such a constant activity. Truth and goodness and the truth of any revelation are confirmed by beauty, but, though each single experience of beauty is a final result, no such result can ever be more than one among many. The mere fact that, whatever result we arrive at, we are still confronted with its interconnected opposite makes it impossible to find any rest apart from the single experiences in which these opposites merge in an absolute value. This, however, is essential, not only because it gives to our thought, by forcing our attention again and again to the opposite facts and possibilities, a richness and fullness that can hardly be found otherwise, but also because these opposites have to lead to the unitary feeling which can only spring from ever renewed experiences. The knowledge that we have had such an experience may give us a deep feeling of a definite security, but even this will eventually vanish unless we experience the unitary feeling again.

We can see now how this feeling is awakened. The interconnected opposites force us to drive our thoughts into those opposite extremes which fully correspond to the division into external and internal reality, and it is the correct experience of this division which makes us feel that we have touched upon absolute primary reality. The opposites must make us see external and internal reality at the same time, so

## CREATION OF FURTHER INTERCONNECTED OPPOSITES

that, stimulated by the tension between them, our feeling embraces the whole of reality.

We experience this feeling most clearly in beauty, when form and content (which have always helped us to understand this division best) come to a final agreement, but it is present in any experience of the absolute values. We must not forget that an investigation of thinking always forces us to divide what may be experienced together. Even the separate discussion of these opposites is up to a point artificial; we are hardly able, for instance, to experience truth without also feeling inner freedom and beauty, nor to realize goodness without feeling that we have recognized truth and experienced beauty. The experience of each such single opposition is sufficient to fulfil the task of these opposites, for it is the tension within the single pair of opposites which creates the unitary feeling. Nevertheless, it remains important to know the different oppositions, for, to create this tension, we have to see in each case which opposites truly correspond to the two realities. It is only half correct to say, 'beauty is truth, truth beauty' [1] because, though we probably experience the two together, they indicate two different ways of approaching the absolute, and it would blur the division into two realities to mix these up. So long as our attention is divided, or our thoughts do not force us to live through one definite contradiction with all its force and pain, but leave us free to neglect or escape it, the synthesis of feeling may still arise, but thinking, in this case, is no longer a help but a hindrance. Only the right opposition can help to make sure that we experience, not an intrusion of feeling, but its unity.

Even the interconnected opposites discovered by investigation may, for this reason, not yet be sufficient in themselves to secure the full experience of such a single pair of opposites. Because they can be discovered by thinking alone, they can also easily become abstract and purely formal; we may discover them without experiencing them. The abstract way of discovering them may also induce us to concentrate too much on their relationship and affinity. Knowledge of them, therefore, should encourage us to create further such opposites which are modelled on these examples, but which are based directly on our actual experience or on the revelation towards which the other interconnected opposites lead.

The oppositions which we have discussed show what is essential for all these opposites. We must not mix up the two realities, but drive our thought into those opposite extremes which become inevitable by the division of reality; we must have the courage to avoid all artificial unifications and to work out the two aspects of reality so clearly that we can express them by one single opposition. The concepts forming the interconnected opposites must not themselves be created by think-

[1] Keats, 'Ode on a Grecian Urn'.

## ABSOLUTE VALUES AND INTERCONNECTED OPPOSITES

ing; they have to refer to facts or conclusions which we cannot possibly deny. All this applies also to those interconnected opposites which are created by thinking, but these are different from the others in so far as they do not consist of fundamental concepts of the two realities, but of the external and internal aspects of the same object, action or event. We have to find, in each particular experience, those aspects which correspond to the two realities and to establish their opposition. We have to become aware of external and internal reality within the same unit and to work out this knowledge so clearly that we can see this fundamental opposition in that single unit. We can never completely transcend internal reality; but that we are appealing to it in the right way can be, and has to be, made sure by the knowledge that it partakes of external reality, for this alone guarantees that we are really laying hold on internal reality itself.

The reality which we actually experience is so pliable that it appears to a quite surprising degree to be determined by our approach; it seems to behave, so to speak, in accordance with what we expect from it. If we presuppose nothing but mechanical laws, we get a mechanical universe; if we presuppose evolution, everything seems to fall in with this idea; if we presuppose persons, and only if we do so, we get a world of persons; if we acknowledge absolute values, we also experience them. This confirms the predominance of internal reality where, as we have seen, anticipation is needed to arrive at any understanding at all.[1] To have a full experience, therefore, we must obviously start from an anticipation which does justice to both the world around us and the world within us, and we must try to experience them in such a way that we can control our anticipation. This can only be reliably achieved if we find, in each single experience, those interconnected opposites which represent the division into two realities.

That it is essential to support the interconnected opposites discovered as the basis of thinking by those created by it can be seen when we remember the opposition between absolute independence and absolute dependence which we have mentioned as connected with morals.[2] Necessity and freedom can easily be taken for purely abstract concepts —for the external reign of mechanical laws and their absence inside internal reality—even when we try to explain morality. The external aspect of any real experience of freedom, however, is absolute independence from any outside influence, which entirely contradicts all our knowledge of external reality, and its internal aspect is absolute dependence, which entirely contradicts all abstract definitions of freedom;

---

[1] Our approach to reality is thus of fundamental importance; as reality seems almost to 'give in' to our ideas, the mere way in which we approach it lays a great responsibility upon us.
[2] See p. 171.

## CREATION OF FURTHER INTERCONNECTED OPPOSITES

we feel completely free from the compulsion of external necessity only when obeying an absolute necessity within us.[1] As soon as we discover this opposition, therefore, we are forced to leave behind all preconceptions and abstractions; we make sure that the opposition between necessity and freedom is kept alive and that it deepens and clarifies our actual experience.

The importance of putting external and internal aspects into opposition can be recognized when we remember the age-old theological controversy about the relevance of faith and works. Whether theologians or not, we are bound to experience some such problem. So long as we toil to obey moral laws and try to put them into practice, we have not yet really experienced the realm of freedom, and it is only when we enter it, quite independently of our efforts or even in spite of them, that we are set free. What is more natural, in such a case, than to turn away from our previous efforts completely and to rely on this inner freedom alone? We are bound to fear that any conscious effort on our part will once more destroy it. Let the fruits come forth naturally and spontaneously; let us do nothing to endanger and falsify them by our intentions! Yet if we thus stop doing anything, we obviously kill that freedom again, for it can find expression only in action. It is perfectly true that it is faith which matters, for the external deed or success may spring from wrong motives; failure and suffering if they are grasped in the right faith may teach us the true meaning of freedom. However, faith remains linked with freedom, for we have no faith unless it is our own, nor can we be forced into true belief; but freedom has to be exercised to remain alive. The problem seems insoluble; so long as we emphasize the works alone we cannot help lessening the importance of faith; but when faith is emphasized alone, be it by St. Paul or Luther, it seems immediately necessary to add that this does not invite us to laziness nor to mere contemplation, but means that actions have to show that the fruits are ripening. Yet we cannot be active without aiming at works.

But is this problem not insoluble because we try to do what we must not do—namely to by-pass the fundamental opposition? When we consider this problem, we first introduce the internal conception of goodness; either faith alone is really good or the works are good in themselves. With faith external reality is completely excluded; with the works external facts enter, but they are not seen as a form of internal reality; any activity of a certain kind, whether or not it springs from the right motives or is fully experienced, is considered as good—that is, the external facts as such are mixed up with internal opposites. Frequently, moreover, success is regarded as reward and failure as punishment. All this makes any clear conception impossible. Would

[1] See H. H. Farmer, *The Servant of the Word*, p. 140.

## ABSOLUTE VALUES AND INTERCONNECTED OPPOSITES

it not be a considerable help, to say the least, to establish faith and action as interconnected opposites?[1]

Faith is based on that truth which we have distinguished from correct statements; on a truth, that is, which cannot be confirmed by external knowledge, but has to be believed, because it has to be experienced as an absolute value.[2] This truth can be neither grasped nor revealed once and for all; it has to be met in constantly renewed experiences. We have also seen that the only way of testing this truth is to put it into action; we can express, develop and confirm our faith, therefore, only by acting according to it. Moreover, because faith belongs to internal reality, we cannot simply state it and preserve it, nor develop it by some further abstract statements; it is only when we act according to it that we are able to give it those external forms which make internal reality more and more real, and only thus can we deepen it. Faith bears fruit because any living faith has to grow and to develop, and as it can only develop in the way just described, it forces us to give it external expression; it is this expression which proves that it is a living force and keeps it in being as such a force. The external aspect of faith, therefore, is action.

On the other hand, the internal aspect of this action, when linked with the search for truth, is the disclosure of it. It is true that we must not see faith as the effect of a cause; nor can we force ourselves into faith; it has to spring spontaneously from the realm of freedom. But if there is this link with our actions, the function of the aims which we have discussed is made to serve faith, for then it is faith which raises certain expectations which anticipate the future.[3] The result of our actions, whether success or failure, will therefore help us to understand how far these anticipations were right or wrong; when we confront the aims with our intentions, our faith will be confirmed and developed, or challenged and transformed. The external opposition—success or failure—will not be linked with internal opposites, for both can serve the same purpose, but the external action will be seen as the expression of our faith, as disclosing the fruits which our faith bears, and thus show us how far the faith we have conforms to, or deviates from, the actual facts. Their agreement or discrepancy will confront us with truth. To see faith as the internal aspect of action and action as the external aspect of faith—that is, to establish them as interconnected opposites—can thus help us to establish the right relationship between them.

Certainly, it is also possible that the results of our actions may rob

---

[1] We use the word 'action' and not 'works' because 'action' is the more fundamental concept, for there are no works which were not produced by action, but there are actions which do not produce works.

[2] See pp. 153-6.   [3] See pp. 52-3.

## CREATION OF FURTHER INTERCONNECTED OPPOSITES

us of our faith. But does not this failure to experience the absolute (which cannot be blamed on the absolute itself, as we have seen) only show that we do not completely realize the internal aspect of our actions and that we take the external results at their face value? Even the scope of this wrong reaction, however, is considerably narrowed when we see, at the same time, that action is also interconnected with suffering.

When I try fully to understand any one of my actions, I am bound to discover that its internal aspect is suffering. Once more it does not matter whether it leads to success or failure; by actively entering the realm of external reality, I produce the impact of its necessity upon me, to which I have to submit. This may take different forms; I see either that my actions have other consequences from those expected, or that these reveal, by confronting my intentions with their external results, characteristics, urges and reactions within me which I did not suspect. Both these discoveries are frequently painful and therefore I may struggle against this compulsion, and I may be successful; but my very success will depend on my submission to both external inevitability and my nature, on my establishing the right relationship between possible action and necessary—even if painful—restriction. I am bound to suffer in both meanings of the word; I cannot avoid remaining passive in front of certain necessities and compulsions and giving in to them, reacting as I am forced to, and by this I experience suffering, I am hurt, I feel pain. Both these meanings of the word are important; I have to see where I must give in and I have to experience it as a painful restriction of my freedom, even if it finally leads to success or joy, for I cannot possibly discover the true realm of freedom if I take everything for granted.

Even if I try to become a powerful man, I have to undergo the painful realization of my external powerlessness before I am able to see what power is within my reach, and I certainly must pay attention to this experience if I want to help others, so as to acquire the humility necessary for successful help. If I strive for power, the task of this suffering probably remains hidden; but when I accept the suffering and recognize in it the significant internal aspect of my actions, these actions are inevitably linked to my faith. I no longer look solely for the external aims towards which I am driving or driven; the impact of each of my steps upon myself can make itself felt; my passive, involuntary reactions and the feelings they awaken in me can be recognized; and it is thus that my external action can disclose its meaning to me, by its relationship to the anticipations based on my faith. For instance, I may concentrate entirely on a good action which thus forms the external aspect of my striving. Yet, even if I am fairly successful, am I not bound to suffer as soon as I am really confronted with the absolute value and

## ABSOLUTE VALUES AND INTERCONNECTED OPPOSITES

forced to realize my own imperfections? If I resist my natural inclination to pass over this feeling for the sake of the action, but recognize its significance, the suffering is bound to lead to a clearer experience and knowledge of the absolute and thus to develop and enhance my faith.

If, on the other hand, suffering is the external experience, if I suffer because I experience pain or failure or defeat or injustice or the suffering of others, the internal aspect of this suffering is action. I react to it; I feel, think and experience and inner urges arise; so long as there is suffering and not merely apathy, my whole being remains active, and I have to appreciate and to understand this inner activity to be able to give meaning to this suffering and to avoid apathy. The meaning of suffering, however, cannot but be related to faith, even if I try to deny any such meaning. I may suffer because there is so much evil in the world and because it seems so much more powerful than the good; I may try to convince myself that this existence of evil destroys the meaning of the good; the suffering, nevertheless, is bound to develop my sensitivity to goodness and to develop knowledge of it, especially if I know that it is this inner activity which has to confront the external experience of suffering. I may remain unable to decipher the meaning of all this external suffering; the inner activity awakened by it, rightly understood, will nevertheless strengthen my faith.

If we say that the interconnected opposite of faith is action, we mean, therefore, both action and suffering which cannot be separated, and this obviously contributes further to the solution of this problem, particularly as it is probably suffering which most frequently brings forth the right fruits.

The Christian revelation abounds in such oppositions, and here it becomes clear that it is essential to experience the opposition as such—that is, the external as well as the internal aspects. To mention once more the Cross—it is only when the external aspect of this event, the complete defeat, the terrible agony, the injustice, the horrible cruelty of man, his lust and his enjoyment of evil, and the unimaginable amount of suffering due to all these single elements, are felt in all their poignancy that the internal aspect can become completely obvious and acquire its full power and profundity. We have to understand what it means for Jesus to shout, 'God, my God, why hast Thou forsaken me.' Or, to give another example—the beatitudes promise blessedness to those who are persecuted and reviled for righteousness' sake and against whom all manner of evil shall be said falsely. How could the weight of this promise and the power of this spirit be understood unless we are really aware of, and fully feel, all the external suffering which is to be turned into joy?

Even when these opposites are not explicitly stated, it is left to us

## CREATION OF FURTHER INTERCONNECTED OPPOSITES

to look for such oppositions and to establish them, for only thus are we able to discern reliably what this revelation means. We have to understand that a revelation which discloses facts which we can neither grasp directly nor ever understand fully has to drive our thoughts into two opposite directions, so that, when we experience the opposite extremes, we also experience that unitary feeling which alone can make real for us, for the moment of this experience, the peace which passeth understanding. We have mentioned before the opposition between judgment and grace;[1] there is also the similar problem of predestination. If God is all-knowing, our destinies must be known to Him from the beginning and cannot be further determined within the relative framework of space and time within which we have to live and to see our lives. Hence belief in predestination. But this belief, taken by itself, remains meaningless, for God cannot have saved 'man' as a kind of abstract generalization, but, in fact, saved only some and condemned others. Moreover, predestination cannot alter the opposite fact that, if our persons matter, our lives must needs be of consequence; they cannot, then, be completely determined, but our choices and deeds must have an influence. Predestination, in other words, cannot exclude freedom of will; and it is by this opposite that it acquires meaning. For it is in both these conclusions that we reach the furthest boundaries to which our thinking can penetrate, and we are meant to do so in order to experience what otherwise could not be expressed in our language at all.

Our understanding always depends on finding the right opposition. There is, to take one more example, the demand that we should not resist evil. There are passages supporting it and others contradicting it, but the comparison of these different passages hardly helps us to solve the problem raised by this command; if we try to assess their relative importance, we never find a way out of merely arbitrary decisions. Certainly, we should renounce the use of force and violence; even if exercised for the sake of love, they only prove that our love is not strong enough to work directly; 'loving humility' is undoubtedly the strongest power of all,[2] and we should be able to rely on it. But can we allow evil to grow unresisted; must we not fight it, especially if it threatens others? Had not even Jesus to use force in the temple? Is the demand really clear in respect to wars? We are hardly able to give a definite answer to all such questions; we have to come to a decision on each single occasion. But it will be much easier to come to a satisfactory decision which transcends mere arbitrariness if we see the fundamental opposition which underlies these contradictory conclusions and if we are thus forced to face them again and again, without evading their contradiction.

[1] See p. 172.   [2] See p. 200, note.

## ABSOLUTE VALUES AND INTERCONNECTED OPPOSITES

We can observe here the constant activity of thinking which is needed. As this command concerns our actions, we have to see it in the light of necessity and freedom. So long as the realm of freedom has not become real within us, we have to apply laws, and laws include the negative; resistance, therefore, cannot be avoided, but it has to be transcended in the end. Yet this is not quite satisfactory, for how can it be transcended? Is not evil too powerful in the world ever to allow non-resistance? If we remain aware of this other extreme, we are driven on and probably see that our actions point also to their other interconnected opposite—faith. This helps us to elucidate the problem further, for the negative fight against evil obviously cannot become that expression of faith which we could call its fruit; this has to be positive. Non-resistance, therefore, leads to a clearer definition of the actions required by faith. We must not resist evil, for this would direct our actions towards it and thus falsify our inner activity; external actions are always determined by what exists, and if our attention is focused on the existence of evil, all our thoughts, feelings and urges are preoccupied with it. We have seen that the negative can entirely dominate internal reality. We must refrain from any external resistance if we are to be able to concentrate on the realization of the good. But what about other people? We cannot expect a complete justification of non-resistance in external terms, for faith must transcend the relationship between cause and effect; the results of our behaviour depend, not on us, but on grace. Yet does this willingness to suffer evil, especially when others are concerned, really contribute to our understanding of grace? It does so if we do not turn away from this suffering, but experience it, for thus we see the interconnection between action and suffering which shows us the fundamental opposition. Even non-resistance must not become an external aim, for then it becomes a weapon of resistance which once more dominates all our endeavours; just like suffering, it has to be seen as the external aspect of inner action. It is the tension between the external non-resistance which seems to allow evil to grow unhindered and our burning desire to strive for the realization of the good—together with the suffering caused by this tension—which force us to make the good completely real within ourselves and thus gradually enable us to replace the use of force by the forceful appeal of loving humility.

Certainly, we are unable to fulfil this demand completely; we are too weak to exclude resistance and compulsion entirely. But if we put these two aspects of non-resistance into a direct and definite opposition, we shall gradually free love and grace from all easy sentimental falsifications. If our actions are determined by love, non-resistance and suffering must be their external aspects, for love cannot be expressed by self-defence, by destruction, by negative endeavours. If we rely on

## CREATION OF FURTHER INTERCONNECTED OPPOSITES

grace, we must have complete trust, which again is bound to have the same external aspect; we must trust that the right deed will have the right consequence, even if external reality seems to contradict this belief and thus causes us to suffer. We cannot avoid suffering by relying on external actions, but must see that external suffering—which again is not an end in itself—remains interconnected with internal activity. Non-resistance has to be understood as purely negative in external reality and yet, at the same time, as the most painful and exacting demand upon ourselves.

The application of these opposites also shows, therefore, that revelation is not concerned with some abstract or abstruse 'religious' problems which do not matter to us, and that it is not simply telling us things which we can neither understand nor do. It is based throughout upon experiences which we continually have, and although, of course, it also transcends them, it has to be related to them, for only thus can it reveal itself to us. But we have also to pay attention to these experiences and to understand them. This will be much easier when we know how to find the right oppositions and how to apply them, for if we apply them correctly we finally arrive at the interconnected opposites which help us to experience that unitary feeling which confronts us with the absolute.

These opposites also make it clear whether or not the necessary tension is really reached, for if we succeed in applying them correctly, we are confirmed in this by meeting the absolute in the experience of an absolute value. There is hardly any awareness of truth more acute than that experienced in confronting judgment and grace, or the two aspects of the Cross, or in opposing either predestination or fate to freedom, if we really succeed in confronting them as opposite and utterly incompatible extremes. Similarly, the opposition between faith and action, between action and suffering, or that between external non-resistance and the inner activity pressing for love, lead to the greatest sensitivity for, and the fullest realization of, that goodness which transcends all moral laws. A man whose love is based on the full awareness of these oppositions will certainly appear beautiful to us; and is not the opposition between 'the starry heaven above' and 'the moral law within' so convincing because it is very beautiful?

Need it be said once more that all such achievements will only be given to us in rare moments of insight and illumination, and they will be given to us, not caused by our endeavours? But the way towards them is indicated and opened by this way of thinking, and though thinking may not finally help us nor be needed in the end, even failure on this way, or staying in the right kind of uncertainty, is more helpful and more rewarding than any neat unitary system of thought or any revelation which is taken as disclosing dead external metaphysical

## ABSOLUTE VALUES AND INTERCONNECTED OPPOSITES

knowledge. Because these moments are given to us, we cannot fight our way to fulfilment; we have to be led there. But we must be ready to receive. We cannot open the door, but we must knock. Thinking is neither the most nor the least important of our endeavours, yet it has been as a result of wrong thinking, after all, that those layers of our existence which we have tried to uncover in this investigation have been buried more and more deeply during the last few centuries.

It is true that the task of philosophy, once we agree that it leads to a constant activity without itself producing final results, may appear much more modest than before. But it will also be more fruitful, for instead of attempting the impossible and thus distorting our lives, it will lead in the right direction; it will awake readiness to believe and provide tests for what we may believe. Both are equally important. The recent centuries have erected enormous barriers against any faith, but we obviously need some kind of belief, for we cannot know the absolute as such; we have seen that even the sciences accept presuppositions which have to be believed. If, however, we cannot dispense with belief, what can be more important than to be able to distinguish between right and wrong belief? The most absurd and disastrous teachings, as our age has shown, are believed most fervently; any faith, therefore, can be seen as meaningless so long as we remain unable to counter errors in this sphere. We must be able to stop the intrusion of feeling which always supports the error; we must become able to show the correct way towards that unitary feeling by which alone we can reach and grasp the unity between ourselves and the whole of the universe, for which we cannot help striving.

These indications may be sufficient to give a clear direction to the work which has to be done and to which this book is only a first introduction—to show that, to distinguish between external and internal reality, we should develop the power of thinking in opposites. This will enable us to discover and to create those fundamental interconnected oppositions which, by leading to a constant activity and by helping us to experience the true meaning of existence, make thinking contribute essentially to a full and complete life, lived in accordance with the absolute primary reality or, as we may probably say now without falsifying the results of this investigation, lived in accordance with the personal will of God.

# INDEX

Abel, K., 11*n*.
Abstraction, process of, 61-2, 85-8, 94, 115-16, 172
Accidental, the, 5-6, 51-2, 133, 192-3, 194-5; and necessity, *see* Necessity and accident
Action, and faith, 234-5; and suffering, 201-2, 235-6
Affirmation, *see* Negation
Aims, and activity, 43-5; and intentions, 117 ff., 133, 198; and the present, 53; and values, 54-5
Analogies, 113
Anticipation, 53-4, 125, 133-4, 232, 234
Art, and morality, 226; works of, 14-15, 28*n*., 131, 214-15, 225-7
Augustine, St., 183*n*.

Beauty, 22, 36, 120-1, 156-8, 161-2, 223 ff.; of God, 162*n*.; as matter of taste, 36, 156; in nature, 157*n*., 215 224; of personal qualities, 227-9; and truth, 190, 231
Belief, 167, 240
Biology, 4, 7, 13, 31, 50, 52, 88-9, 112, 183, 204
Buber, M., 169*n*., 187*n*., 218*n*.
Buddhism, 15-16, 55*n*., 107*n*.

Causality and necessity, 193-4, 195
Cause and effect, 12, 56-7, 60-1, 66, 111, 126, 193
Certainty, 45-6, 165
Christ, 162*n*., 236, 237
Christianity, 15, 52*n*., 55*n*., 172, 236-9
Claim, the inescapable, 198, 200, 219
Colours, 82-3, 89
Concepts, *a priori*, 20*n*., 71*n*.; creation of, 11; transferring of, 56 ff., 66, 93, 113, 125-6

Concepts, constructive, definition of, 62; in both realities, 66 ff.; in external reality, 91 ff.; in internal reality, 125 ff.; and analogies, 113; and interconnected opposites, 70-1, 175 ff., 181, 194-5
Content, *see* Form and content
Contradictions, 3 ff., 73-4, 114, 178, 237 ff.
Cross, the, 15, 236

Dark, *see* Light and dark
Degrees, scales of, 11, 73, 112
Determined, the, and the accidental, 194-5
Deussen, P., 15*n*.
Dialectics, viii
Dostoevsky, 6*n*., 122, 183*n*., 200*n*., 218*n*.
Dualism, viii, 18, 206
Duty, 140, 148

Effect, *see* Cause and effect
Electrons, theory of, 11-12, 85, 86, 209
Eliot, T. S., 139*n*.
Emmet, D. M., 19*n*.
Emotion, 99*n*.
Ends, *see* Means and ends
Events, description of, 12, 26, 34
Evil, *see* Good and evil
Evolution, theory of, 4, 7, 204
Explanation, scientific, 30-2, 114

Faith and works, 201*n*., 233 ff.
Farmer, H. H., 6*n*., 15*n*., 35*n*., 99*n*., 121*n*., 154*n*., 196*n*., 198*n*., 211*n*., 215*n*., 228*n*., 233*n*.
Feeling, concentrating on external reality, 143 ff.; definition of the concept, 99-102; intrusion of, 106 ff., 136 ff.; the nature of, 98 ff.; and opposites,

241

# INDEX

13; as organ of knowledge, 99–100, 102; and repetition, 50–1; splitting up of, 107–8, 146–7; and thinking, 17, 101 ff., 136 ff.; unitary, 17, 147–8, 169–70, 178, 229, 230–1

Feelings, active, and passive reactions, 102 ff.; enjoying one's, 141; and object, 35, 39, 57–8, 103–5; wealth of, 102

Force, the concept of, 12, 30, 56–7, 60, 66

Form and content, definition of, 27–8; in both realities, 166; in external reality, 27 ff., 48, 67, 181, 194; in internal reality, 38 ff., 48–9, 66, 131 ff., 156–7, 159, 220–1, 223; and certainty, 45–6; in thinking, 27n.

Freedom, see Necessity and freedom

Future, its rôle in thinking, 52–3, 113, 197–8

General, the, see Particular and the general

God, 15, 52n., 58, 155, 162n., 164, 172, 181, 193, 201–2, 223, 237, 240

Good, the meaning of, 39, 51, 53n., 59 —, and bad, 128–9; and evil, 6, 76n., 110–11, 205–7

Goodness, 36, 156, 160–1, 162n., 189–90, 203 ff.

Grace, 170, 190–1, 201, 238; and judgment, 172

Haldane, J. S., 10n., 23n., 82n., 89n.
Hegel, 75n.
Heisenberg, W., 82n., 85n., 87n., 90n.
Help, 199
History, interpretations of, 7–8
Humanism, 55n., 167
Hume, David, 57n., 191
Huxley, A., 107n.

Ideals, 129–30, 140–1
Individuality and personality, 212–13
Intentions, 116; and aims, 117 ff., 133, 198
I-Thou relationship, 218 ff.

Jaspers, K., 153n.
Jesus, see Christ

Kant, 4n., 20n., 37, 57, 58, 59n., 71n., 74, 77, 78, 85, 87, 161, 175, 178n., 179, 180, 191; relationship of this book to his teaching, 20n.
Keats, 231n.

Kierkegaard, 43n.
Knowledge, theory of, viii–ix, 18, 20n., 77–8
Köhler's *Gestaltpsychologie*, 217n.

Light, and dark, 9–10, 68, 81–2; scientific explanation of, 30, 86; and seeing, 21
Love, 13, 39, 147, 201–2, 217–18, 222–3, 237
'Lust' and 'Unlust', 103n.
Luther, 233

Macmurray, J., 8n., 24n., 25n., 32n., 37n., 39n., 105n., 106n., 150n., 207n.
Many, the, see One and the Many
Marx, 31n., 75n., 146
Materialism, 31n., 75n., 137, 148
Mathematics, 58–9, 87, 154, 208, 210
Matter, 11, 86
Meaning, and life, 5–6, 8; search for, 61
Means and ends, 66–7, 110 ff., 117–19, 125–6, 136, 159
Metaphysics, ix, 18
Morality, 13, 42, 144, 171, 187, 204–5, 232–3; and art, 226; and religion, 167n.
Moral Laws, 57–8, 59, 198–9, 205; and the universe, 3–4, 74, 178, 186, 239
Motion and rest, 12
Motives, double, 122, 134
Mysticism, 24, 107, 183–4, 187n., 200

Names, 83–4
Nationalism, 106–7, 137–8, 144, 148, 210
Necessity, and accident, 51–2, 66, 192–3; and causality, 193–4, 195
— and freedom, 57, 60, 66, 67, 129, 173–4, 177, 232–3, 238; in external reality, 191 ff.; in internal reality, 195 ff.; temptations of, 202–3
Negation, 54–5, 74–6, 93–5, 137, 145–6, 177
Non-resistance, 237–9
Numbers, 58–9, 208

Oates, Captain, 227–8
Objects, description of, 11–12, 26, 34
Oman, J., 7n., 8n., 11n., 37n., 104n., 125n., 127n., 140n., 154n., 167n., 171n., 206n.
One, the, and the Many, 88, 132–3, 173–4; in external reality, 208 ff.; in internal reality, 211 ff.

# INDEX

Opposite, the meaning of the concept, 71 ff.
Opposites, contradictory, 71–2; as contrasts, 71–2; inherent in thought, 9 ff.; in language, 9n., 11n., 81n.; in nature, 84–5; necessity for different kinds of, 65 ff.; and theory of knowledge, 78–80
—, external, 80 ff., 158; definition of, 69–70, 81
—, interconnected, 164–8, 169 ff.; creation of, 230 ff.; definition of, 69, 70–1, 173–5
—, internal, 110 ff., 159; definition of, 69–70, 110–11
Otto, R., 15n.

Part, the, and the whole, 216–17
Particular, the, and the general, 213, 214–16
Pascal, 3n.
Past, its rôle in thinking, 52, 185
Paul, St., 233
Personality, 9, 200–2, 211, 213
Philosophy, development of, 14; task of, 90–1, 240
Physics, recent developments in, 3, 11, 12, 30–1, 42n., 50, 51n., 54, 77, 85n., 86–8, 90, 94, 135, 181, 192, 209, 210
Physiology, 7
Pictures, appreciation of, 22, 35–6, 214
Planck, M., 135n.
Plato, 169n.
Power, striving for, 138–9, 186, 188, 235
Predestination, 237
Prediction, 46–7
Present, its rôle in thinking, 52–3, 197, 218–20, 221
Principles, 120–3, 126 ff., 139–40, 159; æsthetic, 121, 128, 139
Probability, calculus of, 12, 33–4, 192
Progress, belief in, 4–5, 137, 203
Psychology, 7, 14, 22–3, 25, 26, 27, 31, 50, 89, 96, 183

Qualities, 11, 81–2, 90; and values, 134–5
Quantum theory, 42n., 135n.

Raven, C. E., 7n.
Reactions, passive, *see* Feelings, active, and passive reactions
Realities, agreement between the two, 165–7; mixing up of the two, 55, 75, 76, 95, 143 ff.

Reality, the concept of, 19–20; division of, 19 ff., 46, 47 ff., 55 ff.
—, external, 20, 24 ff., 41–2, 45, 46–7; definition of, 25–6
—, internal, 20, 33 ff., 41 ff., 124–5; definition of, 35–7
—, primary, 20, 55, 62, 65, 135, 178, 222, 240
Relativity, theory of, 12, 42n.
Religion, 15, 46, 239; and morality, 167n.
Repetition, 41–2, 49–51, 56, 60, 128, 212–13
Responsibility, 200, 232n.
Rest, *see* Motion and rest
Revelation, 222–3, 229, 236–9
Romanticism, 104–6

Schiller, 98n.
Schopenhauer, 55n.
Sciences, natural, 7, 23–4, 30–2, 37, 50, 77, 80n., 86–91, 153, 155, 183, 193, 204
Sentimentality, 104–6
Sounds, 26, 83n.
Space and time, 173–5; in external reality, 179 ff.; in internal reality, 182 ff.; temptations of, 184–8
Specialization, 90–1
Statements, correct, 153–6
Suffering, and action, 201–2, 235–6; meaning of, 6
Systems, unitary, of thought, 6 ff., 16–17, 86, 88–90, 93, 146

Tennant, F. R., 19n.
Thinking, activity of, 13; and feeling, 17, 98, 101 ff., 136 ff.; laws of, 20n., 23–4, 61, 77, 92; the major operations of, 158 ff.; in opposites, viii, 16 ff., 78–80, 176–7, 240; relevance of, vii ff., 170; teleological, 112–13
Tillich, P., 99n.
Time, 133; and conscience, 184–5; as fourth dimension, 88n.; and space, *see* Space and time
Truth, 96–7, 153 ff., 160–1, 162n., 188 ff., 196, 234; and beauty, 231; and truthfulness, 128, 161

Unity, longing for, 8, 17, 93, 146–7; its justification, 8–9; its satisfaction, 17–18, 147, 178
Universe, and human existence, 3–4, 74, 178, 186, 239; in modern physics, 3, 54, 86, 210; nature of, 163

# INDEX

Usefulness, 119–20, 126

Validity, general, 25–6, 36–7
Value, the concept of, 119
Values, 8, 54–5, 61, 96; the absolute, 121, 123, 130, 134–5, 148–50, 153 ff.; concentration on, 148–50; hierarchy of, 124, 127, 142–3, 148; and qualities, 134; scales of, 114–15, 118 ff., 127

Whitehead, A. N., 15*n*., 58*n*., 223*n*.
Whole, the, *see* Part and the whole
Wholeness, 212, 214, 216–17
Willing, 13, 39, 98
Works, *see* Faith and works

For Product Safety Concerns and Information please contact our EU representative GPSR@taylorandfrancis.com
Taylor & Francis Verlag GmbH, Kaufingerstraße 24, 80331 München, Germany

www.ingramcontent.com/pod-product-compliance
Lightning Source LLC
Chambersburg PA
CBHW061439300426
44114CB00014B/1755